THE LEGENDARY CHARACTER
OF KAISER MAXIMILIAN

Number Fourteen of the
COLUMBIA UNIVERSITY GERMANIC STUDIES
Edited by Robert Herndon Fife

New Series

THE
LEGENDARY CHARACTER
OF
KAISER MAXIMILIAN

GLENN ELWOOD WAAS

AMS PRESS, INC.
NEW YORK
1966

Copyright 1941, Columbia University Press,
New York

Reprinted with the permission of the
Original Publisher, 1966

AMS PRESS, INC.
New York, N.Y. 10003
1966

Manufactured in the United States of America

PREFACE

IN THE PREPARATION of the following study I have been greatly aided by the advice and help of many kind people. I appreciate deeply the expert services rendered by the staffs of the university libraries of Columbia, Princeton, Rutgers, and Colgate. I wish particularly to thank Miss Alice Guller, Loan Librarian of Colgate University, for her never-failing kindness and assistance in procuring works from other libraries.

A great share of the hard work involved in the typing of the manuscript and reading of the proofs has been done by my wife, Evelyn Waas, who indeed knows how much her help has meant to me.

The entire course of this investigation has been attended and encouraged by the interest, the criticisms, and the practical suggestions of Professor Robert Herndon Fife of Columbia University. His scholarly guidance has made possible its completion and whatever merit it may possess.

G. E. W.

Hamilton, New York
September, 1941

CONTENTS

I. MAXIMILIAN AND THE HISTORIANS	3
II. MAXIMILIAN AS VIEWED BY HIS CONTEMPORARIES	23
A. German Sources	23
1. Contemporary historians and political writers	23
2. Contemporary scholars and poets	35
3. Territorial representatives	48
4. Representatives of the cities	53
B. Foreign Sources	56
III. MAXIMILIAN IN *VOLKSLIED* AND *SPRUCH*	73
A. The *Volkslied*	73
B. The *Spruch*	90
IV. MAXIMILIAN'S SELF-PORTRAYAL	97
V. *TEUERDANK* AND THE MAXIMILIAN ANECDOTES IN THE SIXTEENTH CENTURY	121
A. *Teuerdank* in the Sixteenth Century	121
B. The Maximilian Anecdotes in the Sixteenth Century	135
VI. MAXIMILIAN AND THE FAUST LEGEND	155
VII. THE MAXIMILIAN LEGEND BECOMES LITERATURE	172
VIII. CONCLUSION	187
BIBLIOGRAPHY	191
INDEX	217

THE LEGENDARY CHARACTER
OF KAISER MAXIMILIAN

I

MAXIMILIAN AND THE HISTORIANS

AMONG THE HEROES who are celebrated in German legend there are few who are spoken of with more affection than Maximilian I, German King from 1486 and Holy Roman Emperor-Elect from 1493 to 1519. The easy intimacy of the usual appellation, "Kaiser Max," in itself indicates the popular attitude toward this illustrious prince of the house of Hapsburg. The mass of legendary material with its accompanying variations and additions which has been handed down through the years testifies that many in German lands have told and retold stories of "the last Knight."

As is true in similar cases, a large part of the tradition that grew up about the figure of Maximilian during and after his death was purely oral. It passed from mouth to mouth among the common people until it acquired the color and variety and romance which only the co-operation of innumerable imaginative spirits and the play of generations of folk-minds can produce. The figure of Kaiser Max thus came to shine in a warm glow of feeling. A tradition of this kind becomes not so much a question of certain stories woven about a central character as a way of feeling about that character, a preconceived impression and a warm sensation of familiarity which is aroused when he is mentioned.

In the historical accounts of Maximilian or those in which he appears there are certain problems which always come to the front. He enjoyed the limelight on the stage of European politics for some forty-two years, and it is natural that many historians have sought to describe his life and activities and evaluate his personal character and political importance. He appears first as the young Archduke of Austria who goes to Flanders to become the husband of the variously attractive Mary of Burgundy and thereby an obstacle to French territorial policy; then as King of the Romans he secures the succession for the Hapsburg house; and finally, at the death of his father, Friedrich III, becomes emperor, although with only half a title:[1] at all these stages Maximilian has indeed furnished history with material of an interesting and controversial nature. He has often been praised and often denounced; and although the things he did have long been a matter of record, there has never been complete agreement on why he did them.

While the wider political aspects of Maximilian's reign form only a part of the material from which legends have arisen, they did much to stimulate popular fancy both among contemporaries and later. For succeeding generations the interpretation by historians has been of influence on the creation of the figure of the emperor as he appears in German literature. It is necessary, therefore, to give brief consideration to his personality and character as it has appeared in German history.

The character and motives of Maximilian, like those of Wallenstein, vary widely in the minds of different historians. This was indicated by Leopold von Ranke as early as 1824 when he said: "Maximilian was a prince of whom indeed we possess many portraits, yet in such a way that one seldom resembles another."[2] On the whole two quite different pictures have been drawn. Many well-known historians have been more interested in investigating moot questions of more purely historical interest than in settling what kind of a man Maximilian was. Even in the nearest approach to a biography that we have, Ulmann's *Kaiser Maximilian I*,[3] there is too much reliance on questionable sources;[4] while in other works the suspicion arises that here and there the interpretation of his

---

[1] Maximilian was never crowned emperor by the pope in Rome, but assumed the title of Roman Kaiser-Elect, with the consent of the pope, in Trent on February 4, 1508. Cf. Christoph Friedrich Stälin, "Bericht über die Annahme der Kaiserwürde durch Maximilian im Jahre 1508," *Forschungen zur deutschen Geschichte*, I (1862), 67-73.

[2] "Maximilian war ein Fürst, von dem wir zwar viele Bildnisse haben, doch so, daß selten eines dem andern gleicht." "Geschichten der romanischen und germanischen Völker von 1494-1514," *Sämmtliche Werke* (2. Aufl., Leipzig: Duncker u. Humblot, 1874), XXXIII, 70.

[3] Heinrich Ulmann, *Kaiser Maximilian I*. 2 Bde.; Stuttgart, 1884-1891. Cf. Andreas Walther, "Die neuere Beurteilung Kaiser Maximilians I," *Mitteilungen des Instituts für österreichische Geschichte*, XXXIII (1912), 347; and the review of Ulmann's book by Theodor Lindner, *ibid.*, VI (1885), 166-169.

[4] E.g., the account of J. Grünpeck regarding languages, Ulmann, *op. cit.*, I, 192.

character has been influenced by a desire to prove this or that political theory.[5]

Such differences of historical opinion are observed already in material handed down by writers contemporary with Maximilian. In that day a writer might be strongly influenced by his relationship to the court. A courtier judged differently from a common burgher, and a humanistic poet's point of view varied widely from that of a foreign diplomat. Thus we find only complimentary remarks in the biography of Maximilian by Joseph Grünpeck, a humanistic poet, teacher, astronomer, physician, and secretary, who was at various times in the employ of the emperor. Grünpeck gives a glowing account of the manly disposition and exceptional talents of the child Max. He tells how, in competition with the children of the nobility whom his father chose to play and study with him, the boy Max excelled in all kinds of games, as well as in all lessons, orations, and every sort of memory work.[6]

Grünpeck's work was written during the emperor's lifetime and was read by Max. After the latter's death this picture is completely reversed by Johannes Cuspinianus, likewise a humanistic scholar who spent some time in the employ of the Kaiser. According to his account, Max was not only a poor student, but until he was nine years old he could hardly speak, so that it was thought by many that he would be a mute, to the great sorrow of his mother.[7]

The oratorical powers which Grünpeck lauds in the boy Max evoke still greater praise for the man, whose gift of eloquence was such that Eitelwolf von Stein, the representative of the Mark of Brandenburg at the Diet of Constance in 1507, wrote home a glowing description of his speech.[8] It was said by Fugger, the author of the laudatory work on the house of Austria and distantly

[5] E.g., Ed. Ziehen, *Mittelrhein und Reich im Zeitalter der Reichsreform 1356-1504.* 2 Bde., Frankfurt a. M., 1934, 1937.

[6] Joseph Grünpeck, "Die Geschichte Friedrichs III und Maximilians I." Übersetzt von Dr. Th. Ilgen. *Die Geschichtschreiber der deutschen Vorzeit in deutscher Bearbeitung,* XC (Leipzig, 1891), 33ff. For a detailed account of Grünpeck's account of Maximilian, cf. pp. 23-35, below.

[7] Johannes Cuspinianus, *De Caesaribus atque imperatoribus Romanis* (Basileae, per Ioannem Oporinum, n.d.), p. 602. For further details, cf. pp. 23-35, below.

[8] Quoted by Johannes Janssen, *History of the German People at the Close of the Middle Ages.* Second English Edition, Revised (London, 1905), I, 234.

connected with that house by marriage, that Maximilian could recall deserting soldiers in time of trouble merely by his eloquence, while his personal charm always sufficed to animate his *Landsknechte* on the field as well as win over the princes at the Diets.[9]

These reports are, however, opposed by others which picture Max's eloquence as much less persuasive. Thus it is asserted by the burgher Georg Kirchmair that upon his retreat from Milan in 1516, Max made a speech to his rebellious *Landsknechte*, but that they would not even listen to him,[10] whereupon he fled in the night over the Alps to Germany. Also the same chronicler declares that at Stuhlweissenburg Max' powers were insufficient to keep his victorious soldiers from pillaging the stricken town and deserting back to Germany with their loot.

It is not certain just how good a soldier Max was. A city chronicler tells us that he won the respect and devotion of his men by his open comradeship,[11] and a representative of the nobility, Sigmund von Herberstein, testifies to his refusal to desert his men in trouble.[12] He was a great knight, who often broke lances with any opponent, and almost always won. We hear from Wilwolt von Schaumburg, a knight in Maximilian's service, that at Worms in 1495 Max was the only man who would accept the challenge of the French knight, Claude de Barre, and that although the latter was a man of prodigious strength, Max defeated him.[13] Yet in the *Mémoires* of Olivier de la Marche, an official at Maximilian's Burgundian court, we read of the emperor's indecision and slowness in action, qualities quite out of keeping with good generalship.[14] The Florentine ambassador, Vettori, pictures him as failing

---

[9] Sigmund von Birken, *Spiegel der Ehren des Höchstlöblichsten Kayser- und Königlichen Erzhauses Oesterreich . . . durch . . . Johann Jacob Fugger* (Nürnberg/ Bey Michael und Johann Friderich Endtern, 1668), p. 1368. Referred to hereafter as *Fugger-Birken*, or simply as *Ehrenspiegel*.

[10] "Georg Kirchmairs Denkwürdigkeiten seiner Zeit. 1519-1553." *Fontes Rerum Austriacarum*, I (1855), 437ff.

[11] *Heinrich Hugs Villinger Chronik von 1495 bis 1533*, hrsg. von Ch. Roder. "Bibliothek des litterarischen Vereins in Stuttgart" (referred to hereafter as "Stuttgart. Lit. Ver."), CLXIV (1883), 63.

[12] "Sigmund von Herbersteins Selbstbiographie," *Deutsche Selbstzeugnisse*, IV, 159 ("Die deutsche Literatur," Reihe 25).

[13] *Die Geschichten und Taten Wilwolts von Schaumburg*, "Stuttgart. Lit. Ver.," L (1859), 156f.

[14] "Mémoires de Messire Olivier de la Marche." *Collection complète des mémoires*

in his martial undertakings because of his habit of keeping his plans to himself and not confiding them to his generals.[15]

In addition to the characteristics cited, according to his admirers Max enjoyed about every virtue worth possessing. Wilibald Pirckheimer, the scholarly Nuremberg patrician, describes him as patient and calm of temper, even in the face of defeat.[16] Sebastian Franck, the chronicler from Donauwörth, records that for the preservation of justice he had "einn hitz vnd eyfer" unexcelled among contemporary monarchs.[17] The Augsburg burgher Wilhelm Rem adds that his anger always cooled off so quickly that it did not influence his decisions.[18] He was likewise merciful and forgiving, and, if we believe Jean Molinet, the chronicler and canon from Valenciennes, of a modest and humble disposition.[19] He so loved peace and fought so unwillingly that it became a proverb among the soldiers that "Maximilian would make a good pope, and Julius (II) a good Kaiser."[20] Luther had occasion to speak often of Maximilian's temperance[21] as well as of his great courtesy.[22] And withal Max was a merry fellow, who loved to dance with the burghers' daughters and wives and who could take a joke good-naturedly when one was played on him.[23]

Nevertheless, others say that Max was not so even-tempered. It was a familiar sign of his displeasure, we read in the *Zimmerische*

---

relatifs à l'histoire de France, depuis le règne de Philippe-Auguste, jusqu'au commencement du dix-septième siècle, par M. Petitot (Paris, 1825), Tome X, Sér. 1, p. 450.

[15] *The Historical, Political, and Diplomatic Writings of Niccolo Machiavelli.* Translated from the Italian by Christian E. Detmold (4 vols.; Boston, 1882), IV, 108 (Feb. 8, 1508).

[16] *Wilibald Pirckheimers Schweizerkrieg,* hrsg. von Karl Rück (München, 1895), p. 119.

[17] Sebastian Franck, *Germania* (Bern, 1539), fo. 276.

[18] Wilhelm Rem, "Cronica newer geschichten," *Chroniken der deutschen Städte,* XXV (1896), 71.

[19] "Chroniques de Jean Molinet," publiées par J.-A. Buchon, *Collection des chroniques nationales françaises,* XLV (Paris, 1828), III, 79.

[20] Sebastian Franck, *Chronica: Zeytbuch vnd Geschichtbibel,* etc. . . . (1565), II, fo. 227-b.

[21] *D. Martin Luthers Werke. Kritische Gesamtausgabe: Tischreden* (Weimar), IV (1916), 15; VI (1921), 292.

[22] *Ibid.,* IV, 264, 265.

[23] *Chroniken der deutschen Städte,* XI (1872), 503, 722f.

Chronik, that the veins grew red and stood out on his neck,[24] while we find evidence in the official acts of the day that nothing made him quite so angry as infringements of the hunting laws.[25] Although we learn from Pirckheimer in the reference above that Max could forget quickly a defeat or humiliation, we are led by Machiavelli to believe that it was not so much because of his mild disposition and calm good nature as because of his fickleness and changeableness, for by the time one plan had failed, he was usually already busy with a different one anyway, and had long since lost interest in the first.[26] As for his zeal in administering justice, we read in the *Zimmerische Chronik* how sometimes years would pass with repeated promises from Maximilian to attend to a case; yet such long and inexcusable delays would intervene that the plaintiff might die before anything was done, and his children must renew the plea.[27] The Augsburg merchant Lucas Rem even refused to try to get justice, declaring that he knew beforehand that such an attempt would be useless with Kaiser Max.[28] Merciful and forgiving he might be to some, but a historical folksong describes him also as the stern commander, sentencing a score of men to die by the sword and standing calmly by watching the execution until someone braves his anger and pleads for mercy for them.[29] For even as a young man, an unknown Flemish chronicler tells us, he repeatedly refused to grant pardon, though besought on bended knee.[30] Finally, although temperance was his watchword,[31] his table was always set most sumptuously, as he himself is eager to

---

[24] *Zimmerische Chronik,* IV, 354. In "Stuttgart. Lit. Ver.," XCIV (Tübingen, 1869).

[25] Quoted by H. J. Zeibig, "Der Ausschuss-Landtag der gesammten österreichischen Erblande zu Innsbruck 1518," *Archiv für Kunde österreichischer Geschichts-Quellen,* XIII (1854), 242f. The same characteristic is mentioned by Kirchmair, *op. cit.,* p. 442.

[26] Machiavelli, *op. cit.,* IV, 402f. (1509).

[27] *Zimmerische Chronik,* I, 550 ("Stuttgart. Lit. Ver.," XCI); and II, 59, 72, 90 ("Stuttgart. Lit. Ver.," XCIV).

[28] *Tagebuch des Lucas Rem aus den Jahren 1494-1541,* mitgetheilt von B. Greiff (Augsburg, 1861), p. 20.

[29] Cf. Rochus von Liliencron, *Die historischen Volkslieder der Deutschen vom 13. bis 16. Jahrhundert* (Leipzig, 1865-1869), II, 549-556.

[30] Translated by Octave Delepierre as *Chronique des faits et gestes admirables de Maximilian 1er* (Bruxelles, 1839: quoted hereafter as "Delepierre."), pp. 123, 137.

[31] Cf. Luther, *Tischreden,* IV, 15.

state in his *Weisskunig*;[32] and his death, like that of his father, is reported to have been hastened by partaking immoderately of melons![33]

While his generosity appears a virtue to a Nuremberg chronicler,[34] to the English statesman, Pace, it is not liberality, but prodigality and extravagance.[35] Moreover it frequently happens that the gifts he distributes with lavish hand are given so easily, we hear, because someone else is bearing the expense, like the pension he so magnanimously granted a girl for her services to the city of St. Omer,[36] or the pension and exemption from taxes bestowed upon Dürer in Nuremberg.[37] In both cases it was the city which had to pay. At times confusion arose because property was granted to one person when it already belonged to another.[38]

Grünpeck made much of the Kaiser's ability to tell a man's character at a glance, which enabled him to make the best choice of servants.[39] This claim is denied by countless references to the corruption of his councillors, who cheated and circumvented him at every opportunity.[40] Maximilian himself is accused by English statesmen of that time of being easily accessible to bribery and undependable in the matter of money entrusted to him.[41] Stories by a Flemish chronicler of Max' religious zeal and pious spirit[42] are matched by others from Luther's *Tischreden* concerning the Kaiser's superstition[43] and disregard for human life.[44]

In the appraisal of Maximilian's intellectual attainments there

---

[32] In *Jahrbücher der Kunsthistorischen Sammlungen des allerhöchsten Kaiserhauses* (quoted hereafter as *Jahrb. k.-h. Samml.*), VI (Wien, 1888), 82.
[33] Pontus Heuterus, *Opera* (Lovanii, 1643), III, 178.
[34] *Chroniken der deutschen Städte*, XI (1872), 731.
[35] *Letters and Papers, Foreign and Domestic, of the Reign of Henry VIII*, arranged and catalogued by J. Sherren Brewer (referred to hereafter as *Letters and Papers*), (London, 1862), II, Part I, 570, no. 1964; 594, no. 2016; 598, no. 2024.
[36] Delepierre, *op. cit.*, p. 391.
[37] *Jahrb. k.-h. Samml.* (Wien), X (1889), xxxvi, Reg. 5789; xl, Reg. 5810; xliv, Reg. 5826, etc.
[38] *Zimmerische Chronik*, I, 544 ("Stuttgart. Lit. Ver.," XCI).
[39] Grünpeck, *op. cit.*, pp. 65f.
[40] Wilhelm Rem, *op. cit.*, p. 99; Kirchmair, *op. cit.*, p. 441; Franck, *Germania*, fo. 231-b, 232; etc.
[41] *Letters and Papers*, II, Part I, 517, 531, 570, 598, 721.
[42] Delepierre, *op. cit.*, p. 226.
[43] *Tischreden*, II, 634.
[44] *Ibid.*, V, 31.

is also disagreement. Cuspinianus tells us of his exceptional memory which, in spite of the bad start with a poor teacher, helped him in later years to acquire an excellent education, including a good knowledge of several languages.[45] Philippe de Commines, however, who left the service of Charles of Burgundy for that of Louis XI of France, declared that Max was raised in complete ignorance, so that when he came to Burgundy at the age of eighteen to marry the heiress of that country he knew absolutely nothing.[46] Indeed, while the majority of commentators readily accept as a fact the statement that Maximilian commanded at least seven languages, the emperor's own notes indicate that he may have been over-estimated here also.[47]

With such a variety of opinions on the character of one man, one may well inquire whom to believe. Nor is it strange that there should be many conflicting accounts. Any figure in high position and power is bound to have both friends and enemies, and the friendly or hostile feelings he inspires will leave their imprint on subsequent delineations of his character. In sorting out the material available, the historian has the task of selecting and rejecting until he has assembled a consistent character-picture. Let us see what attitudes some modern writers have assumed toward the character of Maximilian.

As early as 1783 H. Hegewisch, a professor in Kiel, defended Maximilian against foreign historians, no single one of whom, he declared, did justice to the Kaiser, and none of whom was so severe and so unjust as Robertson.[48] William Robertson, a Scotch historian who openly followed the enlightened historical school of Voltaire, succeeded usually in overcoming his Protestant prejudices in his historical writings. In the case of Maximilian, however, these prejudices may have influenced his judgment. In connection with his treatment of the Spanish succession Robertson called Max "always enterprising and decisive in council, though feeble and

---

[45] Cuspinianus, *op. cit.*, pp. 602ff.
[46] *Mémoires de Philippe de Commynes.* Nouvelle édition publiée . . . par B. De Mandrot (Paris, 1901, 1903), II, 16.
[47] *Jahrb. k.-h. Samml.*, VI (1887), 463.
[48] H. Hegewisch, *Geschichte der Regierung Kaiser Maximilians des Ersten* (2 Teile; Hamburg u. Kiel, 1782, 1783), II, 186.

dilatory in execution. . . ." "The emperor, as usual, asserted his rights in a high strain, promised a great deal, and performed nothing."[49] He adds that Max' conduct had always been "feeble and unsteady" (p.70), and finally (p. 69) calls Maximilian's death "an occurrence of small importance in itself, for he was a prince conspicuous neither for his virtues, nor his power, nor his abilities."

Hegewisch, who is important only in that his is the first history devoted specifically to Maximilian, has nothing but praise for the emperor. In his description of the latter's physical and intellectual accomplishments the influence of Grünpeck, Cuspinianus, and Pirckheimer can be clearly seen. He lauds Maximilian's resoluteness, which, he says, was so strong that he would permit damage to himself in order to satisfy his honor. Hegewisch mentions only the fault that Max often halted with a project which he had begun with enthusiasm, merely because a new object had seized his imagination. Also, he says, Maximilian was no economist. But in comparison with a monarch of much greater material resources, such as Francis I of France, Max comes out fairly well.[50] Finally, says Hegewisch:[51]

> In regard to his social character, Maximilian was amiable, condescending, friendly, talkative; he knew how to win all hearts. He liked a joke and could take one on himself. In spite of the vivacity of his temperament, he still let no one about him feel his displeasure, not even at the most annoying occurrences. The impression which bad news made upon him was soon completely eradicated. By his fine manners he distinguished himself markedly from his contemporaries. Drunkenness was intolerable to him.

Hegewisch's characterization is quite representative for subsequent historians. These are the traits which first arrest their attention: Maximilian's splendid talents; his excellent education, gained chiefly by himself; his surpassing excellence in all physical exercises of the time; an equal excellence in all intellectual fields, and the works which he himself wrote or inspired others to write;

---

[49] William Robertson, *The History of the Reign of the Emperor Charles V* (London, 1774), II, 23. This was written in 1769.
[50] Hegewisch, *op. cit.*, II, 186.
[51] *Ibid.*, II, 187.

his proficiency in military technic; his bold deeds, especially on the hunt; and finally his personal virtues.[52]

Not only Hegewisch rose to protect the memory of Maximilian from the criticism of Robertson. A countryman of the latter, William Coxe, a quarter of a century later (1807) in a popularly conceived *History of the House of Austria*[53] also declared that the Kaiser had been too much depreciated by modern historians, that both Robertson and Hume[54] had treated the character of Max with unmerited contempt, and that Roscoe, misled by these authorities and by the prejudices of the Italian historians, had described him without a single virtue or good quality and stamped his character as a compound of vanity, imbecility, and bigotry.[55] Maximilian, Coxe declares, was in spite of these reports a remarkable person, and so superior to his age that he was the admiration of many of his contemporaries. If his means had equaled his abilities and if his spirit and active mind had been more guided by judgment and discretion, his reign would have been a very brilliant one in the history of the house of Austria.

---

[52] Among the sources which Hegewisch used for his picture of Maximilian there are several which form the regular stock-in-trade for historians down through the Nineteenth Century. To mention only the most pertinent, he refers to Pontus Heuterus, Fugger-Birken, Machiavelli, and Guicciardini. However, there is only a faint trace mentioned of the adverse Italian criticism, i.e., that he often left one project for another. Practically everything said about Max here can be found either in Heuterus, *Historica Omnia: Bvrgvndica, Avstriaca, Belgica*, etc. (Lovanii, 1643), III, 179-180, 364ff., or in *Fugger-Birken, op. cit.*, pp. 766ff., 1367-1383, who used Heuterus also. Heuterus in turn used Cuspinianus and Grünpeck, among others.

[53] Third Edition; London, 1847, I, 397.

[54] David Hume, in *The History of England* (A New Edition, 8 vols.; London, 1802) in 1759, had spoken in some ways not too unkindly of Maximilian (e.g., III, 415, 434); but he had also mentioned his "levity of character" (III, 415), that of money he was "very greedy, very prodigal, and very indigent" (IV, 11); and in describing his death called him "a man who, of himself, was indeed of little consequence" (IV, 18).

[55] William Roscoe, a pupil of Hume, and like him and Robertson a follower of the school of Voltaire in England, speaks of Max in *The Life and Pontificate of Leo the Tenth* (4 vols.; Philadelphia, 1805-1806) as "that mean and crafty sovereign" (II, 243); and after berating him for his "weak and fluctuating character" (IV, 26), he adds (IV, 27): "An ostentatious vanity, and an inordinate desire of fame, were accompanied by an imbecility of mind that frustrated all his purposes, and rendered his magnificence contemptible, and his pretensions to heroism absurd. His whole life was employed to demonstrate how insignificant the first monarchy in Christendom might be rendered by the want or the misapplication of the personal talents of the sovereign; and his death was of no other importance than as it opened the way to a successour, who might vindicate the imperial dignity from disgrace, and restore to it that influence in the affairs of Europe which Maximilian had lost."

In this same year (1807) Maximilian was made the subject of one of a series of historical essays on Austrian men of note by Joseph Freiherr von Hormayr.[56] Hormayr's writings follow the patriotic purpose of glorifying his Austrian home-land, but the fact that they were very popular justifies his mention here. His account is not different from that of Hegewisch, except in that he goes to greater lengths and uses much more flowery terms in the description of Maximilian's virtues. Thus he expands on the Kaiser's regal appearance (pp. 149f.), his ardent temperament (p. 150), and his tremendous energy (p. 151). The failure of many well thought-out plans of Max he lays to the lack of money, which in turn he ascribes to a virtue, his generosity (p. 155). He tells with relish several familiar adventures of the Kaiser (pp. 156f.), lauds his ability to speak nine different languages (p. 171), praises him for improvements and reforms (pp. 172-176), and finally defends him vigorously against foreign historians who accused Max of fickleness in his unions and treaties (pp. 185f.).

In the descriptions by Ranke[57] a generation later we meet more historic prudence and in general a more careful statement of facts based on a scholarly examination of a greater range of material. Whereas Hegewisch, for instance, had used only printed materials, Ranke's use of unpublished sources has earned for him the name of the greatest master of the philological-critical method in the writing of history.[58] Still, Ranke's account of Maximilian's character is also entirely favorable, for his adverse criticism is directed toward political and not personal characteristics. Indeed, he even attributes to these personal qualities of Maximilian the fact that he so long enjoyed the fame of having founded the constitution of the empire;[59] and he says that Max' reputation came from these characteristics: his health, strength, memory, intelligence, inventiveness, ability to pick servants, the right feeling for every situation—"a personality in general which awakened admiration and

---

[56] No. 10 of his *Österreichischer Plutarch* (Wien, 1807), V, 86-186.
[57] Ranke, *op. cit.*, pp. 70ff.; and *Deutsche Geschichte im Zeitalter der Reformation* (Gesamt-Ausgabe, hrsg. von P. Joachimsen; München, 1925), I, 253-257. The latter was first printed in 1839-1847.
[58] Eduard Fueter, *Geschichte der neueren Historiographie* (München u. Berlin, 1936), pp. 478ff. Cf. Franz X. Wegele, *Geschichte der deutschen Historiographie seit dem Auftreten des Humanismus* (München u. Leipzig, 1885), p. 919.
[59] *Deutsche Geschichte im Zeitalter der Reformation*, I, 253.

devotion and which gave the people something to talk about."⁶⁰ Ranke does deny the truth of the point of view which sees Max as the organizer of national reforms.⁶¹ But while he must admit that the emperor served rather dynastic than national ends, he excuses him by calling it an unavoidable result of the political situation.⁶² It is plain that Ranke is warmly sympathetic with the figure of the Kaiser, and in spite of his criticism of the latter's political policies, a slightly romantic hue tinges his picture of Max the man.⁶³

In the same year as the first volume of Ranke's *Deutsche Geschichte im Zeitalter der Reformation* (1839) there appeared in Paris a collection of the correspondence between Maximilian and his daughter, Margaret of Austria, to which was appended by the editor, Le Glay, a biographical sketch of the emperor.⁶⁴ In this *Notice* the author, although a Frenchman, appears as one of the first to assemble a more complete picture of Maximilian. He too is familiar with the sources of Hegewisch and Ranke, and he recounts most of the things that they have said in favor of the Kaiser. But he knows also the sources which have unfavorable things to say; and although Ranke knew them also,⁶⁵ Le Glay does not skip over them. Thus he quotes Machiavelli at length (II, 419) and dwells in detail on Maximilian's illegitimate children (II, 415). Yet he presents both sides fairly, even protesting that the historians of his own nation had judged Max too severely, for he was able, after all, to hold his own among the clever and unscrupulous monarchs of his time (II, 419). Here too we read more anecdotes about Maximilian than we are accustomed to meet assembled in one place, and we find a quotation from the librarian of the Royal Court Library, Lambecius, on the long list of books which the emperor himself is supposed to have written.

---

⁶⁰ *Ibid.*, I, 254.
⁶¹ *Ibid.*, I, 85, 134f., 253.
⁶² *Ibid.*, I, 356.
⁶³ Wegele pointed out this tendency, *op. cit.*, p. 1044.
⁶⁴ André J. G. Le Glay, *Correspondance de l'empereur Maximilien Ier et de Marguerite d'Autriche, etc.* (Paris, 1839). Cf. II, 385-421: "Notice sur Maximilien Ier, Empereur d'Allemagne."
⁶⁵ Ranke refers, but casually, to the unfavorable details mentioned by Machiavelli. Cf. *Geschichte der romanischen und germanischen Völker*, p. 72.

Interest in Maximilian outside of Germany was further manifested in this year by a staunch defender of the Kaiser, the Fleming, Octave Delepierre. In 1839 he published a French translation of a Flemish chronicle of 1577, which had recently been brought to the attention of the public because of its extreme rarity;[66] and in his introduction he defends Maximilian stoutly against most of the things that had been said in his disfavor.[67] In the eyes of Delepierre, Max was unfortunate in having to follow in Burgundy the grand figure of Charles the Bold and to fight Louis XI. His "nobles sentiments" themselves were the source of what have been called his faults, says the author (p. ii); his financial difficulties were the result of the conditions he found in Burgundy (p. iii). He refers to his piety, to his touching grief at the death of his young wife (p. vi), and to proofs that he was a man of courage and honor (p. vii). In the end, he says, "all accusations directed against him are reduced to this, that he was prodigal, that he deserved the name of *sans-argent*, that he had a romantic and improvident spirit." And these accusations he calls futile in view of the grave events of his reign (p. vii).

The more properly Flemish view, however, and contrary to that of Delepierre, is expressed by the Fleming Kervyn de Lettenhove, who in his *Histoire de Flandre*[68] in 1850 does about everything he can to disparage the emperor's character. When necessary to admit anything complimentary, concerning Max' courage for example, he does so grudgingly or else he qualifies his praise in some way.[69] In portraying the struggles between Flanders and Max, his sympathies are always with the former,[70] which of course can be considered only natural in view of the author's nationality; and in a

---

[66] By M. Auguste Voisin, *Notice sur le seul exemplaire connu d'un livre intitulé: Die wonderlycke oorloghen van den doorluchtighen hooghgheboren prince, keyser Maximiliaen, hoe hy hier eerst int landt quam, ende hoe hy vrou marien trowde. Édition de 1577.* (Without date or place.)

[67] Delepierre, *op. cit.*, Introduction, pp. i-xi.

[68] Vol. V, "Ducs de Bourgogne" (Bruxelles, 1850).

[69] E.g., *op. cit.*, p. 310, concerning the battle of Térouane: "Il avait montré du courage dans cette journée; mais la faiblesse et l'incertitude qui formaient l'un des traits principaux de son caractère se reproduisirent presque aussitôt, trop promptes à étouffer les inspirations d'une énergie momentanée."

[70] Thus in describing Max' captivity in Bruges, *ibid.*, V, 400ff.

question of who was to blame he does not hesitate a moment to attack the "bad faith of the King of the Romans."[71]

German authors, however, continue to emphasize the good side of the Kaiser. Two works purporting to be histories of Kaiser Maximilian appeared within twenty years of each other, in 1850 and 1870, both unmistakably in the romantic tradition. The first of these is the *Geschichte des Kaisers Maximilian des Ersten* by Karl Haltaus, a book quite devoid of all adverse opinions. This writer gives Maximilian credit for all the virtues ever claimed for him and in addition he uses some of the stories told about the Kaiser as if they had actually happened, not bothering to indicate their anecdotal nature. If he was acquainted with the Italian sources at all, he was at least uninfluenced by them, for he gives no space to the Kaiser's faults whatever.[72] The second work, by Karl Klüpfel, is a popular treatment, in which the author acknowledges that he can not boast about Maximilian's political successes nor their consequences for Germany;[73] but he dwells with pleasure on the emperor's figure, tells some of the tallest stories of the *Teuerdank* as if they were fully authenticated (p. 73), and clearly indicates his sympathy for the romantic Kaiser, whom he calls "the last heroic figure of the Middle Ages" (p. 202).

In historical works from now on Max is considered in varying lights. Droysen, the founder of the Prussian school of historians,[74] speaks of Maximilian's splendid spirit, his pleasure in all sorts of ventures, large or small, of his "incomparable talent for handling and winning people."[75] To Droysen this is important in that Max used his power to raise national and patriotic hopes and to direct all forces toward fulfilling his dynastic ambitions.[76] Thus, says Droysen, it is uncontested that his influence in the empire was

---

[71] *Ibid.*, V, 454.
[72] Karl Haltaus, *Geschichte des Kaisers Maximilian des Ersten*, Leipzig, 1850. This book is in keeping with Haltaus' conception of Max some years earlier in the introduction to his edition of the *Teuerdank* (Quedlinburg u. Leipzig, 1836), p. 95, where he speaks of "sein, für alles Gute und Edle glühendes Herz." Also cf. p. 107.
[73] Karl Klüpfel, *Kaiser Maximilian I.* (neue Ausgabe; Berlin, 1870), p. 202.
[74] Cf. Fueter, *op. cit.*, pp. 492ff.
[75] Joh. Gust. Droysen, *Geschichte der preussischen Politik* (Leipzig, 1868), II, 1. Abt., 362.
[76] *Ibid.*, II, 1. Abt., 362.

greater than that of any Kaiser for a long time before him; but having influence is not the same as ruling, and the hopes awakened in the people could never be satisfied by Maximilian's policies.[77]

The Kaiser's romantic nature is emphasized by Victor von Kraus, an Austrian specialist in the history of Maximilian's time, who declares that he "was and remained all his life an impractical dreamer who never, or at least never at the right time, understood how to reckon with the material needs of the world or with the people about him."[78]

Gothein, a student particularly of the history of the Reformation and of the popular movements of that period, sees Maximilian as one of the true children of the Renaissance in his desire to develop and express his individuality. Max considered the only permanent aim of all his striving to be the purely personal fame which would remain after his death.[79] To this end, says Gothein, he used and publicized every conceivable opportunity: the so-called *Kreuzwunder*,[80] the miraculous story of two stags and a pheasant coming to pay him homage,[81] the terrible plague of the "bösen Blätter."[82] All were used in a continuous campaign to win public opinion. Just this, declares Gothein, was the trouble with Maximilian's popularity. It was not the popularity of a statesman among his people, *dem Volk*, but with a sum of separate individuals, *dem Publikum*.[83]

A romantic-nationalistic point of view and an uncritical method of writing cultural history were placed in the services of confessional tendencies in the writings of the historian Johannes Janssen.[84] To the Catholic Janssen, the Catholic Kaiser appears to have been much less egoistic than the picture by Gothein would indicate. "The most gratifying thing about this activity," says Janssen,

---

[77] *Ibid.*, II, 2. Abt., 24f.
[78] Victor von Kraus, *Maximilians I. vertraulicher Briefwechsel mit Sigmund Prüschenk Freiherrn zu Stettenberg* (Innsbruck, 1875), p. 20.
[79] Eberhard Gothein, *Politische und religiöse Volksbewegungen vor der Reformation* (Breslau, 1878), p. 54.
[80] *Ibid.*, pp. 89, 96f.
[81] *Ibid.*, p. 97. Cf. Jos. Chmel in "Stuttgart. Lit. Ver.," X, 185.
[82] v. Kraus, *op. cit.*, p. 103.
[83] *Ibid.*, p. 56.
[84] Cf. Fueter, *op. cit.*, pp. 571ff.

referring in particular to Maximilian's contributions to historical research, "was that everything which he did, untiringly and self-sacrificingly, for the dissemination and extension of historical-antiquarian knowledge followed the higher purpose: to arouse patriotism and 'to make the native land dear to all.' "[85] In like strain Janssen paints with only the brightest colors the character of the Kaiser.[86] Often he quotes from the humanists, Max' most avowed admirers,[87] who never had aught but good to say of him. When he does refer to authors of less complimentary remarks, he quotes only the favorable things they said, or else softens their reproaches by emphasis on their more laudatory passages.[88]

By far the most comprehensive work on Kaiser Maximilian I is the two-volume biography by Heinrich Ulmann, an industrious historian of the philological school. Here is assembled the majority of the opinions, favorable and unfavorable, of Maximilian's character. In his delineation of Max' political life, Ulmann presents rather the unfavorable aspects, a circumstance which in its turn caused much criticism of the author.[89] In considering Maximilian's relation to art, literature, and science, however, Ulmann's praise is not stinted. He does still give both sides of the picture; but he also allows credence to those reports which we know to be not the most reliable[90] and thus by his very comprehensiveness leaves the picture more blurred than clear.

A short time after Ulmann and in the same vein as that writer, Friedrich von Bezold, a highly regarded student and historian of

---

[85] Johannes Janssen, *Geschichte des deutschen Volkes* (17. u. 18. Aufl.; Freiburg i. B., 1897), I, 159.

[86] *Ibid.*, I, 591-598.

[87] E.g., Trithemius, I, 157, 593; Wimpheling, I, 157, 159; Scaliger, I, 162; Coccinius, I, 598; Brant, I, 597, etc.

[88] Thus Machiavelli, Vettori, I, 594f. Moreover he achieves an undue effect by quoting Anshelm as "ein Gegner des habsburgischen Hauses," I, 593. Anshelm, writing as an old man for the Bernese council, was after all born a Swabian and often expresses his own opinions. Cf. Wegele, *op. cit.*, pp. 292f.

[89] E.g., by A. Bachmann, cf. A. Walther, *op. cit., Mitteilungen des Instituts für österreichische Geschichtsforschung*, XXXIII (1912), 322 and note 2. The first volume of Ulmann's work was also criticized sharply by Th. Lindner, *ibid.*, VI (1885), 166-169, and the second volume even more severely by H. Huber, *ibid.*, XII (1892), 349-352. The latter's objection to the complicated style, by the way, is well justified.

[90] E.g., Grünpeck, I, 192, 197; *Weisskunig*, I, 192f.

the Reformation in Germany, expressed the greatest admiration for Maximilian as a popular figure,[91] for his abilities in military affairs (I, 69f.), and for his many and varied interests and true powers of observation (I, 224). But he likewise uses the strongest language in illustrating his faults: his unreliability in all political matters (I, 66); his unscrupulous use of any land or party for dynastic interests; and finally his " incomprehensible faithlessness" (I, 68), which led him to falsehood and even to forgery, in fact, to anything which would raise more money (I, 69).

The principal impression created by Ulmann and Bezold was, on the whole, to emphasize Maximilian's unfavorable characteristics. A monograph on the emperor by Eduard Heyck followed the lead of Ulmann but sought a new point by emphasizing Maximilian's vivacious nature as an inheritance from his Portuguese mother.[92] This in turn was the cause of his changeableness and his tremendous energy, the despair of his councillors and all foreign ambassadors (pp. 26f.). This vivacity, says Heyck, served to create for Max a kind of popularity, while it really concealed his lack of inner superiority (pp. 29f.).

These later depreciations of Maximilian called forth new champions in the style of Johannes Janssen. Even in the United States, a devout churchman, William Stang, arose to defend the Kaiser's reputation in a romantic and panegyrical effusion, which however probably left no effect on historical opinion.[93] In a school *Programm* in Brixen in 1892 Professor Hartmann Ammann objected to Ulmann's representation[94] and sketched a laudatory picture of his own, although not forgetting to temper it somewhat with an appraisal of the other side of the question.[95] In 1905 Max Jansen published in the collection *Weltgeschichte in Karakterbildern* a monograph[96] which treated the Kaiser in a popular manner and

[91] *Geschichte der deutschen Reformation* (Berlin, 1886), I, 63.
[92] Eduard Heyck, *Kaiser Maximilian I.* (Bielefeld u. Leipzig, 1898), p. 25. In *Monographien zur Weltgeschichte*, V.
[93] William Stang, "Emperor Maximilian I." *Catholic World*, XLII (1886), 660f.
[94] Hartmann Ammann, "Versuch einer Charakteristik Kaiser Maximilians I., seiner Regierungsthätigkeit und äusseren Politik," *XLII Programm des K. K. Gymnasiums zu Brixen* (Brixen, 1892), p. 1.
[95] *Ibid.*, pp. 4ff.
[96] Max Jansen, *Kaiser Maximilian I*, München, 1905.

which gained considerable significance in scholarly circles because of its public endorsement by a more important scholar of the Middle Ages, Kurt Kaser.[97] In his own delineation of Maximilian's character Kaser combined scholarly research with all the romantic enthusiasm of Ranke and Janssen.[98]

Several works in English mark a continued interest in Maximilian in the Twentieth Century. An essay by R. W. Seton-Watson is a popular and romantic treatment in the tradition of Janssen and leaves no doubt of the author's intention of glorifying his hero.[99] The interpretation of Ulmann is also echoed by Paul Van Dyke, who sets out in his *Renascence Portraits* to sketch Maximilian as a figure of the Renaissance.[100] Mrs. Marian Andrews likewise follows the Ulmann tradition in a romantic mood with her *Maximilian the Dreamer, Holy Roman Emperor 1459-1519* (London, 1913).

In latest times Maximilian's character has been presented to us in a work on the problem of the *Reichsreform* in Germany by Eduard Ziehen.[101] Since the author is definitely prejudiced in favor of Berthold von Mainz, with whose history he fills a major portion of his pages, he has nothing good to say for the Kaiser. Here, as Baron has remarked,[102] are "all the unfavorable opinions concerning Maximilian which have ever been expressed." In a way it is refreshing to see even an unfavorable viewpoint consistently maintained; it produces a bracing effect after reading one of the purely laudatory accounts. Nevertheless, the absence of any saving grace from the delineation of the Kaiser makes Ziehen appear too emphatically one-sided and too assiduously concerned with proving his thesis at Maximilian's expense.

This variety of opinions right up to our day demonstrates the influence of each writer's viewpoint on the resultant conception of Maximilian's character. This was indicated long ago by Gothein,

---

[97] In the *Mitteilungen des Instituts für österreichische Geschichtsforschung*, XXVI (1905), 616, in an article, "Die auswärtige Politik Maximilians I." (pp. 612-626).
[98] Kurt Kaser, *Deutsche Geschichte zur Zeit Maximilians I. (1486-1519)*, (Stuttgart u. Berlin, 1912), cf. pp. 11-17. This is Vol. 2 of *Deutsche Geschichte im Ausgange des Mittelalters (1438-1519)*.
[99] R. W. Seton-Watson, *Maximilian I. Holy Roman Emperor*, Westminster, 1902.
[100] Paul Van Dyke, *Renascence Portraits* (New York, 1905), pp. 259-375.
[101] Eduard Ziehen, *op. cit.*
[102] Hans Baron in the *American Historical Review*, XLIV (1939), 293-303.

who in reply to the accusation that he was idealizing the Kaiser, declared that one's judgment of Max must be different depending upon whether one considers him in connection with cultural movements of his time or as a statesman.[103] Most historians have been concerned with portraying him in the latter capacity. The accounts of Ranke and others show, however, that even the historians could maintain a sympathetic attitude toward the Kaiser's character while denying him certain political aptitudes. How much more distinct then is the halo about Maximilian's head to those who have no historical axe to grind! The common people who preserved the figure of Kaiser Max in their memory soon forgot his bad points while remembering his good ones, a circumstance not unusual after the death of a popular hero. From them we hear only of the great Kaiser Max, the strong fighter in battle against Germany's traditional enemies, or of Max as the greatest of all hunters, chasing the stag, the boar, or the bear, and following the chamois to dizzy heights which professional hunters dare not reach; a friend of the common burgher, who loved to take part in their dances and feasts and who knew how to work and play on familiar terms with them; who, in spite of his numberless activities, his wars and restless journeys, still had time for the great new movement in arts and letters, making its principal representatives his friends and councillors and contributing greatly to it himself—for his intellectual gifts were many, his knowledge universal.

As the foregoing indicates, the figure of Kaiser Maximilian is by no means fully clarified in German historiography. The differences of opinion concerning him can be traced back to his contemporaries and persist when he is viewed in the perspective of more than four centuries. His characteristics of personality were such as to both attract and repel the observers of his time. It seems evident that he possessed a certain romantic magnetism which made an objective judgment of his character difficult even for those who knew him best. Furthermore, he lived in an age when the humanists cultivated a style of exaggerated expression and were adept at weaving

---

[103] Eberhard Gothein, "Die Lage des Bauernstandes am Ende des Mittelalters, vornehmlich in Südwestdeutschland," *Westdeutsche Zeitschrift*, IV (1885), p. 20, note. Gothein was defending himself against Ulmann.

a nimbus about the head of one whom they sought to glorify. We have seen that even so cool and objective a historian as Ranke was not able to escape altogether the decorative picture drawn by these writers.

It is evident then that the legendary character in which the great Renaissance emperor appears in later centuries had its beginnings in his own lifetime. Before proceeding to investigate the development of these elements it will be desirable to examine in detail contemporary statements, both German and foreign, regarding his personal characteristics. We cannot expect that this will bring us to the real Maximilian, for he was evidently one of those personalities whose essence lies hidden even from intimate acquaintances; but we shall seek to approach the real figure as closely as the accounts of contemporaries permit and thus uncover the bases which served as a foundation for later conceptions of the Kaiser. Further light will then be sought in the *Volkslied* and *Spruch* of his time. We can then turn to Maximilian's works, for there is a strong suspicion that Max himself had considerable influence upon the genesis of his romantic portrait and its transmission to posterity. These are the materials out of which the legend of Maximilian was woven. Its extension will then be examined as it was developed in the anecdotes and similar literature of the Sixteenth Century. After investigating the origins and the formation of the Maximilian legend, we shall finally illustrate by examples its vitality, persistence, and further treatment in German literature.

II

MAXIMILIAN AS VIEWED BY HIS CONTEMPORARIES

A. German Sources

1. Contemporary historians and political writers

ONLY A RELATIVELY SMALL GROUP of contemporary historians and political writers contribute materially to form the picture of Maximilian. For although more and more scholars were beginning in just this period to devote their talents to historical studies, the majority gave but sketchy accounts of current events and seem to have had no interest in depicting personalities. There are among the emperor's contemporaries especially two men who form our main source of information, merely because they wrote the most: Joseph Grünpeck and Johannes Cuspinianus.[1] Judged by modern standards of history their works can not be considered of great value.[2] We are nevertheless interested in them here as contemporary accounts. Although both Grünpeck and Cuspinianus were in the employ of the Kaiser at various times, and without question created idealized images of their royal patron, their close acquaintance with him placed them in an excellent position to observe

---

[1] Joseph Grünpeck (cf. p. 5, above) was born at Burghausen am Inn in the third quarter of the Fifteenth Century; in 1497 he was private secretary to Maximilian and *Historicus kais. Majestät;* later he wandered about teaching humanistic subjects, dabbled in medicine and astrology, and wrote prophetic pamphlets. He died about 1532. Cf. the biographical sketch in the introduction to Grünpeck's *Die Gesch. Fried. III. und Max. I.*, pp. v-xix; and A. Czerny, "Der Humanist und Historiograph Kaiser Maximilians I. Joseph Grünpeck," *Archiv für österr. Gesch.,* LXXIII (1888), 315-364.

Johannes Cuspinianus (Spiessheimer) (cf. p. 5, above) was born 1473 at Schweinfurt and died 1529 at Vienna, where in 1508 he had succeeded Celtis as professor at the university. Cf. Hans Ankwicz von Kleehoven, *Johann Cuspinians Briefwechsel,* München, 1933.

[2] Grünpeck's work was *Die Geschichte Friedrichs III. und Maximilians I.* (ca. 1514-1516); that by Cuspinianus was *De Caesaribus atque imperatoribus Romanis* (ca. 1512-1522), both mentioned in the previous chapter. Eduard Fueter, in his *Geschichte der neueren Historiographie* (3. Aufl.; München und Berlin, 1936), p. 189, calls the former "unbedeutende Elogien," and Cuspinianus' work "die durchaus mittelmäßigen *Caesares.*"

Max and to describe him. Grünpeck wrote his work sometime between 1514 and 1516 as an example for Maximilian's grandson, the Archduke Karl, to whom the book is dedicated. Maximilian saw the completed manuscript and made some notations on it. Grünpeck's hope that the Kaiser might have it printed was never realized, however, and it was first published by Joseph Chmel in 1838.[3] Cuspinianus' *De Caesaribus* is supposed to have been nearly finished in 1522, but it was not published until 1540, eleven years after the author's death.[4] Of the two authors, Grünpeck is probably the more informative; but the account of Cuspinianus is composed in a more restrained style and usually appears more credible. Grünpeck's history, with some of the most ecstatic passages omitted, was still used by such well accredited scholars as Ulmann; while the writings of Johannes Cuspinianus furnish the basis for practically every German historian of any importance in evaluating Maximilian's character.

These writers portray Maximilian as a wholly lovable character. According to them he had such a pleasing personality that everyone naturally liked him, even his enemies, if they but had an opportunity to talk with him.[5] He was the kindest prince of his time and affable toward everyone with whom he conversed, putting at ease those who were bashful or timid so that they spoke with him quite freely.[6] He endeared himself to those about him by little acts of kindness; when his court servants were married he liked to dance before them in the costume of some part of the country, and thus he won the favor of the ladies, noble and otherwise.[7] Because of his popularity he never had to fear poison, since no one wished him ill or would want to harm him.[8]

Max was also a very courteous prince. According to George Spalatin, the intimate friend of Luther and historian at the Saxon court, Friedrich the Wise of Saxony declared that he had never

---

[3] Cf. Grünpeck, *op. cit.*, pp. vi, xi-xiv.
[4] Cf. Simon Laschitzer, "Die Genealogie des Kaisers Maximilian I.," *Jahrb. k.-h. Samml.*, VIII (1888), 2f.
[5] Cuspinianus, *De Caes.*, p. 614; Grünpeck, *op. cit.*, pp. 52f.
[6] Cuspinianus, *op. cit.*, pp. 610, 613.
[7] Grünpeck, *op. cit.*, pp. 57f.
[8] *Ibid.*, pp. 52f.

met a politer man in all his life;[9] and although Max did not get what he wished from Friedrich, he still preserved his friendliness toward him.[10] These good manners he had exhibited even as a youth, reports Grünpeck,[11] showing the greatest consideration even to the lowest servants. In affairs of state he never refused to hear a petition, and certain hours were set aside each day to hear private people.[12]

Here for the first time we encounter a contrary opinion in a letter from Cuspinianus. Writing in 1514 to Laurenz Saurer, the Kaiser's *Rentmeister,* Cuspinianus speaks of the minister of King Sigismund of Poland, Raphael Leszczynski, whom Max "so spöttlich abgefertigt habe mit großen straichn."[13] But this is only one exception and does not greatly disturb our picture thus far.

As a rule, we hear from Grünpeck, Maximilian was of a calm and even temper, was never angry for long, and could hide his ill-will so cleverly that only a reddening of the neck, a biting of the lip, would betray him.[14] In petty affairs of state he might occasionally become impatient and irritated, as the councillor Cyprian von Serntein complains in a letter of April 3, 1509, to Paul von Lichtenstein.[15] In more important matters, however, such as the trouble which descended upon him in Flanders at the death of his young wife, he bore adversity calmly.[16] When certain princes were once meeting for the purpose of taking the management of the government from him, Cuspinianus tells us, Max walked cheerfully into the castle of the prince who had instigated the meeting and with undaunted good spirits, had luncheon with the prince's wife.[17]

---

[9] Georg Spalatin, "Friedrichs des Weisen Leben und Zeitgeschichte." *Georg Spalatin's historischer Nachlass und Briefe.* Aus den Originalhandschriften herausgegeben von Chr. Gotth. Neudecker und Ludw. Preller (Jena, 1851), I, 45.

[10] *Ibid.,* I, 38, 39, 50, 51.

[11] Grünpeck, *op. cit.,* pp. 40f.

[12] *Ibid.,* pp. 61f.

[13] *Johann Cuspinians Briefwechsel.* Hrsg. v. Hans Ankwicz von Kleehoven (München, 1933), p. 61, no. 30.

[14] Grünpeck, *op. cit.,* pp. 53f.

[15] Victor von Kraus, *op. cit.,* p. 121.

[16] Cuspinianus, *op. cit.,* p. 604.

[17] *Ibid.,* p. 613. Cuspinianus does not tell us the name of the prince. "Ita enim eos elusit, ut quum olim Principes conuenticulum celebrarent contra eum, quo administrationem Imperij illi auferrent, in castrum illius principis sponte ingressus,

He could, to be sure, be momentarily aroused by the negligence or cowardice of his men. Pirckheimer describes, from personal observation, such an occasion when in the Münsterthal on the Malserhaide during the war with the Swiss a shameful retreat followed a costly defeat.[18] Yet after an even more disastrous collapse, the rout at Dorneck, near Basel, in which the responsible commander, Graf von Fürstenberg, lost his life, Max complained only of the Graf's folly. In spite of the seriousness of the loss, his features betrayed no trace of distress; and as night approached he turned the conversation to the stars and spoke of their nature and relation to one another. The next day Max went by boat from Lindau to Constance and spent the day in joking, gay conversation, and games. "When I saw and heard this," says Pirckheimer, "I could not help considering him happy who could so quickly get over such deeply felt and irreparable losses."[19]

This equanimity in the face of misfortune may have been partly the result of a volatile disposition which passed easily from one experience to another. Maximilian's energy was unbounded. His official business alone was enough to keep him occupied through such a long day that he got much less than the normal amount of sleep; but his endurance was great and he would sacrifice needed rest for hunting or hawking. Then too he bothered about small things around the house and the kitchen; he saw to the wine cellar, inspected the stables, and kept in touch with every department of the household.[20]

This restless energy was not always a blessing to those about him, however. One of his councillors, Cyprian von Serntein, complains, in the letter above, that Max wants to give all the orders, that he insists on looking over and correcting everything himself. Because of the diffusion of his interests, it is hard to get him to come to any firm decision.[21] Cuspinianus, on a mission to King Wladislaw of Hungary, writes of his audience with the king and

---

qui autor factionis erat, cum uxore eius pransus est hilariter & intrepide."
[18] *Bilibald Pirckheimers Schweizerkrieg und Ehrenhandel mit seinen Feinden zu Nürnberg*, hrsg. durch Ernst Münch (Basel, 1860), p. 156.
[19] *Ibid.*, pp. 184f.
[20] Grünpeck, *op. cit.*, pp. 63f.
[21] V. v. Kraus, *op. cit.*, pp. 120-125. Letter of April 3, 1509: "ir mt. feirt nit und zeucht fur und fur, ligt nit stil."

Archbishop Thomas Bakács: "At first they would only say, why should we deal with him, who is so inconstant, and who begins so many things and finishes nothing?"[22] Cuspinianus himself defends Max for forsaking many great undertakings favorably begun with the excuse that he lacked the necessary money. He might have helped himself from the large Hapsburg family treasure and thus avoided countless difficulties; but he refused to touch this, regarding it as his duty to hand it on to his grandsons intact.[23]

Some writers attribute Maximilian's difficulties, mainly his military failures, to his reticence and unwillingness to share his plans with his councillors or even with his generals. He was careful to keep his designs to himself, especially in military affairs, so that a minister at his court once wrote home in despair that no one could act, because no one knew what the Kaiser wanted.[24] Nevertheless, Cuspinianus praises the Kaiser's wisdom and particularly his habit in difficult matters of seeking the counsel and opinions even of persons of the lowest degree.[25] There are accounts, of course, of Max' suffering diplomatic defeats in spite of the great sagacity attributed to him, as when the King of England made a separate peace with France and, in the words of a Danzig chronicler, "zoch in sein heimot in Engelandt und ließ den Romischen konig zwischen 2 stole dael siczen."[26] Still the only contemporary reference to actual incapacity on the part of Max is supposed to have come from his father, who, when approached by some of the electoral princes about electing Max king, is said to have remarked: "No one knows our son better than we; we know that he is not fit to rule." The Strasbourg writer who records this, Caspar Hedio, adds that Kaiser Friedrich liked less to speak of this matter than any other.[27]

---

[22] Cuspinianus, *Briefwechsel*, p. 62.

[23] Cuspinianus, *De Caes.*, p. 613.

[24] "Auszug aus dem Bericht des v. Westerstetten d. d. Gengenbach 8. August 1504." *Baiersche Landtags-Handlungen in den Jahren 1429 bis 1513* (München, 1825), XIV, 728; and cf. v. Kraus, *op. cit.*, pp. 120-125.

[25] Cuspinianus, *De Caes.*, p. 613.

[26] "Caspar Weinrichs Danziger Chronik." *Scriptores Rerum Prussicarum. Die Geschichtsquellen der preussischen Vorzeit bis zum Untergange der Ordensherrschaft.* Hrsg. v. Th. Hirsch, Max Töppen u. Ernst Strehlke (Leipzig, 1870), IV, 791.

[27] Caspar Hedio, *Ein Auszerleszne Chronick von anfang der welt bisz auff das jar nach Christi vnsers eynigen Heylands Geburt M. D. vliij.*, etc. (Strassburg, 1549), p. 662.

When Maximilian was a child he would give his toys to anyone who asked for them, which Grünpeck interprets as an omen of his future great generosity.[28] When he reached manhood his extreme kindness and good nature were still joined with the greatest liberality.[29] Like Alexander and Charlemagne, he helped the children of poor parents and sent them to the university, some to Vienna and some to Freiburg, as we learn from the Bavarian historian, Aventinus.[30] The revolt of 1488 in Bruges in Flanders, where the citizens seized Max and held him prisoner for several months, was really caused by his generosity, Grünpeck would have us believe; for it was this and the corruption of his head-steward, over whom his control was too mild, which brought about the shortage of funds; and the anger of the people was directed not so much against Max as against his officials.[31]

Along with these testimonials to his generosity we hear that Maximilian found it easy to ask for what he wanted in return for favors he had granted. According to Kanzow's chronicle, Duke Bugslaff of Pommerania discovered this to his sorrow when, after enjoying Max' hospitality and generosity during a visit to Innsbruck, he was calmly asked by his host for his most cherished possession, a magnificent stallion, the Duke's favorite mount.[32] The stallion is supposed to have died mysteriously on the very night before Max' servant arrived to take it to his master, and the Duke did not answer later appeals from the Kaiser for substantial military aid.[33]

Such asides, however, did little to dim Maximilian's reputation. Nauclerus describes him as a kind and merciful prince,[34]

[28] Grünpeck, *op. cit.*, p. 35.
[29] Cuspinianus, *De Caes.*, p. 613.
[30] *Johannes Turmair's genannt Aventinus BAYERISCHE CHRONIK.* Herausgegeben von Dr. Matthias Lexer (München, 1882), IV, Teil 2, pp. 912f.; V, 157.
[31] Grünpeck, *op. cit.*, pp. 48f.
[32] *Thomas Kanzow's Chronik von Pommern in hochdeutscher Sprache.* Aus der Handschrift des Verfassers herausgegeben von Fr. L. B. von Medem (Anclam, 1841), pp. 315ff.
[33] *Ibid.*, p. 326.
[34] Johannes Nauclerus, *Memorabilivm omnis aetatis et omnivm gentivm chronici commentarii* (Tubingae, Anno M. D. XVI.), fo. 298-a. Nauclerus (Johannes Verge or Vergenhans) was born between 1425 and 1430. He was tutor to Graf Eberhard, son of Graf Ludwig I. von Würtemberg-Urach; from 1477, professor and later Rektor of the university at Tübingen, where he died in 1510.

while Carion calls him just and magnanimous to the enemies whom he has conquered.[35] Hedio praises his love of peace,[36] and Nauclerus acclaims his zeal in upholding justice.[37] In the latter quality Cuspinianus says that he imitated Alexander, who always gave just as ready a hearing to the accused as to the accuser.[38] In the war with the Swiss, where it might appear that he acted unjustly, Pirckheimer believes that the fault actually lay with his advisers, who instigated strife while he was away in the Netherlands and deceived him with false information when he returned.[39]

Maximilian was also considered unusual in that he preserved the greatest temperance, not only in food and drink, but in all things, taking as his motto the words: "Mediocritas optimum."[40] Thus he disliked any unusual degree of attention, and as much as he was pleased to have his deeds celebrated by posterity, he nevertheless sought to avoid being praised to his face. "This I am able to swear on oath," says Cuspinianus,[41] and gives an illustration. Several eloquent and learned men were once praising the Kaiser in the latter's presence. Max ordered Cuspinianus to tell them to stop it immediately, because personal flattery of that kind becomes soiled while still in the mouth.[42] In Grünpeck's biography there is a note in Maximilian's handwriting: "Lyber laudis post mortem," which we may suppose applies to the entire book.[43] Still Max was probably not wholly displeased at such praise. Konrad Peutinger of Augsburg, antiquarian and councillor

---

[35] *Chronica Ioannis Carionis miro artificio ab orbis conditi exordio res gestas continentia, ex lingua Germanica in Latinam, ab Hermanno Bono optima fide transfusa*, etc. (Antverpiae, 1540), fo. 154-a. But cf. Andreas Felix Oefelius: *Rerum Boicarum Scriptores* (Augustae Vindelicorum, 1763), II, 471f., regarding the Kaiser's profit from the Bavarian quarrel, to which Johannes Carion refers. It seems that Max could afford to be kind. Carion was born at Bietigheim in Wurttemberg in 1499, studied at Wittenberg, later became court astronomer to Kurfürst Joachim I von Brandenburg, and died in 1537. Melanchthon went over his work before it was printed.
[36] Hedio, *op. cit.*, pp. 672, 695.
[37] Nauclerus, *op. cit.*, fo. 298-a.
[38] Cuspinianus, *De Caes.*, p. 614; *Pirckheimer's Schweizerkrieg*, ed. Münch, p. 152.
[39] Pirckheimer, *op. cit.*, pp. 120f.
[40] Cuspinianus, *De Caes.*, pp. 613f.
[41] *Ibid.*, p. 614: "id ego sancte deierare possum."
[42] *Ibid.*, p. 614: "Caue, inquit, ne me laudes, sordescit enim in ore laus illa propria (ut uulgus loquitur)."
[43] Grünpeck, *op. cit.*, pp. 56f., and *Einleitung*, p. xv.

to Max in political and diplomatic affairs as well as his agent for artistic and historical hobbies, related to the Kaiser's secretary how he had obtained privileges for his father-in-law, the merchant Anton Welser, by pointing out to Max that he would be the first German king to send German merchants to India.[44]

The Kaiser was always extremely virtuous in his relations with women, our accounts inform us. When he invited matrons and their daughters to a banquet or a dance, he entertained them most respectably and in their presence produced plays which would fit everyone's sense of decency and decorum. No matter of what degree a woman might be who approached him, he always spoke modestly to her. Nor was he like other princes, says Cuspinianus, from whom parents must fear for their daughters.[45] Indeed, Max always carried in his heart the image of his first wife, Mary of Burgundy; and the anguish which he had felt at losing her was revived whenever he thought of her, so that he could never mention her name without sighs and tears.[46]

When the citizens of Bruges finally released Max from captivity in 1488, they extracted from him a promise that he would not attempt to take revenge upon them but would leave the country. Friedrich III did not feel himself bound by Max' word, however, and continued the war against them for some time longer. Bruges claimed that Max broke his word and helped his father. Most German writers of the time deny this, and even use this incident as an example of Maximilian's faithfulness to his given word.[47] Nevertheless, one source at least, differs from this opinion, the Danzig chronicle of Caspar Weinrich. It declares that Max gave his word and broke it.[48]

A sufficient number of pictorial representations of Maximilian has been preserved to afford us a fair idea of his personal ap-

---

[44] "Ein Brief Dr. Conrad Peutingers an den Kaiserl. Secretär Blasius Hölzl. ddo. 3. Januar 1505." In *Tagebuch des Lucas Rem aus den Jahren 1494-1541.* Ein Beitrag zur Handelsgeschichte der Stadt Augsburg. Mitgetheilt von B. Greiff (Augsburg, 1861), *Studien und Darstellungen aus dem Gebiete der Geschichte,* hrsg. von Dr. Hermann von Grauert (Freiburg i. Br., 1919), IX (Heft 1 u. 2), 107f.
[45] Cuspinianus, *De Caes.,* p. 614.
[46] *Ibid.,* pp. 604, 612.
[47] Grünpeck, *op. cit.,* pp. 49ff.; Hedio, *op. cit.,* p. 664.
[48] Weinrich, *op. cit.,* p. 769.

pearance. We have in addition various descriptions by contemporaries which agree quite well with the pictures we have of him. Grünpeck's claim that he was more exquisitely formed than any prince before him,[49] is of course a bit of extravagant flattery. Grünpeck further describes him as a powerfully built man of great physical strength, who could lift a lance of ten-ells' length with one outstretched hand and carry it thus. His body had been steeled by all exercises of knighthood, to which he had devoted much time since boyhood; he had begun early to evade his teachers and play at jousting with his companions.[50] Thus he grew up adept in the games of the tournament, indeed, according to Grünpeck, he was more the inventor than the cultivator of the sport, making rules for it for all German princes.[51]

In military matters Max was said to be equally skillful. He revived and revised military training, and with wonderful talent devised new machines of war, against which no fortification could stand.[52] According to Aventinus, he is to be credited with the organization of the first regular German foot-soldiers, the *Landsknechte*, who originated under him in the Netherlands.[53] Among all learned emperors Pirckheimer rates him as the most valorous, as well as the most learned among the valorous.[54] Not only was he an excellent general, but he could dismount from his horse during a review and show his captains that he was the best shot of all.[55]

This military prowess, Grünpeck says, was partly the reason for Max' popularity among his soldiers. He also gave his men kind words in hard times and helped them forget their cares by furnishing them with clowns and jesters. Thus he made himself

---

[49] Grünpeck, *op. cit.*, pp. 67f.
[50] *Ibid.*, pp. 40f.
[51] *Ibid.*, pp. 56f.
[52] *Ibid.*, pp. 66f.; Cuspinianus, *De Caes.*, p. 614; Werner Rolewinck, "Fascicvlvs temporvm omnes antiqvorvm chronicas complectens." *Rerum Germanicarum Scriptores* of Joannes Pistorius (Ratisbonae, 1726), II, 576; and Hartmann Schedel, *Libri Chronicarum* (Nuremberg, 1493), fo. 258-a.
[53] Aventinus, *op. cit.*, IV (Teil 1), 212.
[54] Bilibald Pirckheimer, *Opera*, ed. Goldast (Francoforti, 1610), p. 51 of the *Historica*.
[55] Pirckheimer, *Schweizerkrieg*, ed. Münch, p. 193; ed. Karl Rück (München, 1895), p. 126.

so well liked by them that the best soldier would rather serve him for no pay than any other prince for a tremendous salary. Moreover, his men seldom had to be punished for mutiny.[56] Nevertheless, the same source furnishes us with an illustration of Maximilian's holding back a group of mutinous soldiers, inadvertently showing that mutinies did occur.[57] Furthermore, Pirckheimer relates that during the Swiss War Max' *Landsknechte* and army ran out of food and left him.[58]

Another reason for Maximilian's popularity with his men was his personal bravery. Grünpeck is not the only one who declares that he was always in the front line, driving the enemy before him by the ardor of his attack.[59] How we are to judge his conduct while he was a captive in Bruges then, is hard to say; for according to Hedio he did more weeping than talking before the deputation of citizens who came to negotiate with him.[60] There seems to be little doubt, however, that Maximilian's reputation in another line of physical endeavor was generally recognized. Grünpeck says that as a child he showed inclinations toward the hunt by chasing the barnyard fowl about the castle courtyard against the strict orders of his father.[61] As a man he hunted all kinds of animals at all times of year, in the hottest or coldest weather, so that the foresters and beaters would sometimes steal back to their huts while he went on. He used to hunt even when he felt badly; at such times he would go all day without eating or drinking. He always killed his own game single-handed and others were forbidden to help him.[62] He was often criticized, too, by those who thought he indulged too much in hunting and exposed himself to too many dangers. The cost of his dogs and falcons attracted unfavorable criticism. But such people, Cuspinianus remarks, did not consider that these were the exercises of kings and princes and that hunting was much to be preferred to the usual occupa-

[56] Grünpeck, *op. cit.*, pp. 51f.
[57] *Ibid.*, p. 62.
[58] Pirckheimer, *Schweizerkrieg*, ed. Münch, p. 170.
[59] Grünpeck, *op. cit.*, pp. 43ff., 67; Felix Faber, "Historia Sueuica," in M. Goldast, *Rerum Alamannicarum Scriptores* (Francofurti et Lipsiae, 1730), IV, 70.
[60] Hedio, *op. cit.*, p. 664.
[61] Grünpeck, *op. cit.*, pp. 66f.
[62] *Ibid.*, pp. 55f.

tions of princes, that of leading innocent girls astray. This most chaste emperor was far from such wicked deeds.[63]

The extraordinary thing about Maximilian, however, was held to be his combination of moral and physical excellence with outstanding mental capacities. These were all the more remarkable because until his ninth year he was almost unable to speak, so that many thought him dumb, to the great grief of his mother. But later he became as fluent as he had been backward before. Friedrich III was surprised to hear the princes at Frankfort in 1486 praising his son's fluency and told them that until Max was twelve years old they thought he would grow up either a mute or a fool. His apparent slowness in learning was partly the fault of his teacher, Peter Engelbrecht, who often beat him cruelly for not understanding his dialectical subtleties and thus instilled in him a hatred and aversion for learning.[64]

The account just cited from Cuspinianus is confirmed by the other intimate biographer, Grünpeck. The latter declares that as a boy, Max excelled in everything; that his quick comprehension and excellent memory enabled him to outshine all his classmates, whom he would then scold and berate as blockheads.[65] Cuspinianus, too, praises the Kaiser's wonderful memory, which never let him forget the face of a person to whom he had once talked.[66] It was indeed so retentive that, considering his great ability and judgment, had he been properly instructed from boyhood, he would have quickly learned all the arts and sciences.[67] In spite of his late start, Maximilian's intellectual attainments were considered unusual and varied. He was especially interested in geography and history and was angry at those princes who had no interest in preserving records of their reigns, since these were the sources of virtue and their neglect was the cause of the decay of the state.[68] On his deathbed he chose to have Jacob Manlius, the genealogist and historian, read to him from Hapsburg history to

---

[63] Cuspinianus, *De Caes.*, p. 614.
[64] *Ibid.*, p. 602.
[65] Grünpeck, *op. cit.*, p. 39.
[66] *Ibid.*, pp. 59ff.; Cuspinianus, *De Caes.*, p. 613.
[67] Cuspinianus, *De Caes.*, p. 603.
[68] Grünpeck, *op. cit.*, pp. 58f.

while away the sleepless nights, and during these last days he showed his knowledge of medicine and mathematics in learned discussions with two noted physicians from Vienna, Wilhelmus Polymnius (i.e., Püelinger) and Georgius Collimitius (i.e., Tanstetter).[69] Some of his many experiences he had set down in writing; as noted a scholar as Pirckheimer declared that no German historian had so pure a style as he.[70] Aventinus says that he was tireless in his efforts to trace his own genealogy,[71] and that he extended his interests in antiquity to include investigations of old coins, inscriptions, or anything else which might throw light on the past.[72] Beatus Rhenanus calls him "studiosus antiquitatis" and relates that anyone who gave him information about a rare old book was sure to be well rewarded.[73]

In his desire to exchange ideas with others, we read, Maximilian had also acquired a fluency in other tongues. Besides German, he spoke Latin, French, and Italian very well, in fact the princes at Frankfort in 1486 praised his Latin.[74] Grünpeck adds to this repertory Spanish, Illyrian, Flemish, and English.[75] Cuspinianus' reference to Max' command of Latin must be accepted with reserve, for we find the same author apologizing in a letter to one of Maximilian's councillors because he had sent Max a report in Latin without knowing that there was no councillor at court to receive it. He hopes that the Kaiser will not be angry with him for not having written in German.[76]

Our sources inform us that although Maximilian was slow in learning to express himself, he developed later into one of the most eloquent speakers of his time. Those who at home spoke angrily against him were pacified by a single word in his presence. In war, when the soldiers were clamoring for their overdue pay, he spoke kindly to them and quickly quieted them.[77] At the con-

---

[69] Cuspinianus, *De Caes.*, p. 610.
[70] Carion, *op. cit.*, p. 153; Hedio, *op. cit.*, p. 709; Grünpeck, *op. cit.*, pp. 59f.
[71] Aventinus, *op. cit.*, IV (Teil 1), 21, 361.
[72] *Ibid.*, IV (Teil 1), 19f., 704, 713; Beatus Rhenanus, *Rerum Germanicarum* (Basileae, 1551), p. 131.
[73] Rhenanus, *op. cit.*, p. 113.
[74] Cuspinianus, *De Caes.*, p. 602, who says he spoke them "eleganter."
[75] Grünpeck, *op. cit.*, pp. 60f.
[76] Cuspinianus, *Briefwechsel*, pp. 43f., no. 21, Apr. 13, 1513.
[77] Cuspinianus, *De Caes.*, p. 614.

gress of kings in Vienna in 1515 his words drew tears from many a listener;[78] and at the same congress, according to Hedio, he spoke so wisely and so well that

> everyone was amazed at him, and also many who were not of the Kaiser's party were changed in their opinions and declared freely that they would never have expected such kindness, good sense and sincerity from Maximilian. They also openly praised the Kaiser, his deeds and all his words.[79]

There are, finally, one or two other qualities which attract the praise of Max' admirers. He is said to have been able at a glance to estimate a person's abilities, so that he could immediately assign each servant to the task for which he was best fitted.[80] His appreciation and knowledge of music was such that musicians flourished at his court as in a fertile field the mushrooms spring up after a rain.[81]

2. *Contemporary scholars and poets*

The portrait of Maximilian as we have tried to paint it from the accounts of contemporary historians and political writers certainly flatters the original, but also undoubtedly reflects a good deal of sincere admiration. Among the scholars and poets of Humanism, the New Learning in Germany which looked to the princes and especially to Maximilian as its patron, the characterization of Max swells into a chorus of adulation, of panegyrical exaggeration. Not that the members of this group say any more about the Kaiser than has already been said. Praises are re-sung for his mercy and liberality. Even Swiss authors describing the Swiss War of 1499 style him a lover of peace;[82] and one of these, Nicolaus Schradin, "Schreiber zu Luzern," in "the most tedious of all Swiss rimed chronicles,"[83] speaks of his generosity and calls him (1500),

---

[78] *Ibid.*, p. 608.
[79] Hedio, *op. cit.*, p. 699.
[80] Grünpeck, *op. cit.*, pp. 65f.
[81] Cuspinianus, *De Caes.*, p. 614.
[82] Simon Lemnius, *Raeteis. Heldengedicht in acht Gesängen.* Im Versmasz der Urschrift ins Deutsche übertragen von Placidus Plattner (Chur, 1882), p. 4. The father of Simon Lemnius (Lemm Margadant) had taken part in the war of 1499.
[83] Thus called by Th. v. Liebenau in *Anzeiger für schweiz. Geschichte.*, n. f., V (1888), 244.

..... ein fromer fürst
Den nach eren vnd der gerechtigkeit dürst
Alß man zu ziten vil vnd dick hat gespürt.[84]

The Swabian Johannes Faber, who after Max' death became bishop of Vienna (died 1541), gave a funeral oration in Wels in Austria before the removal of the Kaiser's body to Neustadt in which he credited the departed monarch with every virtue and in particular called him courteous and thoughtful of others right up to his last hour.[85] A funeral oration is hardly the place to look for objective characterizations of the deceased, to be sure; but whether living or dead, Max commanded the gratitude of humanists and poets for his patronage of letters and they were inclined to see him in a glorified light. Max' skill as a hunter and a knight is celebrated in the plain German verses written for the *Ehrenpforte* of 1515 by Johannes Stabius (Stöberer), once a famous mathematician, the crowned poet, and favorite of Celtis:

In Weydwerck er sich sorglich wagt/
Gantz dürstiglich vnd vnuerzagt/
Nach Gembsen/ Eber/ Hirsch vnd Bern/
Mit den er hat sein kurtzweil gern/
Die auch gezügelt in seim Landt.
Gefangen mit sein selbes Handt.

. . .

Er hat getrieben Ritterspiel/
Darinn erzeigt auch kurtzweil viel/
Mit Warheit ich das sprechen kan/
Als vormals nie kein Fürst gethan/
Das alles doch mit solchem Schimpff/
Darauß jm kam Lob/ Ehr vnd Glimpff.[86]

---

[84] Nicolaus Schradin, "Kronigk diß Kriegs gegen den Allerdurchlüchtigsten Herrn Romschen Konig, etc. . . ." *Der Geschichtsfreund* (Einsiedeln, 1847), IV, 39f.

[85] Johann Faber, "Oratio Funebris, etc.," in *Rerum Germanicarum Scriptores* of Marquard Freher, ed. Burcard Struve (hereafter referred to as *Freher-Struve*), (Argentorati, 1717), II, 741. Cf. Struve's notes on Faber, *ibid.*, II, 718.

[86] "Porta Honoris, hoc est, descriptio Portae Honoris qvondam Caesareae Maiestati Maximiliano primo, anno 1515. erecta, per Ioannem Stabivm Viennensem Maiestatis illius bidem historiographum," found in Pirckheimer's *Opera*, p. 188. The New York City Public Library has a copy of the *Ehrenpforte* woodcuts (fourth edition; Vienna, 1799). Stabius was crowned poet by Celtis in 1502, received through the latter's help the position of professor of mathematics and astronomy at the university of Ingolstadt; later he was made the head of the new mathematical division of the *Collegium poëtarum* in Vienna. After the death of Celtis he was engaged

The number of languages which he could speak readily seems to have been agreed upon as seven,[87] and he is praised for his interest in instruction in languages and in science.[88]

There is practically no criticism to be found among this group. Most of them had been recipients of his favor or wrote in expectation of reward. The only discordant note comes, in private correspondence, from Reuchlin, who wrote of Max very shortly after his death: "Slow and hesitating, he was governed more than he himself governed."[89] Reuchlin had criticized this trait of the Kaiser many years before, when he wrote to the Markgraf Friedrich von Brandenburg: "No one who is near the king knows what is going on. I do not believe he himself knows what he is doing."[90] Again, when he was *Orator* for the Markgraf at Cologne in 1486,[91] Reuchlin took apparent pleasure in describing Maximilian's efforts to find somebody to joust with him against his father's orders, and how, after forging permission from the Kaiser, Max was unseated by the Pfalzgraf to his own discomfort and the amusement of the Kaiser.[92]

Reuchlin is the exception, but his views are of some importance since they were contained in private letters and were therefore likely to be sincere. The rule, however, is unadulterated praise. It is a very difficult task to discover a clear picture of Maximilian in the writings of the humanists. Their odes and their elegies, their *panegyrica*, their *staurosticha*, and the many profusely worded dedications and orations contain an abundance of flowery

---

by Max in historical and genealogical research. Cf. Gustav Bauch, *Die Anfänge des Humanismus in Ingolstadt* (München u. Leipzig, 1901), pp. 28, 105; and Joseph Aschbach, *Geschichte der Wiener Universität im ersten Jahrhunderte ihres Bestehens* (Wien, 1865), II, 365, who calls him J. "Stab."

[87] Stabius in Pirckheimer's *Opera*, p. 188. Cf. Johann Geiler von Keisersberg to Wimpfeling concerning Maximilian, letter from Fiessen, Aug. 2, 1503: "Latinus bonus, sed scripto melior quam verbo." *Freher-Struve*, II, 767.

[88] "Eine Gedächtnisschrift von Johannes Faber über die Erbauung der Augsburger Dominikanerkirche," von P. Dirr. *Zeitschrift des historischen Vereins für Schwaben Neuburg*, XXXIV (1908), 171.

[89] Letter to Questenberg of Feb. 12, 1519. Quoted by L. Geiger in "Maximilian I. in seinem Verhältnisse zum Reuchlinschen Streite," *Forschungen zur deutschen Geschichte*, IX (1869), 216.

[90] Füssen, March 28, 1492. *Johann Reuchlins Briefwechsel*. Gesammelt und hrsg. von Ludwig Geiger. "Stuttgart. Lit. Ver.," CXXVI (1875), 33.

[91] Cf. Bauch, *op. cit.*, pp. 22f.

[92] Quoted by Ziehen, *op. cit.*, I, 234f.

expressions but very little that is definite. As Geiger has pointed out, humanistic poetry differs from the popular especially in its more general character and its praise of the person who is celebrated without helping to characterize him. "Even when the humanists speak of a certain battle or of an event important for the life of the Kaiser and for the history of the empire," continues Geiger, "they use such customary expressions that at their celebration of the *Böhmenschlacht* one could think just as well of the Battle of Thermopylae, and at their glorification of the Kaiser as Maecenas, of Augustus."[93]

Thus the majority of the panegyrics on Maximilian read like a list of the more important virtues, plentifully interspersed with classical and mythological allusions. Stabius even attempted to arrange the virtues of his prince in a symmetrical pattern as an adornment for the *Ehrenpforte*,[94] just as Albrecht Dürer was given the difficult task of crowding as many as possible into his sketches for the *Triumphzug*.[95]

The usual form of praise, however, is the panegyrical Latin poem. Such a poem is the *Encomiastica* of Quinctus Aemilianus, in 1504,[96] in which Maximilian's election as Roman King and his imprisonment in Bruges are used as the framework for his verses. Its style is characterized by the apostrophe:

> Maximiliane, tui decus & verissima secli
> Gloria.[97]

Henricus Glareanus on the occasion of his coronation as *poeta laureatus* in Cologne in 1512 was "inspired" to write a *Panegyricon* on Max, which in lauding the Kaiser's various virtues becomes almost a catalogue of names.[98] Again a background of classical

---

[93] Ludwig Geiger, *Renaissance und Humanismus in Italien und Deutschland* (Berlin, 1882), p. 345.
[94] "Porta Honoris," in Pirckheimer's *Opera*, pp. 176-179.
[95] Franz Schestag, "Kaiser Maximilians I. Triumph." *Jahrb. k.-h. Samml.*, I (1883), 154-181.
[96] *Freher-Struve*, II, 417-444. Cf. Gustav Bauch, *Die Reception des Humanismus in Wien* (Breslau, 1903), p. 168.
[97] *Freher-Struve*, II, 444.
[98] *Schardius redivivus sive rerum Germanicarum scriptores varii, olim ad. Simone Schardio, in IV. tomos collecti*, etc. (Giessae, 1673), p. 335. Also in *Freher-Struve*, II, 482f. A sample:

references is used for the *Panegyricus* of 1502 by Vincentius Longinus, another *poeta laureatus,* of Freistadt in Silesia, in praise of Max for the erection of the College of Poets and Mathematicians in Vienna.[99] Wolfgang Lazius lavishes praises for the same reason;[100] and Jakob Locher (Philomusus), pupil, friend, and successor to Celtis at the university of Ingolstadt, gives expression to his devotion in still another *Panegyricon* (1497).[101]

One of the most frequent occasions for lauding the Kaiser's virtues was in connection with an appeal for unity of action within the empire and against the arch-enemy of Christendom, the Turk. Sebastian Brant seized every opportunity to bring this need before the princes and the Kaiser. In the *Narrenschiff* (1494) he summons the former to support their brilliant ruler:

> Aber jr herren, künig, land,
> Nit wellen gstatten solch schand
> Wellent dem Rômschen rich zů stan
> So mag das schiff noch vff recht gan.
> Ir haben zwor eyn künig milt
> Der üch wol fürt, mit ritters schiltt,
> Der zwyngen tůg all land gemeyn
> Wann jr jm helffen wendt alleyn.
> Der edel fürst Maximilian
> Wol würdig ist der Rômschen kron
> Dem kumbt on zwifel jnn sin handt
> Die heilig erd, vnd das globte landt
> Vnd wůrt sin anfang thůn all tag
> Wann er alleyn üch trüwen mag.[102]

The news of a strange birth, two children with one forehead and one brain, prompts Brant to a comparison with the unity among

---

> Denque Marmaricis ubi murmurat Auster in oris,
> Imbriferas cogens nubes Gaetulia, Psylli,
> Æthiopes, Elephantophagi, & Garamantica proles
> Ambigua, & Numidae, Massyli, & corniger Hammon,
> Saepe tuas laudes, saepe audivere procellas. etc.

Heinrich Loriti, of Glarus (1488-1563), humanist, poet, wrote on music and geography.
[99] *Freher-Struve,* II, 489-492.
[100] *Ibid.,* II, 488f.
[101] *Der Briefwechsel des Konrad Celtis.* Gesammelt, hrsg. und erläutert von Hans Rupprich (München, 1934), p. 343.
[102] *Sebastian Brants Narrenschiff.* Hrsg. von Friedrich Zarncke (Leipzig, 1854), no. 99, "von abgang des glouben," p. 95, ll. 151-164.

the princes which he supposes Maximilian has newly gained.[103] He praises Max upon his election as Roman King,[104] and defends him hotly when he is detained at Bruges.[105] The fall of a meteorite near Ensisheim, or the sight of a strange flock of falcons, is used for promoting the idea of Maximilian's journey to Rome to receive the imperial crown.[106] The alleged miraculous appearance of crosses on people's clothing, which so seized the imagination in Alsace about 1501, he interprets as another call to Maximilian to lead a crusade against the Turks.[107]

Thomas Murner's *Narrenbeschwörung* (1512), one of the works stimulated by Brant's *Narrenschiff*, mentions Maximilian several times. Murner berates the fools who like to sit over their wine, tell tall tales of their battles in distant lands, and complain of Maximilian because he cannot pay them. These same fools, he says, would slander "den frommen man" if he did pay them.[108] Murner makes it clear that he intends to spare no one in his criticisms; even the pope and the emperor are Adam's children and not free from sin, as they would themselves admit.[109] In the lines that follow, however, Murner is careful to say nothing more specific than this. Finally he asks, who is responsible for the bad conditions in Germany? He declares that if the princes were obedient, Germany's sufferings would be less, for, he concludes:

> Ein künig ist ein einzig man,
> Wann kein fürst will bi im stan,
> So ist es bis an in getan;
> Darum ich fürsten, grafen, herren
> Redlich dapfer will beschweren,
> Das sie den frummen künig lon
> Und so schlechtlich bi im ston
> Zu schand der tütschen nation.[110]

---

[103] *Ibid.*, p. 163.
[104] *Ibid.*, *Varia Carmina*, p. 184, no. 44.
[105] *Ibid.*, *Varia Carmina*, p. 186, no. 47. Cf. Charles Schmidt, *Histoire littéraire de l'Alsace à la fin du XV° et au commencement du XVI° siècle* (Paris, 1879), I, 283, note 109.
[106] *Narrenschiff*, ed. Zarncke, *Varia Carmina*, p. 186, nos. 48, 49, 52, 53.
[107] *Ibid.*, p. 187, no. 56.
[108] *Deutsche National-Litteratur*, hrsg. von J. Kürschner, XVII, 83, ll. 713-721.
[109] *Ibid.*, XVII, 285, ll. 7991-8009.
[110] *Ibid.*, XVII, 286, ll. 8045-8052.

One is impressed by the number of poets who are continually calling on Maximilian to defend the faith.[111] Pallas Spangel in his welcoming words to Max on behalf of the university of Heidelberg, in 1489, expresses his confidence in "your power to bring together Christians in a bond of peace, . . . so that you may destroy the enemies of Christ, curb the savageness of the Turks, . . . and finally lead the wandering sheep into the sheepfold of Christ."[112] This is also the plea of the author of the *Welschgattung* of 1513, who tells the heads of Christendom that it is time to stand together and especially to support the Kaiser.[113] Pamphilus Gengenbach, the printer and dramatist of Basel, preaches the same thing in *Der Buntschu* in 1513;[114] and in *Der Nollhart* of 1517 he has Maximilian himself complain of the lack of support and unity.[115] Finally in the same work the author prophesies to "the Turk" that Max will punish him sevenfold. The Turk asks at what time he may expect the Kaiser to begin and receives the answer, "As soon as all Christendom is living in good peace together." Thereupon the Turk disdainfully replies:

> So han ich worlich noch lang frist
> Fur wor ein schlechter wysag bist![116]

Thus, although these appeals to Maximilian to save Christendom are always couched in most polite and laudatory terms, we can see that their authors are beginning to wonder when they will bring results. Johann Adelphus (Muling), who was employed in 1505 in Strasbourg as physician, after 1514 in Schaffhausen, and who translated a number of humanistic works, said in his preface to an edition of a poem on the history of Alexander the Great,

---

[111] It is difficult nowadays to appreciate the reality and the imminence of the danger from the Turks which was felt by the Germans at that time. Cf. Richard Ebermann's *Die Türkenfurcht, ein Beitrag zur Geschichte der öffentlichen Meinung in Deutschland während der Reformationszeit* (Halle a. S., 1904).

[112] ". . . tua potentia Christianos ad pacis vinculum cogere, . . . ut . . . hostes Christi elidas, Turcorum immanitatem compescas, . . . ac tandem in Ouile Christi ouiculas errantes perducas." *Freher-Struve*, II, 465.

[113] "Die Welsch-Gattung," von Friedrich Waga. *Germanistische Abhandlungen*, 34. Heft (Breslau, 1910), 180, 210. Text on pp. 170-272.

[114] *Pamphilus Gengenbach. S R F.* Herausgegeben von Karl Goedeke (Hanover, 1856), p. 26, ll. 116-121.

[115] *Ibid.*, p. 89.

[116] *Ibid.*, pp. 104ff.

published in 1513, that he thought that Alexander should serve as an example to Max. Alexander was always prompt in executing designs, while Max thought he could save the empire by procrastination. Since the Kaiser does great things every day, concludes Adelphus, he would do even greater things if he but had more resolution and if he found more support from his princes.[117]

These expressions are, for the most part, nothing more than the conventional humanistic mode of laudatory address, which as we have seen, deals in generalizations and is lavish in superlatives. Even a poem by Brant, *De Caesaris Maximiliani virtutibus,* and another, *De nobilitate Caesaris,*[118] say no more than that Maximilian excells in virtue Alexander the Great, Pompey, Justinian, Constantine, Aeacides, Charlemagne, Otto, Dagobert, Hector, etc. Thus we can pass over many others of the same kind. The Tübingen professor, Heinrich Bebel, whose writings did much to raise the standards of humanistic Latin, made a speech before Max in Innsbruck in 1501 in which he extolled enthusiastically the Kaiser's patronage of scholars.[119] Three years later he praises, in the usual style, Max' courage and skill on the occasion of his defeat of the Bohemians near Regensburg.[120] Conrad Celtis owed a good deal to the patronage of Maximilian, who called him from Ingolstadt to Vienna in 1498 as the first lector to be appointed especially for poetry and rhetoric. With every reason to be grateful to the emperor, Celtis now writes complimentary verses to accompany pictures of Max in the Aula of the university at Vienna.[121] In his *Quattuor libri amorum* he describes a meeting with Maximilian in a passage which develops into a eulogy of the emperor for his encouragement of learning and especially for the establishment of the College of Poets and Mathematicians:[122]

---

[117] The publication of the poem on Alexander the Great, which was by Gaultier de Chatillon, was placed in charge of Adelphus, who then used the opportunity to air some of his own views in the preface. Cf. Schmidt, *op. cit.,* II, 142.

[118] Brant, *Narrenschiff,* ed. Zarncke, p. 197, nos. 13, 14, 15.

[119] Th. Muther, *Aus dem Universitäts- und Gelehrtenleben im Zeitalter der Reformation* (Erlangen, 1866), pp. 78-83.

[120] *Freher-Struve,* II, 511-514.

[121] Gustav Bauch, *Die Reception des Humanismus in Wien* (Breslau, 1903), p. 90.

[122] *Conradus Celtis Protucius. Quattuor libri amorum.* Ed. Felicitas Pindter (Lipsiae, 1934), Liber IV, Elegia 14, pp. 94ff. Quoted here pp. 94f., ll. 153-166.

> Vel tibi quod melius, Brixnam vel adito Tridentum,
>   Musarum pater hic Maximilianus agit.
> Qui dudum Almanas concepit ferre sub oras
>   Pegasides nymphos Pieridumque choros.
> Is tibi perpetuo donabit tempore census
>   Et paupertatis non sinet esse metum
> Collegio sacras statuens donare Camenas
>   Atque mathematicos iunget in aede duos,
> Hic ubi nunc tollit sua moenia clara Vienna
>   Et Cetius Bacchi munera largus alit.
> Teque huic domui rectorem praeesse iubebit
>   Caesareasque vices te gerere ipse iubet,
> Scilicet ut lauro poteris decorare poetas
>   Et qui succedent post tua fata tibi.

In a *Ludus Dianae,* which was produced before Maximilian, the Empress Bianca Maria Sforza, and the court at Linz in 1501,[123] and which ended with a *Carmen Saphicum* on Max by Stabius,[124] Celtis celebrated the Kaiser's fame particularly as a hunter; and in another *Ludus* he commemorated a victory over the Bohemians.[125] In gratitude to Maximilian for his support in the establishment of the Collegium, Celtis gave his pupils in poetry as a theme the praise of the Kaiser; had these poems publicly declaimed on February 1, 1504; then collected and published them in the *Rhapsodia* the following year in Augsburg.[126]

Whether it is the poetic praise of the *Amores,* or the encomiastic phrases of a prose dedication,[127] this type of writing weighs us down with its wealth of generalities, and because of its very lavishness leaves a pale and confused picture of its hero. The humanists' desire to please in return for favors granted or expected is so obvious that we can not take them too seriously. There is, to be sure, a certain sincerity in their words, in as much as they were genuinely fond of anyone who would further their principal interest, and Max was their great benefactor *in re* and *in spe.* Their

---

[123] The *Ludus Dianae,* edited by Virginia Gingerich, has now been reprinted for the first time since its second printing in Nuremberg in 1502, in *The Germanic Review,* XV (October, 1940), 159-180.

[124] Celtis' *Briefwechsel,* pp. 91, 121.

[125] Gustav Bauch, *Die Reception des Humanismus in Wien,* p. 144.

[126] *Ibid.,* p. 144.

[127] E.g., to "Epitoma in utramque Ciceronis rhetoricam," cf. Celtis' *Briefwechsel,* pp. 43ff.

enthusiasm carried them away, and they saw in him the ideal Kaiser.[128] It was, then, no mere rhetorical convention but something like real feeling that prompted Johannes Tolhopf of Kemnat, a friend of Celtis, in a letter to the latter to write thus of the emperor: "gloriosissimi, victoriosissimi et invictissimi nostri Salvatoris et paratoris orbis terra(rum) nostri Maximiliani."[129] It is not altogether the usual mock-modesty of the humanist when Glareanus professes that in his writing he is unable to follow even the shadow of the Kaiser.[130] These men were, to be sure, concerned for their livelihood; but even in such cases it is possible to be sincere.

It might be taken as some indication of sincerity that they continued to write in this way about Maximilian even after his death. It is customary to praise the dead, and eulogies of a prince who passed away are not without hope of reward. Nevertheless, there is a unanimity and a fervor in those devoted to Maximilian that is impressive. Johann Faber's funeral oration in Wels, delivered four days after Max' death, assembled, as we have seen, a list of his characteristics[131] which resembles a roll-call of all physical and moral virtues. Practically the same sort of oration was given by Georgius Sauromanus;[132] and there was still another by Ulrich Zasius,[133] who had welcomed Max to the university of Freiburg ten years before in an adulatory address in which he stressed the Kaiser's generosity.[134] Philipp Gundel spoke for the university of

---

[128] Ludwig Geiger, *Renaissance und Humanismus in Italien und Deutschland*, p. 342.
[129] Celtis' *Briefwechsel*, p. 368, no. 221. Nürnberg, July 16, 1499.
[130] Letter to Joh. Caesarius, Basel, 1514. *Freher-Struve*, II, 481.
[131] Cf. above, p. 36. *Freher-Struve*, II, 721-743. E.g., p. 722: "Nam quo magis animo ipse mecum repeto singulares ac heroicas virtutes tuas, quam fueris videlicet mitis, placidus, lenis, prouidus, aequus, humanus, patriae pater, magnanimus, pecuniae contemptor, nemini magis quam tibi ipsi imperans, voluptates subiiciens, affectibus nullis prauis obnoxius, magna cogitans, pro nobis quibus imperabas sollicitus, ad beneficentiam omnium promptissimus, ad vindictam lentus; propensior ad iustitiam, facilis aditu, comis in congressu, cunctis (alioquin volentibus) blandus, strenue bella agens, nullum tamen per te affectans, pacis amantissimus, cuius & tenax esses, & quidem natus visus es ad bene merendum de genere humano, ac humani generis vt esses delitiae."
[132] "Oratio Georgii Sauromani," *Freher-Struve*, II, 743-760.
[133] "Vdalrici Zasii Oratio," *Freher-Struve*, II, 770-773.
[134] *Freher-Struve*, II, 466ff.

Vienna, where he was professor.[135] Then there is a long Latin lament for Maximilian written by Petrus Aegidius,[136] who also composed an epitaph in his honor;[137] while still another epitaph was written by Joseph Pinicianus.[138] In his *Epicedion* Sebastian Brant mourned in Max the collapse of all his hopes for the future.[139] Bartholomaeus Latomus (Steinmetz), professor in Cologne, Freiburg, and Paris, in a long Latin poem celebrated the dead hero in sonorous verse.[140]

The number of orations delivered before Maximilian in his honor would be difficult to determine. Aschbach mentions twenty-two Latin speeches of greeting at the Vienna congress of princes in 1515 alone, the first of which was by Joachim Watt (Vadianus), the physician and later Bürgermeister of St. Gallen.[141] A good example of the type which might be expected from a scholar who had risen from the peasant or burgher class is the *Oratio* of Heinrich Bebel *De ejus atque Germaniae laudibus* of 1504,[142] in which the

[135] Cuspinianus, *De Caes.*, p. 611.
[136] *Freher-Struve*, II, 761-764.
[137] *Ibid.*, II, 765f.
[138] *Ibid.*, II, 769.
[139] Brant, *Narrenschiff*, ed. Zarncke, p. 198, no. 18.
[140] "Vita et obitvs Maximiliani I. imperatoris auctore Bartholomaeo Latomo." In *Vitae summorum dignitate et ervditione virorum ex rarissimis monumentis literato orbi restitutae*, cura Johannis Gerhardi Meuschenii (Coburgi, 1735), I, 1-25. E.g., p. 4:

> Justitiae custos, tutor probitatis & aequi
>   Praeque aliis semper religionis amans:
> Sive sacer mystes, seu jura sacrata patronum
>   Optassent, potior nemo petendus erat.
> Hoc duce tuta fuit pietas, defensaque virtus,
>   Hoc duce sacratis est data cura focis:
> Caesaris officium templis monstratur & aris
>   Caesareo superum munere crevit honor,
> Auctaque spectantur magno coenobia sumptu
>   Quae pollent titulis Maxmiliane tuis.

[141] Aschbach, *op. cit.*, II, 135.
[142] Schardius, *op. cit.*, I, 94-104. E.g., p. 94: "Mihi igitur te adeunti, *Sacratissime Rex*, incessit & laetitia & timor; Laetitia quidem vel incredibilis, quod ego adolescens infimae conditionis humilimoque locô natus, tanti viri affandi copiam sim nactus, Regis scilicet terrenique Dei, quique talis & tantus TU sis, ut omnium judicio non solum praesentes orbis terrae Reges, & in hunc usque diem viventes animi magnitudine, disciplina militari, singularique prudentia longe excellas; verum etiam in omni genere laudis, & gloriae, omnes superiores Reges quacunque tandem hi aetate floruerint, si non exuperaveris, aequasti tamen omnino, adeo ut Clementia Caesari, Justitia Trajano, Pietate Antonino, Gravitate Alexandro Severo nunquam cedas." etc.

flattered vanity of the lower class and genuine patriotism combine in a grateful effusion. Chapter LXIII of Jacob Wimpfeling's *Epitoma Germanicarum Rerum* (1505), which bears the heading "Ad Maximilianum Romanorum Regem," certainly resembles a laudatory address more than it does history.[143]

There is one humanist who does not fit so readily into the classifications that have gone before: Ulrich von Hutten. Some of his Latin poems fall into the same humanistic categories with those we have discussed, but with him they appear somehow more incidental.[144] In the tumultuous soul of Hutten there was little room for anything which did not directly concern the events of the moment. Everything he did, he did with tremendous energy and with all his heart. During the time that Germany was involved in strife in Italy, Hutten was continually haranguing the princes to promote the war,[145] encouraging Maximilian,[146] while abusing the Venetians.[147] Every victory called forth rejoicing;[148] a defeat evoked only renewed calls to battle.[149]

His attitude toward Maximilian is that which sees in the Kaiser the potential liberator of the nation, the man who may finally and decisively assert the integrity of the empire against France, in Italy, and against the Turks. Max' differences with the pope are seized upon and magnified; and his words are still quoted after his death to emphasize the division between the spiritual and temporal heads of the world.[150] Hutten's complimentary remarks

[143] Schardius, *op. cit.*, I, 197. E.g., the chapter ends: "Tu etenim Regnorum terrarumque potentia, militari gloria, experientia rerum, diversarum linguarum notitia, Sapientia, laborum & vigiliarum tolerantia, omnes Imperatores, quantumvis egregios vincis, superas, excellis."

[144] *Ulrichs von Hutten Schriften.* Hrsg. von Eduard Böcking, Leipzig, 1859-1869. E.g., *De Magnitudine Maximiliani ad Germaniam*, III, 210f.; *De Caesaris Magnitudine*, III, 247, no. 104.

[145] "Ritter Ulrichs von Hutten Vermahnung an die teutschen Fürsten, die Türken mit Krieg zu überziehen," in *Des teutschen Ritters Ulrich von Hutten auserlesene Werke.* Übersetzt und hrsg. von Ernst Münch (Leipzig, 1822-23), III, 236-302.

[146] *Schriften*, ed. Böcking, III, 123ff.

[147] Whose city he calls "the arrogant frog," *ibid.*, III, 216, no. 21; and cf. *ibid.*, III, 220, nos. 31, 32; 221, no. 34.

[148] *Ibid.*, III, 243f., nos. 95, 96.

[149] *Ibid.*, III, 216, no. 20; 232, no. 3; 234, no. 71.

[150] *Ibid.*, II, 384, reports that Max said of Pope Leo: "Nun ist dieser Bapst auch zu einem Bösewicht an mir worden; nu mag ich sagen daß mir kein Bapst, so lang ich gelebt, je Treu oder Glauben gehalten hat; hoffe, ob Gott will, dieser sol der

about Maximilian are mostly in the conventional style. Occasionally, however, we find a reference which lets us glimpse the Kaiser through his eyes for just a moment. He is to Hutten a just emperor, whom his princes respect, but do not fear. Therefore scarcely half of them obey him.[151] He is easy-going and completely duped by his secretaries, who have become rich and prodigal at his expense[152] and who actually rule him.[153] Nevertheless, Max is a fair and upright prince who hates tyrants and tyrannical deeds.[154]

The first three of the four statements cited above were made, as might be suspected from their lack of restraint, after Maximilian's death. The last characterization, however, was made during Max' lifetime. It was more a hope on Hutten's part than anything else. Duke Ulrich of Wurttemberg had offered a deadly insult to the house of Hutten,[155] and the dialogue *Phalarismus* was written to expose his tyranny and to stir up sentiment against him. In several long *Reden* Ulrich tries to arouse Maximilian to action in the case: he tells him how his mercy has been abused by the Duke[156] and declares that all hope for justice lies with him. Repeatedly he calls upon him for justice:

Give us a hearing then, Kaiser! Give us thine ear, protector of innocence, maintainer of justice, defender of freedom, to whom every duty is dear! May he hear us, successor to Augustus' throne, Trajan's worthy follower, ruler of the world, regent of the human race! Banish the fear of all! Preserve the remains of Germany! Avenge and save thy century, thy reputation, thy respect. Avenge the righteous, punish the miscreant![157]

Here we find ourselves back among the humanists where we

---

lezte seyn." Cf. *ibid.*, V, 363-384: "Eiñ trewe Warnung, Wie die bâpst allwegen wider die Teutschen Keyser geweßt," where the statement above is repeated. And cf. *ibid.*, IV, 427-457: "F. A. F. Poetae Regii Libellus de obitu Iulii Pontificis Maximi," p. 441.

[151] *Inspicientes*, or *Die Anschawenden* (1520), *ibid.*, IV, 288.
[152] *Febris Secunda* (1519), *ibid.*, IV, 138.
[153] *Praedones* (1520), *ibid.*, IV, 378.
[154] *Phalarismus* (1517), *ibid.*, IV, 9.
[155] He had conceived a passion for the wife of his *Stallmeister*, Hans von Hutten, and murdered the latter while he was unarmed and unsuspecting.
[156] *Werke*, ed. Münch, III, 74.
[157] *Ibid.*, III, 183f.

started. Even Hutten's encomiums end with a personal request. For our picture of Maximilian, he too has given us little beyond glittering generalities. We must conclude that we do not know just what these scholars and poets really thought of Maximilian. We do know that they had many reasons for wanting him to believe that they thought highly.

3. *Territorial representatives*

It is natural that Maximilian should be judged differently in the eyes of his fellow nobility than by the scholars and poets of Humanism. The nobility for the most part was made up of men of action, not students and dreamers; and they saw in Max the hunter, the soldier, the diplomat, rather than the patron of learning. At most they would know the story of how he had been turned against study through the poor methods of his teacher, just as had the young Duke of Wurttemberg.[158] It was more important to them that Max was a humane and friendly prince who could understand a joke.[159] They told with gusto the story of how Meister Albrecht stopped young Max as he was running away from a battle, and the latter turned about without resentment and conducted himself creditably.[160] They praised him for coming to the aid of faithful soldiers.[161] Among his men he did not dress nor conduct himself pretentiously, but he often wore such unassuming costumes that the soldiers might not even know that he was the Kaiser, unless some one, as in the case of Götz von Berlichingen, recognized him by his large nose.[162] To have served under him, to

---

[158] *Zimmerische Chronik*, III, 5. Hrsg. v. K. A. Barack, "Stuttgart. Lit. Ver." (Tübingen, 1869), Bd. 93.

[159] *Ibid.*, IV, 354, in "Stuttgart. Lit. Ver.," Bd. 94.

[160] *Ibid.*, IV, 355. "Fuegt sich uf ein zeit, das der kaiser ein trefen thette aigner person mit seinen feinden des kaisers volk wardt geschlagen, das sich der kaiser in die flucht wolt begeben. So schreit ine diser maister Albrecht an mit disen worten: 'Herr, flucht nit! das euch botz leicham schende! es ist kain herr von Österreich nie geflohen.' Der kaiser kert geschwindt wider umb, nams zu kainer ungnad oder misfallen uf, sonder sprach: 'Nun, nun ist kein herr von Österreich nie geflohen, so will ich auch nit der erst sein,' und man sagt, der kaiser hab sich in solcher schlacht wol gehalten."

[161] "Aus der Selbstbiographie Sigmunds Freiherrn von Herberstein (1486-1553)." *Die deutsche Literatur, Reihe 25, Deutsche Selbstzeugnisse*, IV, 159.

[162] *Lebens-Beschreibung Herrn Gözens von Berlichingen, Zugenannt mit der Eisern Hand*. Ed. *Verono* Franck von Steigerwald (Nürnberg, 1731), pp. 35f.

MAXIMILIAN VIEWED BY CONTEMPORARIES 49

judge by Sebastian Schertlin von Burtenbach, was considered a fine recommendation for a Reichsritter.[163] We hear from the companion of the young Archduke Philipp, Antoine de Lalaing, of his excelling his hunters in agility in 1503 as he clambered up the rocks after chamois,[164] or we read how he entertained his friends in good spirits after a successful hunt.[165] It is recorded too that he took great pleasure in the company of beautiful ladies and that he sometimes fled from business to enjoy their society.[166] Again we are told of his oratorical powers and how he could sway an audience to his will, as at the Diet of Constance in 1507, from which the representative from the Mark of Brandenburg, Eitelwolf von Stein, wrote home in glowing terms.[167] His knowledge of men was said to be so great that he could tell which of his servants were faithful to him and which were not.[168] His motto, "Halt Maß!" reminds us of his admirable temperance in all things.[169] The question of his fidelity, in relation to the Bruges imprisonment, is decided definitely in his favor by Wilwolt von Schaumburg, a knight in the Kaiser's service.[170]

Nevertheless, we also find a darker side of Maximilian exposed among the nobility. A vassal who had been wronged might look in vain to him for redress. His reputation as a just Kaiser is not upheld in the case of Johann Wörnher and his sons, who tried for years to get a settlement in the matter of some lands taken from them. Max promised repeatedly to adjust the difficulties; but with his habit of procrastinating and forgetting a sour duty in favor of more novel and pleasant occupations, he allowed the

---

[163] *Sebastian Schertlin von Burtenbach und seine an die Stadt Augsburg geschriebenen Briefe.* Mitgetheilt von Theodor Herberger (Augsburg, 1852), p. 243.

[164] Antoine de Lalaing, "Voyage de Philippe le Beau en Espagne, en 1501." (Premier Voyage) *Collection des voyages des Pays-Bas,* publiée par M. Gachard (Bruxelles, 1876), I, 312.

[165] *Zimmerische Chronik,* II, 59, in "Stuttgart. Lit. Ver.," Bd. 92.

[166] *Ibid.,* IV, 301.

[167] Report of Eitelwolf von Stein, quoted in Johannes Janssen, *History of the German People at the Close of the Middle Ages* (Second Eng. ed., revised, translated by M. A. Mitchell and A. M. Christie; London, 1905), II, 234.

[168] *Zimmerische Chronik,* IV, 150.

[169] *Ibid.,* II, 244.

[170] *Die Geschichten und Taten Wilwolts von Schaumburg.* "Stuttgart. Lit. Ver." (Stuttgart, 1859), I, 79.

matter to drag on over a long period of years.[171] So it went too with the quarrel between the Duke of Wurttemberg and the Huttens; Max had a dislike of offending the nobility in general, the knights in particular.[172] The Hutten affair was finally settled by Duke Ulrich paying *Maximilian* a sum of 27,000 florins; no mention is made of indemnity to the Huttens.[173]

The Kaiser's weak financial situation was well known to everyone. He borrowed so often and his credit was so poor that he was continually in difficulties, a position scarcely becoming to the dignity of Holy Roman Emperor. Letters from the royal councillors at Worms in 1496 stating that the feeding of courtiers has been suspended and that the same will happen to the queen and her ladies if no money is found within four days;[174] appeals from Wolf von Polheim and Marquard von Breisach describing the financial misery at the Dutch court, where the burghers of Malines have demanded the imprisonment of the most well-to-do courtiers until full payment of the royal debts;[175] discouraging reports from Martin von Polheim and Florian Waldauf von Waldenstein in 1493 that they can not get money from the Widow Wirsing, evidently of Innsbruck—in spite of all their offers of security she declares that she has no money, and that she would lend none to Max on any security:[176] these and other contemporary sources give some idea of Max' reputation as a debtor.

Concerning the political situation within the empire, Max had, of course, much opposition and the motives for his actions were

---

[171] *Zimmerische Chronik*, I, 550; II, 59, 72, 90; IV, 354.

[172] Cf. "Cronica newer geschichten," von Wilhelm Rem (1512-27), *Chroniken der deutschen Städte* (Leipzig, 1896), XXV, 71, where Rem tells us that the Kaiser placed a ban on Franz von Sickingen; but his anger soon cooled off and nothing came of it, and soon afterwards he took Franz into his employ. And *ibid.*, XXV, 91f., when v. Sickingen does more damage to Worms, Max does nothing, although he is a protector of Worms and Franz is his servant. He is loath to punish Götz von Berlichingen, who tells of his delight at hearing the Kaiser's answer to the Nuremberg merchants who wished the empire to take their part against Götz. Cf. Götz' *Lebens-Beschreibung*, pp. 125ff.

[173] Rochus von Liliencron, *Die historischen Volkslieder der Deutschen* (Leipzig, 1866), III, 190ff.

[174] Letter to Maximilian, Worms, May 27, 1496. Quoted by Kraus, *op. cit.*, pp. 108f.

[175] Letter to Maximilian, *ibid.*, pp. 103-107.

[176] Letter to Maximilian, Innsbruck, April 24, 1493, *ibid.*, p. 83.

questioned then and are still a subject of debate among historians. That he was hampered by jealousy of the territorial princes, is obvious, but they seem to have had grounds for believing that he played for the interests of the Hapsburg dynasty rather than those of the empire. It is, indeed, in the matter of the *Reichsreform* that Maximilian incurs the most severe criticism. It is for others to decide how much he is to be credited for what was accomplished in this regard or to what extent he is to be blamed for what failed.[177] In any event, there were many who placed themselves on the side of the energetic Berthold von Henneberg, Archbishop of Mainz,[178] and raised their voices in loud protest. All of the attacks did not come from those whose material interests were threatened. We have evidence of this in an interesting contemporary document which no doubt expressed the views of many at that time. An unknown Rhenish writer who attended the Reichstag at Worms in 1495, hoping to put through his reform-plans, was at first full of hope in the new Kaiser. A gradual estrangement arose between him and Max, however, no doubt because of the failure of the would-be reformer's plans. In anger he withdrew the dedication of his work to Maximilian and dedicated it instead to the Virgin Mary. With many bitter remarks about the blindness and stubbornness of rulers, he voiced his anger at the Kaiser's foreign policy as well as at his indifference to religious and political inroads on the empire.[179] The Kaiser's union with France and the pope in the League of Cambray was the last straw for the author, who

[177] Cf. Eduard Ziehen, *Mittelrhein und Reich im Zeitalter der Reichsreform 1356-1504* (2 vols.; Frankfurt a. M., 1934, 1937), who is decidedly unfavorable toward Maximilian. For the other side of the question, cf. Bernhard Schmeidler, "Die Bedeutung des späteren Mittelalters für die deutsche und europäische Geschichte," *Historische Vierteljahrsschrift*, XXIX (1934), 93-108; and by the same author, "Das spätere Mittelalter als ein Zeitalter der Auflösung und der Vorbereitung," *Welt als Geschichte*, II (1936), 349-367.

[178] Cf. Ziehen, *op. cit.*, who devotes much space to Berthold.

[179] "Ein oberrheinscher Revolutionär aus dem Zeitalter Maximilians I," reported by Hermann Haupt, Oberbibliothekar of the University of Giessen, in *Westdeutsche Zeitschrift für Geschichte und Kunst*, Ergänzungsheft VIII (Trier, 1893), 76-228. Cf. pp. 99-102. Haupt states that he found this account in an unknown manuscript of the Colmar Stadtbibliothek, Miscellanhandschrift nr. 50. It is the only copy of which he knows. One can only conjecture who the author was; he may have been from Alsace (cf. p. 89) and he was born about 1438 (cf. p. 92). He was definitely not a cleric (cf. p. 95).

even went so far as to demand his deposition.[180] Deeds which others praised, such as the beheading of Hans Pienzenauer, this critic censures as being as bad as those of Abimelech. He criticizes Max for his conflict with the Swiss, for making useless plans, for undertaking things he could not finish, for leaving his own land to win a foreign one. Max, he declared, is cheated by his councillors and badly influenced at court. He takes money from sharpers, usurers, and adulterers and ennobles them, while faithful old servants are plotted against and their names blackened until he consents to their execution.[181] When a king ceases to rule well, he continues, he should be chased out and the reform carried on in the hands of the people.[182] For this critic, the pope, the King of France, and Maximilian are "die drei unreinen Menschen."[183]

Another political declaration of the year 1495 is the Latin *Dream* of Hans von Hermannsgrün. Here the writer attacks the character of Max even more bitterly. In an imagined oration, Friedrich Barbarossa is made to call the German people to action, declaring that Max is more fitted for the distaff than for the sword. Sunk in luxury, he had allowed the King of France to conquer Burgundy, Picardy, Brittany, and the Duchy of Milan, as well as insult his daughter and seize his wife. The princes, the writer declares, should disregard this weak and spiritless king, take counsel together, and save their country.[184]

These, to be sure, are but two voices raised against Maximilian, but they are indicative of a feeling that possessed not only certain of the territorial representatives but also others who were striving with desperate earnestness to administer a saving dose to a weak and ailing empire. They show that to some earnest patriots in this crisis Max appeared to be a weak and selfish personality.

---

[180] *Ibid.*, p. 104: "Man wird dem Kaiser ein Bauernhütlein aufsetzen und ihn in das Elend schicken!"
[181] *Ibid.*, pp. 124f.
[182] *Ibid.*, p. 160.
[183] *Ibid.*, p. 206.
[184] "Der Traum des Hans von Hermannsgrün. Eine politische Denkschrift aus d. J. 1495." Mitgetheilt von Heinrich Ulmann. *Forschungen zur deutschen Geschichte*, XX (1880), 67-92. Latin text, pp. 78-92. Cf. Paul Van Dyke, *Renascence Portraits* (New York, 1905), p. 302.

4. Representatives of the cities

From the time that he had gone as "ein hubscher jungling"[185] of fourteen with his father to Trier to meet the mighty Duke Charles the Bold of Burgundy, Maximilian seems to have been regarded quite generally in the German cities with a spirit of almost fraternal good will. With increasing wealth and power and a consequently heightened sense of independence, the free burghers associated with their Kaiser in a way which sometimes appears a little patronizing on their part. Max' predilection for the city of Augsburg was well known.[186] Here the merchants were glad to see him come, especially when he called a Reichstag there, for then, by bribery of the right councillors, they were sure to make a nice profit.[187] Such occasions, however, were a mixed blessing for the city; and pious complaints arose because of the bad influence of wealth and courtly morals on the citizens, especially the young girls.[188]

The city of Nuremberg probably was second choice in Max' affections, and here he liked to entertain and be entertained by the ladies with banquet and dance. When they hid his boots and spurs to keep him beyond the time set for his departure, he good-naturedly entered into their fun and danced on into the evening, keeping the Count of the Palatinate waiting another day for him at Neumarkt.[189] For he was very fond of female company and would do favors for women which no other influence could extract from him, as when, in 1491, at the plea of the women of Nuremberg, he released the condemned captain of the mutinous Stuhlweissenberg troops.[190] It is recorded that at a certain dance in Augsburg, Max asked the women not to wear veils unless they were over 50 years old, so great an admirer was he of womanly

---

[185] "Die Chronik Erhards von Appenwiler 1439-1471." *Basler Chroniken*, hrsg. v. der historischen und antiquarischen Gesellschaft in Basel (Leipzig, 1890), IV, 358 ("Fortsetzung von unbekannter Hand").

[186] "Paul Hektor Mairs I. Chronik von 1547-1565." *Chroniken der deutschen Städte*, XXXII (Leipzig, 1917), 77.

[187] Wilhelm Rem, *op. cit.*, p. 101.

[188] *Zimmerische Chronik*, II, 303.

[189] *Chroniken der deutschen Städte*, XI, 503 ("Tucher'sche Fortsetzung der Jahrbücher bis 1469-1499"); XI, 722f., 731 ("Etliche Geschichten").

[190] *Ibid.*, XI, 731f. ("Etliche Geschichten").

charm.[191] He was always most polite to all women, and it was never heard of him that he had dishonored any girl.[192]

These features of the popular, amiable Max are the most favorable that appear in the picture of the Kaiser as drawn by burgher contemporaries. We hear also that he disliked flattery,[193] that he was brave and fearless in battle,[194] although not without moments of almost extreme caution.[195] His reputation as a hunter is also known to city chroniclers, who note that his anger is never so easily aroused as by infringements of the hunting laws.[196] His interest in learning, especially in history, was repeatedly emphasized by his calling on the cities for material in their archives.[197]

But the independent spirit of the burghers allows them to show other less complimentary characteristics of Maximilian such as we find, for instance, in no humanistic writer, except perhaps Reuchlin. We hear that he was always out of money, although he spent great sums on his secretaries and on the hunt, and that he had pawned nearly everything he possessed.[198] His attempts to extract money from the cities gave them opportunities enough to discover his lack of financial soundness. The city of Basel forced him to resort to humiliating requests for a loan of two thousand gulden; finally they gave it to him with very bad grace and wrote it off

---

[191] Wilhelm Rem, *op. cit.*, pp. 83f., February 1, 1518. But when the Fuggers and the Adlers began wearing veils like noble women, people said they had persuaded the Kaiser to make the request.

[192] "Georg Kirchmairs Denkwürdigkeiten seiner Zeit. 1519-1553." *Fontes Rerum Austriacarum*, I, 442.

[193] *Ibid.*, I, 421.

[194] *Ibid.*, I, 424f.; and "Iacobi Vnresti, theologi et sacerdotis Carinthiaci chronicon Avstriacvm," in D. Simonis Friderici Hahni, *Collectio monumentorum, veterum et recentium*, etc., Brunsvigae, 1724, I, 618.

[195] *Chroniken der deutschen Städte*, XI, 634 ("Heinrich Deichslers Chronik").

[196] Kirchmair, *op. cit.*, I, 441f. H. J. Zeibig quotes an official act which takes into account this latter characteristic of the Kaiser. "Der Ausschuss-Landtag der gesammten österreichischen Erblande zu Innsbruck 1518," *Archiv für Kunde österreichischer Geschichts-Quellen*, XIII (1854), 242f.

[197] *Christophori Lehmanni Chronica Der Freyen Reichs Stadt Speier*, (first published in Frankfort, 1612) (Franckfurth am Mäyn, 1698), fo. 169-a, tells how Max offered a large reward and honor to anyone who could find a letter written in German five hundred years before; and on Dec. 18, 1498, he asked Speyer to lend him the oldest German writings in the original in its archives. Max also intended to have a general chronicle of Germany written, for he especially favored history.

[198] Kirchmair, *op. cit.*, I, 443.

MAXIMILIAN VIEWED BY CONTEMPORARIES 55

as a loss to the city.[199] In the matter of the administration of justice it was the sad but usual experience that the imperial councillors took money from both sides and favored the highest giver—and, according to Wilhelm Rem, Max allowed this to go on.[200] He himself let men out of prison instead of punishing them, because he or his councillors were paid for it. The cities' prisoners sometimes got out by paying councillors, although Maximilian did not always know this.[201] It was so commonplace a fact that it took money to get a favorable hearing that in 1518 Lucas Rem would not even try to press his case against Bartolomaeus Welser, since he "neither hoped nor expected to get any justice, neither here, nor from His Royal Majesty."[202]

Other attempts to praise Maximilian raise a doubt as to their sincerity, for they produce the opposite effect on the mind of the reader. The Carinthian preacher Unrest defends him from the accusation of having broken his word to Bruges by the naïve argument that Max had promised only to leave the country within a certain time, but that he had not said he would not come into it again.[203] Kirchmair mentions Max' mercy and kindness to the captured Italian cities, but adds that he was merciful to them with the hope of winning their affections.[204] Max' oratorical powers were of no help against the rebellious *Landsknechte* at the retreat from Milan in 1516; they called him "Strohkönig" and "Apfelkönig"[205] in mockery of his weakness.

While Anshelm gives Maximilian all possible credit for attempting a peaceful agreement with the Swiss in 1499,[206] the more accurate view of the cities is probably that of Wilhelm Rem, who declared that Max "always wanted to wage war and yet had no money."[207] Rem complains that the princes never sent their share

---

[199] Peter Ochs, *Geschichte der Stadt und Landschaft Basel* (8 vols.; Basel, 1786-1882), IV, 433-442.
[200] Wilhelm Rem, *op. cit.*, p. 99: "Er hett rätt, die waren laurbůben, die regnierten in gar."
[201] *Ibid.*, p. 100.
[202] *Tagebuch, op. cit.*, p. 20.
[203] Unrest, in Hahn, *op. cit.*, I, 774f.
[204] Kirchmair, *op. cit.*, I, 428.
[205] *Ibid.*, pp. 437ff.
[206] *Die Berner-Chronik des Valerius Anshelm*, hrsg. vom Historischen Verein des Kantons Bern (6 Bde.; Bern, 1884-1901), II, 98f.
[207] Wilhelm Rem, *op. cit.*, p. 100.

of men when the *Bund* and the cities had sent theirs, and so from insufficient preparation and bad management five or six hundred thousand men from the cities died because of the Kaiser.

Finally, Maximilian's indecisiveness arouses criticism. The Esslingen ambassador complains of his childish inability to make up his mind;[208] and Max' slowness, or neglect, in going to the aid of Anne de Bretagne in 1491 earns him the epithet "dilatory" from the same source.[209] Even less favorable is the report of his seizing and hanging the captain of Malannoy during his wars in Flanders—this "unprincely deed and revenge," as Anshelm calls it.[210] Although it probably was not intended by the chronicler as a stain on his memory, Unrest's account of his accepting large sums of money from Styria and Carinthia for permission to drive out the Jews[211] shows Maximilian just as lacking in tolerance as most of his contemporaries.

Thus the attitude of the representatives of the cities is one of admiration for Maximilian's popular character, but it does not prevent full recognition of his limitations in other respects. In spite of all his fraternizing with them, he never fooled them. They gave him respect; and when they could not refuse, they gave him money and men. But they did not approve of what he did with these, and they said so as loudly as they dared. In comparison with the brilliant figure created by the humanists, the Maximilian of the city historians and other burgher-scribes is a Maximilian with most of the glamor removed. Only the traditional glory of the imperial office clings to his figure and commands respect and attention.

B. Foreign Sources

The Italians whose comments on Maximilian have been examined can be divided into two groups: humanists and political writers.

In their treatment of the figure of the emperor the Italian

---

[208] Quoted by Peter Diederichs, *Kaiser Maximilian I. als politischer Publizist* (Heidelberg, 1932), p. 67.
[209] *Die Berner-Chronik des Valerius Anshelm*, I, 375-382.
[210] *Ibid.*, I, 158.
[211] Unrest, in Hahn, *op. cit.*, I, 795f.

MAXIMILIAN VIEWED BY CONTEMPORARIES 57

humanists do not differ from the Germans in subject-matter, style, or purposes. A good example is Ludovico Ticiano's "Concerning the Praise of the Kaiser and the Germans."[212] He calls Maximilian "King of Kings and Duke of Dukes," great in peace and war, excellent in understanding and mind as well as in body; so skillful in peaceful government and in military affairs that it is hard to tell whether he is dearer to the citizen or the soldier. He extolls his simplicity, his kindness, his chastity, and especially his faithfulness to his men and his unshakable love for the Church. He mentions that people reproach Max for sloth, for the buying of peace with money, and for his poverty; but, he declares, the first two accusations are unfounded, and as for the last, poverty is no disgrace, since both Cyrus and Alexander were poor and still their names are honored.

We find similar extravagant praise repeated in the *Austriados* (1515)[213] and in the *Hodoeporicon* (1515)[214] of Ricardus Bartholinus of Perugia (Perusinus), and in the *Epicedion* (1494) of Paulus Amaltheus, who was trying to get a position at the university of Vienna;[215] in the panegyrics of Girolano Balbi (Accellini) of Venice,[216] and in the *Carmen* of the Umbrian Ioannes Antonius Modestus.[217] In an oration before Maximilian and Blanca Maria at Innsbruck in 1494 Jason Maynus lauded Max for his extraordinary knowledge of languages;[218] Pandolphus Collenutius, legate from the Duke of Ferrara, speaking before the emperor in Innsbruck in 1494, praised him for all virtues, for his illustrious family, for his extensive empire, and for his universal fame;[219] Hermolaus Barbarus, legate from Venice to Friedrich III and Maximilian in Bruges in 1486, brought his

---

[212] Ludwig Geiger, *Renaissance und Humanismus in Italien und Deutschland*, quotes Ticiano, p. 346. Geiger says that this work is as yet unprinted and unmentioned.
[213] Justus Reuberus, *Veterum Scriptorum*, I, 469-734.
[214] *Freher-Struve*, II, 613-672.
[215] Gustav Bauch, *Die Reception des Humanismus in Wien*, pp. 33-38. Cuspinianus was his pupil and may have been influenced by him in his *De Caesaribus*.
[216] *Ibid.*, p. 38.
[217] *Briefwechsel des Beatus Rhenanus*, gesammelt und hrsg. von Adalbert Horawitz und Karl Hartfelder (Leipzig, 1886), pp. 578, 596.
[218] *Epithalamion*, Freher-Struve, II, 470.
[219] *Oratio, ibid.*, II, 476-481.

Signory's congratulations to the new king and recited all the virtues he then possessed and all those he was expected to acquire in the future.[220] In his *Staurostichon* in 1509[221] and in the dedication to Max of his work "On the Imagination" (1500), Pico della Mirandola lauds the Kaiser for his attainments in peace and war. In the latter work he eulogizes especially Max' "keenness of mind," his "strength of body," his "knowledge of affairs and languages," his "foresight, justice, bravery, self-restraint, liberality, kindness" and "piety." Like the majority of these writers, Pico hopes that Maximilian will restore liberty to the Christian State.[222]

As was pointed out in connection with the writings of the German humanists, we can not make much use of these accounts in the construction of a picture of Maximilian as the Italians saw him. Such indiscriminate praise marked the conventional way in which a legate or a poet addressed the emperor. A distinction must be made between what a poet said to him and what a political representative said about him.[223]

The Italian statesmen looked at Maximilian with a cool and calculating appraisal, and what they found good in him can all the more be considered their sincere opinion since they more often saw the bad. In 1508 Machiavelli commends his affability and graciousness in his audiences,[224] but adds that he will grant an audience only when it suits him.[225] Quirini also mentions his kindness and cordiality,[226] while Francesco Vettori says: "But he is

---

[220] *Oratio Gratulatoria, ibid.,* II, 408-414.

[221] "Staurostichon Ioannis Francisci Pici Mirandulae Domini, et concordiae comitis, heroicum carmen de mysteriis dominicae crucis nuper in Germaniam delapsis: ad Maximilianum Aug. Romanorum Regem." *Ibid.,* II, 497-506.

[222] *Gianfrancesco Pico Della Mirandola On The Imagination.* The Latin Text with an introduction, an English translation, and notes, by Harry Caplan (New Haven and London, 1930), pp. 18f. "Cornell Studies in English," XVI. Ed. by Lane Cooper.

[223] Caplan, *op. cit.,* p. 16, note 2, says: "Abject humility of this sort in communications addressed to Roman Emperors is to be regarded as rhetorical commonplace, the practice having its historical roots in the Panegyrists of the Empire."

[224] *The Historical, Political, and Diplomatic Writings of Niccolo Machiavelli,* translated from the Italian by Christian E. Detmold (4 vols.; Boston, 1882), IV, 397 ("Second Report on the Affairs of Germany. Made 17 June, 1508").

[225] *Ibid.,* IV, 402f. ("Discourse on the Affairs of Germany and on the Emperor").

[226] "Relazione di Vincenzo Quirini, Tornato Ambasciatore dall'imperatore Massimiliano nel Decembre 1507." *Le Relazioni degli Ambasciatori Veneti al Senato Durante il Secolo Decimosesto.* Raccote ed Illustrate da Eugenio Albèri (Firenze,

MAXIMILIAN VIEWED BY CONTEMPORARIES 59

so good and humane a gentleman that he has become too easy and too credulous."[227] Machiavelli even goes so far as to maintain that if Max could get over two qualities, *weakness* and his *easy nature,* "he would be a most perfect man."[228]

Here we see a characteristic of the Italian attitude. Everything adduced in Maximilian's favor has a "but" attached to it. He is kind, *but* he is too kind for his own good. He is generous, but being too liberal, he gets into one financial difficulty after another.[229] One report tells of Max' popularity among his soldiers, whom he never abandons in danger.[230] But from other sources we hear of his troops leaving him in Italy and going back to Germany because of their lack of confidence and respect.[231] Machiavelli even accuses him of plain desertion of troops, to be slaughtered by the Venetians.[232] Vettori exonerates him from this charge, however, in what seems to be a more accurate account.[233]

The point upon which the Italians seem to feel most strongly, since they mention it most often, is Maximilian's chronic poverty. This is easy to understand, since they were most interested in the Kaiser's plans in Italy, and these depended entirely upon his ability to find support. Max' inconstancy and extravagant ideas, "in conjunction with an immense prodigality, and dissipation of money," declares the Florentine historian, Guicciardini, "interrupted all his successes and lost him all his opportunities."[234] To this Machiavelli brings confirmation: "There is not, and perhaps

---

1862), Serie I, Vol. VI, p. 26: "Per quanto spetta all'animo, è umanissimo, piacevole, affabile con ognuno."

[227] Letter from Trent, Feb. 8, 1508. Machiavelli, *op. cit.,* IV, 109.

[228] *Ibid.,* IV, 397 ("Second Report, etc.").

[229] Vettori, letter of Feb. 8, 1508. Machiavelli, *op. cit.,* IV, 109.

[230] Quirini, *op. cit.,* p. 26: "Ha un credito inestimabile tra tutte le sorte di soldati tedeschi, avendo a tutti per molte esperienze dimostrato non fuggir alcun pericolo, e mai abbandonar i suoi nella battaglia."

[231] Vettori, Trent, June 8, 1508. Machiavelli, *op. cit.,* IV, 150. "In fact, their going home at this time seems to me proof of their having little affection, and still less respect, for the emperor." And Machiavelli, "Second Report," IV, 396, says: "And the little estimation in which he is held causes his feeble resolutions and their still more feeble execution."

[232] *Ibid.,* IV, 393 ("Second Report").

[233] Innsbruck, March 22, 1508. *Ibid.,* IV, 126.

[234] Francesco Guicciardini, *The History of Italy, from the Year 1490, to 1532,* translated into English by the Chevalier Austin Parke Goddard (London, 1753), VII, 117.

never has been, a prince more wasteful than he is. This is the reason why he is always in want, and why he never has money enough, no matter in what situation he may find himself."[235] Many instances are cited which tend to prove that Max should have more money than he has. He collects money in Flanders, we hear; receives 150,000 ducats from the pope, 100,000 more from France, and still he sits in Innsbruck letting slip the opportunity for a magnificent victory in Italy, "all the sums he had received in so many places not being sufficient to answer his prodigality."[236] His expenses, it is reckoned, actually should not be very large, while his resources and revenues are quite sizeable; thus he should be able easily to take Italy. "But the emperor, with all this income, never has a penny; and what is worse, no one knows what becomes of all his revenues."[237]

Some of the Italians, at least, made guesses as to where Maximilian spent his money. Giustinian, Venetian ambassador at the court of Henry VIII of England, contends that Max spent money intended for one thing in a very different way; and we may assume that he means on personal pleasure.[238] Pope Julius II was more definite in ascribing the low state of the Kaiser's finances to his passion for hunting;[239] while Machiavelli suggests, less specifically, that "the emperor's frequent needs of money are the consequences of his frequent irregularities."[240] Unless Max changed his ways, Machiavelli declares, "if all the leaves on all the trees in Italy had become ducats, they would not suffice him."[241]

[235] Machiavelli, *op. cit.*, IV, 402f. ("Discourse, etc.").
[236] Guicciardini, *op. cit.*, IV, 281.
[237] Machiavelli, *op. cit.*, IV, 395 ("Second Report"); cf. Quirini, *op. cit.*, p. 26, who calls Max "prodigo più tosto che misero."
[238] *Four Years at the Court of Henry VIII. Selection of despatches written by the Venetian ambassador, Sebastian Giustinian, and addressed to the Signory of Venice, January 12th 1515 to July 26th 1519.* Translated by Rawdon Brown (London, 1854), I, 259, and note 5, p. 262.
[239] *Letters and Papers, Foreign and Domestic, of the Reign of Henry VIII.* Arranged and catalogued by J. Sherren Brewer (Referred to hereafter as *Letters and Papers.*) (London, 1862), II, Part 1, 539, no. 1877: "Imperator est levis et inconstans, alienae pecuniae semper mendicus quam male consumit in venandis camuciis, et tamen conciliandus nomine diaboli et pecunia ei semper est danda."
[240] Machiavelli, *op. cit.*, IV, 396 ("Second Report").
[241] *Ibid.*, IV, 395.

This last remark, however, should not be construed as too harsh a statement. It has been said that in view of the fact that Maximilian's bad financial condition was such common knowledge, Machiavelli's words are mild and scarcely injurious.[242] The Florentine, indeed, admits that Max needs much more money than the King of Spain or any other sovereign for carrying on war, as the Germans are a free people and will not serve unless overpaid.[243] There is, however, biting scorn in the words of a papal nuncio to Francis I of France, which the latter repeated in the presence of the Venetian minister, that when the Kaiser had no money he was accustomed to leave his wife in the inns as a pledge.[244] This sort of unkind ridicule was common in Venice and Florence. The representative of Venice in London received complaints from "German lords of account" that an abusive work had been printed in Venice against Maximilian.[245] Many years later Luther tells his table companions[246] of a *Fastnachtspiel* in Venice in which Max in a hunter's costume and with an empty purse followed the Prince of Venice and the King of France, whose purses were full; while the Florentines expressed in vulgar but forceful fashion their disdain for "Maximilian of the empty purse."[247] These Venetian *Ludibilia* had been mentioned in Germany by Kirchmair[248] and Hutten.[249] In Milan Lodovico il Moro

---

[242] Moritz Brosch, "Machiavelli am Hofe und im Kriegslager Maximilians I." *Mitteilungen des Instituts für österreichische Geschichtsforschung*, XXIV (1903), 98.

[243] Machiavelli, *op. cit.*, IV, 396f. ("Second Report").

[244] Brosch, *op. cit.*, p. 98.

[245] Giustinian to the Doge, Nov. 1, 1516. *Letters and Papers*, II, Part 1, 781, no. 2499.

[246] *D. Martin Luthers Werke. Kritische Gesamtausgabe: Tischreden.* 6 Bde.; Weimar, 1912-21. References to the play by the Venetians alone are found in I, p. 4, no. 5; II, 609, no. 2709-b; while references to this and also to the picture of the Florentines are found in III, 193, no. 3149-a, 194, no. 3149-b, 559, no. 3717; V, 160, no. 5449.

[247] As late as 1754 Christoph Freiherr von Bartenstein used the Italian nickname, "Massimiliano di pochi denari," as an evil example to be avoided by his pupil in history, the Archduke Joseph. Cf. Matthias Koch, "Aus dem zum Unterrichte Kaiser Josephs II. bestimmten Lehrbuch der deutschen Reichsgeschichte, verfasst vom Staatssecretär Baron Bartenstein," *Kais. Akad. d. Wissenschaften, Phil. Hist. Classe, Denkschrift* (Wien, 1850), I, Teil 2, 168-186. Cf. p. 174.

[248] Kirchmair, *op. cit.*, I, 424.

[249] *Schriften*, ed. Böcking, II, 167ff.; 250, no. 113.

bragged that Max was his condottiere, who came and went as he pleased.[250]

Nevertheless, if we look beyond this universal opinion of the emperor's incompetence in money matters we can find more favorable traits for his character-sketch. In spite of his unfavorable judgment in other respects, Guicciardini sees Max as "merciful, bountiful,"[251] and a lover of peace.[252] However poor his opinion of the Kaiser as a manager of his finances in Italy, Machiavelli says that Max "governs his country with great justice."[253] In a land where Maximilian's arms practically never met with good fortune, all these writers agree with one assent that he was a good general, skillful and successful in war.[254] He is described also as a man inured to fatigue as well as any soldier, courageous in danger,[255] and doggedly persistent in carrying out his plans.[256] Reports of his turning back from certain projects[257] might seem to indicate fearfulness or over-caution, if we did not know of the need for vigilance when the Signory of Venice, for example, was carrying on wholesale attempts to poison people of note, Maximilian among them.[258]

The same writers, however, point out fundamental weaknesses in his character as a military leader. Vettori speaks of his habit

---

[250] Jacob Burckhardt, *Die Kultur der Renaissance in Italien. Ein Versuch* (9 Aufl. hrsg. v. Ludwig Geiger; Leipzig, 1904), I, 44, quotes from Malipiero, *Ann. Veneti, Archiv Stor.* VII, I, 492.
[251] Guicciardini, *op. cit.*, VII, 117.
[252] *Ibid.*, I, 69.
[253] Machiavelli, *op. cit.*, IV, 397 ("Second Report").
[254] *Francesco Vettori*, Trent, Feb. 8, 1508. Machiavelli, *op. cit.*, IV, 109: "It cannot be denied that he is an active and careful man, most skillful in the art of war, laborious and of great experience; and more reputed than any of his predecessors for the past hundred years."
Machiavelli, *op. cit.*, IV, 402f. ("Discourse, etc."): "On the other hand he is most warlike, and knows how to maintain and conduct an army well, preserving justice and discipline . . . and as a general is not inferior to any man of the present day."
Guicciardini, *op. cit.*, VII, 117: "He was otherwise a prince very knowing in the art of war."
Quirini, *op. cit.*, p. 26, calls Max "esperto nelle guerre e nel governo degli eserciti più che null'altro capitano di Alemagna. . . ."
[255] Machiavelli, *op. cit.*, IV, 402f.
[256] Guicciardini, *op. cit.*, IV, 153.
[257] Vettori from Trent, Feb. 8, 1508. Machiavelli, *op. cit.*, IV. 108.
[258] Burckhardt, *op. cit.*, II, 350f.

MAXIMILIAN VIEWED BY CONTEMPORARIES 63

of wanting to carry through everything in person, although he might entrust much to others.[259] While unwilling to share his plans with others, he was unable to come to any firm decision by himself. In describing the Kaiser's military movements in Italy, Guicciardini is again and again struck by his instability,[260] by his love of novelty,[261] and by "his fickleness and ill-digested councils."[262] This indecision and unreliability in the Kaiser's behavior causes much comment.[263] "He is very fickle," writes Machiavelli,[264] "wanting one thing today, and next day caring nothing about it; he takes counsel from no one, and yet believes everybody. He desires what he cannot have, and leaves that which he can readily obtain; and therefore he always takes contradictory resolutions. . . . He is extremely reticent; he lives in a constant state of agitation of mind and body, and often undoes in the evening what he has concluded in the morning. This makes the missions near him very difficult. . . ."

It was no doubt Maximilian's reticence which caused much of the diplomatic criticism both from friendly and hostile quarters. Their task was to discover information; the Kaiser's secrecy thwarted them.[265] At all events, they find much to criticize. They speak severely of Max' gullibility; it is said that anyone can deceive him at least once.[266] He is accused of implacability,[267] of arrogance,[268] dilatoriness,[269] and vanity.[270]

[259] Machiavelli, *op. cit.*, IV, 108.
[260] Guicciardini, *op. cit.*, II, 131.
[261] *Ibid.*, IV, 83.
[262] *Ibid.*, IV, 163; and cf. IV, 284, 286; V, 203; VII, 117, etc.
[263] Cf. Machiavelli, *op. cit.*, IV, 395, who quotes the priest Lucas; and the oft cited passage by Quirini, *op. cit.*, p. 27.
[264] Machiavelli, *op. cit.*, IV, 402f. ("Discourse, etc.").
[265] Machiavelli, *op. cit.*, IV, 87, quotes Disviri, Jan. 17, 1508: "The emperor observes the greatest secrecy in everything he does; if he but changes his lodgings, he sends his cook only after he has himself been for an hour on the way, so that no one may know where he is going." Cf. Vettori's letter of Feb. 24, 1508, *ibid.*, IV, 98; and Machiavelli's letter of Dec. 12, 1509, *ibid.*, IV, 218; also Guicciardini, *op. cit.*, IV, 153; VII, 117.
[266] Machiavelli, *op. cit.*, IV, 397; cf. Vettori, *ibid.*, IV, 109; and Giovio, quoted by Guicciardini, *op. cit.*, VI, 404f., note.
[267] Giustinian to the Doge, Nov. 1, 1516, *Letters and Papers*, II, Part 1, 781, no. 2499.
[268] Giustinian, *op. cit.*, I, 226.
[269] Guicciardini, *op. cit.*, VI, 399, 404.
[270] Machiavelli, *op. cit.*, IV, 392 ("Second Report").

Altogether, the most serious accusations seem to be those of prodigality and indecision. The Italians were interested in Maximilian as a potential political ally, or, more often, as a possible enemy. Thus it is that they regard him; when his fortunes or his plans shift, so do their opinions and their actions. The minister of Venice gives a stirring address to the new King of the Romans in 1486 and is full of admiration and congratulations.[271] In the same city shortly afterward the Venetian agent whispers into the ears of the king's captors: "Homo mortuus non facit guerram."[272]

The Italian picture of the Kaiser does not lack kind features. But these are in the minority. There was no longer alive in Italy any great enthusiasm for a Holy Roman Emperor. There was, on the other hand, an eager desire to use the German ruler to further dynastic and other political ambitions. The politicians and political writers therefore looked at Max with realistic eyes. They found him very much a mortal man, a man with good qualities, but weak and wavering, and usually involved in troubles of a very earthly sort.

The attitude toward Maximilian in France was comparable in part to that in Italy; but it never reached the degree of seriousness that it did in the latter country, where Max and his armies had become a familiar sight. After his entrance upon his duties as the new Duke of Burgundy in 1477 Maximilian had been kept busy, either defending his boundaries from French attacks, or worrying about greater attacks to come. The French, on the other hand, although repulsed in parts of Burgundy and in Flanders, were quite safe within their borders. With the help of French money properly distributed they had no fear of Max' getting enough help from the princes to become a menace to their country. Confident in a larger and more professional army and with coffers well filled with cash, Charles VIII had even had the temerity to seize Anne of Brittany, who had already been married by proxy to Maximilian, and marry her himself. Then, to add insult to injury, he refused for some time to send home Max' daughter Margaret, to whom he had been legally affianced when they were

---

[271] *Freher-Struve*, II, 408-414.
[272] "Ex Trithemii chronicorum Hirsaugiensium." *Freher-Struve*, II, 418.

both children.²⁷³ When the French finally sent Margaret home, they ridiculed Max by making a straw figure of him and dragging it in derision through the puddles.²⁷⁴

The constant need for money which plagued Max was well known across the French border. Even when he became their ally, the mood in the French court and camp is probably correctly described by Gian Giacomo Trivulzio, the famous Milanese in French service, who said, "The Kaiser is building castles in the air, and would be able to dry up a sea of gold."²⁷⁵ An English spy, writing from Malines on June 10, 1516, declared of the French: "They are afraid of none but England. The King of Castile has not a farthing, and the emperor has even less."²⁷⁶

Maximilian's main contact with France was by way of Burgundy, and at least a partial picture may be had of this phase of his life and the impression he left there. When Max came to Flanders in 1477, Philippe de Commines sourly remarked that he knew nothing: partly because of his youth, partly because he was a foreigner in a strange country, and partly because he had been too poorly brought up to have knowledge of much.²⁷⁷

A quite contrary picture, however, is that sketched by Jean Molinet in his *Chroniques*.²⁷⁸ To him Max is prudent in deed, discreet in counsel, sober in conversation, gracious of bearing, inventive, devoutly Catholic, charitable to the poor, kind, skillful at arms, pleasing to the ladies, and chaste and pure of soul and body. "In short, he is endowed with so many precious gifts, so

---

²⁷³ Margaret was still a child of eleven years at the time of the *Brautraub* (1491).
²⁷⁴ Anshelm, *op. cit.*, I, 381.
²⁷⁵ Quoted by Brosch, *op. cit.*, p. 109.
²⁷⁶ *Letters and Papers*, II, Part 1, 600, no. 2027.
²⁷⁷ *Mémoires de Philippe de Commynes*. Nouvelle édition publiée avec une introduction et des notes . . . Par B. De Mandrot (2 vols.; Paris, 1901, 1903), II, 16.
²⁷⁸ "Chroniques de Jean Molinet," publiées par J.-A. Buchon (5 vols.; Paris, 1827-1828), *Collection des chroniques nationales françaises*, vols. 43-47. Molinet lived in the second half of the Fifteenth Century as canon in Valenciennes, therefore he was a contemporary of the Burgundian-French wars and in the center of the fighting area. He is so highly eulogistic in his writings on Maximilian that we must take what he says with a large grain of salt. Cf. Hermann Klaje, *Die Schlacht bei Guinegate vom 7. August 1479* (Greifswald 1890), p. 6. Molinet even goes so far as to draw a long and tiring comparison between the three temporal heads—Kaiser Friedrich, King Maximilian, and the Prince Philip—and the Trinity in Heaven. Cf. *op. cit.*, III, 99-117, Chapter 149: "Le Paradis terrestre."

much knowledge and good manners, acquired and natural, that the people of the country count themselves fortunate to have such a prince and master." Physically he is a man such as any woman would be content to have as a husband, "a Narcissus brought to life." In the matter of generosity, who can be compared to the archduke, who is able to say: "I am the son of the emperor and king"?[279] Max soon became a popular youth among his soldiers too, we hear. Often he was in the saddle with them for twenty-four hours at a time.[280] Olivier de la Marche, a French chronicler at the Burgundian court, declares in his memoirs that the young duke did not disdain to take a pike on his shoulder and march with his footsoldiers.[281] The men-at-arms admired his courage at the battle of Guinegate, when he fought fiercely in the front line, and himself vanquished two of the enemy and captured a third.[282] Still, in spite of his popularity, they would sometimes abandon him for lack of pay.[283] If his officers and men in the Swiss War had had their leader's courage and temperance, de la Marche thinks that the Swiss and not the Germans would have been defeated.[284] The same observer also praises his great energy. In Flanders he prepared attacks both on land and water so diligently that his enemies were confounded and knew not where to expect him next.[285] Moreover, he was a great knight in single combat. He met "Claude de Vaudre, Signeur de L'Aigle," a Burgundian and his subject, a strong man and very experienced in arms on foot and on horse, and in the encounter Max conducted himself chivalrously and finished with honor.[286]

[279] Molinet, *op. cit.*, II, 85ff.
[280] *Ibid.*, II, 217.
[281] "Mémoires de Messire Olivier de la Marche," *Collection complète des mémoires relatifs à l'histoire de France, depuis le règne de Philippe-Auguste, jusqu'au commencement du dix-septième siècle;* etc., par M. Petitot (Paris, 1825), Série I, X, 443. This writer, who composed his memoirs in 1501 (cf. p. 470), was in the service of the Burgundian court and may therefore be expected to be prejudiced in favor of Max. However, he emphasizes his intention of describing only those things which he himself saw or had heard at first-hand from the very best authorities (p. 465); and the fact that he is not always complimentary encourages confidence in his report.
[282] Molinet, *op. cit.*, II, 201f., 204, 212; de la Marche, *op. cit.*, p. 428, says of Maximilian, who is not yet 19 years old, that he "avoit courage de prince et d'homme chevaleureux"; and p. 472 he calls him "cœur-d'acier."
[283] de la Marche, *op. cit.*, p. 442.
[284] *Ibid.*, p. 471.
[285] *Ibid.*, p. 443.
[286] *Ibid.*, p. 469.

Other arts than fighting were not neglected at the Burgundian court. The chapel-music, which had enjoyed a good reputation under Duke Charles the Bold, had suffered during the Duke's later wars and the musicians had been dispersed. Maximilian had them brought together again, and sought out besides the best musicians and singers, many of whom had enjoyed great honors at various courts of Europe.[287]

The fatal trait of character which later caused so much criticism from the Italians, also plagued Max as a youth in Flanders. One of his ministers would advise him one way, a second minister would advise a contrary course; until, torn between two counsels, he would not know what to do and so put off the decision until a later date.[288] He was not to be entirely excused from blame when Charles VIII seized his intended bride. "I do not believe," says de la Marche mildly, "that the King of the Romans exercised as much diligence in aiding and succoring the Duchess of Brittany as he should have."[289]

The attitude toward Maximilian in France is rather difficult to establish. Those who were more Burgundian than French, or who depended in some way on Max, are naturally full of his praises, but did not altogether overlook his faults. French scholars are not unacquainted with the influence of Maximilian on learning in Vienna and they are favorably impressed.[290] Others in France seem to have regarded him with light derision, as scarcely worth their comment; but if we may believe a story current in Germany which Hutten put into Latin verse,[291] one very competent French

[287] Molinet, *op. cit.*, III, 2f.
[288] de la Marche, *op. cit.*, p. 450.
[289] *Ibid.*, p. 432.
[290] Janssen, *op. cit.* (English ed.), I, 160, quotes from Pierre Froissart's *Lettres*, pp. 14ff.
[291] Hutten's *Schriften*, ed. Böcking, III, 211: "De Divo Maximiliano Imperatore Germanico Lvdovici Regis Gallorvm Testimonivm."

> Rex invitarat quondam ad convivia Gallus
>   Insigni quosdam nobilitate viros,
> Qui cum de variis loquerentur Regibus, unus
>   Maxmilianaeas extenuavit opes,
> Dixit et esse Augustana hunc modo Consulem in urbe,
>   Nec formidandum Regibus ergo aliis.
> Sed cum Caesareas ita vires extenuari
>   Audiret, sapiens Rex Ludovicus ait
> "Certe ego Consulem eum nolim contemnere, namque is
>   Tympana si pulsat, Gallia tota tremit."

judge of rulers thought otherwise. The story runs that some one in the presence of King Louis of France, thinking he would please the king, declared that Maximilian was nothing more than mayor of Augsburg. "Yes," Louis wisely replied, "but every time that mayor rings the bell, he makes all France tremble!"[292]

In Maximilian's Burgundian duchy, as in France, there were divided opinions of his character. To the praises of Molinet and de la Marche there may be added those of the anonymous author of "Die wonderlycke oorloghen,"[293] to whom all Max' deeds seem marvelous, and the chronicle of Despars,[294] which is scarcely less laudatory. Nevertheless, the picture we get of Maximilian from these Flemish sources is not entirely eulogistic. His bravery in battle is unquestioned;[295] it inspires his soldiers, as do his eloquent words and pious gestures.[296] His energy and persistence in resisting France during the first years after his marriage[297] appear in bright relief in contrast with the slight esteem which Louis XI at first had of his powers.[298] Whether these chroniclers intended to or not, however, whether naïvely or ironically, they nevertheless reveal unfavorable qualities of Max along with favorable. His generosity, for instance, is illustrated by his liberality with money which his captains have acquired;[299] and the pension he so magnanimously gave to the savior of St. Omer must be paid by

---

[292] As told by A. J. G. Le Glay; *Correspondance de l'empereur Maximilien I*ᵉʳ *et de Marguerite d'Autriche* (Paris, 1839), II, 420. Notice the different ending in Hutten's poem.

[293] Called to public notice by M. Auguste Voisin, *Notice sur le seul exemplaire connu d'un livre intitulé: Die wonderlycke oorloghen van den doorluchtighen hooghgheboren prince, keyser Maximiliaen, hoe hy hier eerst int landt quam, ende hoe hy vrou Marien trowde. Édition de 1577.* (Without date or place.) The French version: *Chronique des faits et gestes admirables de Maximilien I*ᵉʳ *durant son mariage avec Marie de Bourgogne*, translatée du Flamand en Français pour la première fois, et augmentée d'éclaircissements historiques et de documents inédits, par Octave Delepierre, Bruxelles, 1839.

[294] *Cronijcke van den Lande ende Graefscepe van Vlaenderen*, gemaect door Joʳ Nicolaes Despars, Poortere ende Inboorlinck der Stede van Brugghe, Bacelier in die Rechten. Van de jaeren 405 tot 1492. Tweede Uytgaef, Vierde Deel; Brugge & Rotterdam, 1840.

[295] *Ibid.*, IV, 193.

[296] Delepierre, *op. cit.*, pp. 222f., 226f., 232f.

[297] *Ibid.*, p. 161.

[298] Commynes, *op. cit.*, II, 47.

[299] Delepierre, *op. cit.*, p. 213.

MAXIMILIAN VIEWED BY CONTEMPORARIES 69

the town itself.[300] Likewise his great courtesy to a prisoner of war is the subject of approbation; but it is noted that he is thus polite only because he expects to exchange the prisoner for an officer of his own.[301] Quite contrary are his actions with respect to Guillaume de Liège,[302] or a French spy in Ghent,[303] or Sadet, the captain of Mollennoy.[304] Their pleas for mercy all meet a deaf ear. At Bruges it was told that Fransoys Roels, a carpenter, was sitting drinking in a tavern as Max and his court rode by. When someone asked Roels if he was not going to get up and watch the Roman King go past, he answered without considering: "The devil take the Roman King, with all those who like him and wish him well! I'll not move a foot for him!" For this speech he was denounced and lost his head.[305]

Such events as the last contributed to the rise of the rebellious factions in Bruges, Ghent, and Ypres. Encouraged by French money, the bold Flemish burghers had seized Maximilian's daughter in 1482 and sent her to the French court as the future wife of the Dauphin, had dictated terms to Archduke Philip and King Maximilian, and finally in 1488 they seized Maximilian and held him captive for several months. It was said, Despars reports, that Max' councillors were to blame for the shortages of money and the indignities to Flemish citizens. But there is no doubt that the burghers of at least these cities held Max personally responsible for many of their grievances.

Nevertheless the impression made upon them by the young king need not have suffered too much. They still remembered the "Kaiser and King" as the dashing young archduke, the husband of their native queen, the leader of their armies. They still told of his skill in the tournament, when he would unseat a doughty knight to the delight of the crowd, or when he entertained the onlookers and himself with a shooting match.[306] Only when their

---

[300] *Ibid.*, p. 391.
[301] *Ibid.*, p. 213.
[302] *Ibid.*, p. 123.
[303] *Ibid.*, p. 137.
[304] *Ibid.*, pp. 272f.
[305] Despars, *op. cit.*, IV, 305.
[306] *Ibid.*, IV, 185f.

personal liberties were infringed upon, when they thought their *Privilegien* were in danger, the sturdy clothmakers could forget their admiration for the popular figure and come quickly to grips with hard facts.

Across the Channel, in England, the news of Maximilian was mostly second-hand, coming from the English ministers who were in Germany on affairs of state. Only during the brief period in 1513, when Germany and England combined forces and routed the French army in the "Battle of Spurs," did Max come into personal contact with Henry VIII and his court. The clerk of the Parliament, John Taylor, who was an eye-witness of events in Calais in 1513, writes of Max: "He is of middle height, with open and manly countenance, pallid complexion, has a snub nose [Max' Roman nose is emphatic in the portraits!] and a grey beard; is affable, frugal, an enemy to pomp."[307] The picture, too, which Sir Robert Wingfield sent home was highly enthusiastic about the virtues of the emperor.[308]

Nevertheless, most of the reports from Germany by English observers are bitter and uncomplimentary. Maximilian is blamed for his slowness and the habit of delay which costs him otherwise easy victories.[309] Instead of being temperate, Colman declares, "the Emperor Maximilian . . . tipples up wine and he tipples up all the money he can get."[310] It is the money question which determined practically the whole English viewpoint. Max is depicted as insatiable in his demands for cash, unscrupulous in his methods of obtaining it, dishonest in his manner of disposing of it. Pace complains repeatedly to Wolsey that money sent to Maximilian is just the same as thrown away;[311] and the Lord High Treasurer in London tells the Italian minister that England would never think of sending Max any money, for the same reason.[312] It

---

[307] *Letters and Papers*, I, 625, no. 4284.
[308] *Ibid.*, II, Part 1, 517, no. 1817, Pace complains to Burbank, Apr. 3, 1516: "Sir Rob. Wingfield takes him for a *God,* and thinks that all his deeds and thoughts do proceed ex (Spirit)u Sancto. It was only for this purpose that he wished a commission."
[309] *Ibid.*, II, Part 1, nos. 1816, 1844, 1854, 1942, 2014, 2019.
[310] *Ibid.*, II, Part 1, 166, no. 606, Th. Colman to Wolsey, June 22, 1515.
[311] *Ibid.*, II, Part 1, 570, no. 1964; 594, no. 2016; 598, no. 2024.
[312] Giustinian, *op. cit.*, I, 150.

is charged that money sent by England for payment to the Swiss went through Max' hands and that the Swiss never saw it;³¹³ and that he always managed to get possession of some of any money near him "by force or false promises of restitution."³¹⁴

Maximilian's expeditions into the eastern part of his empire were, until 1515, never on a peaceful mission. It is no wonder then that a Bohemian writer on the affairs of his country, Dubravius, looking back nearly a century later on this period, calls him "experienced in the adverse fortune of battle," and censures him soundly for the cruel slaughter and pillage at Stuhlweissenburg, where the soldiers plundered the churches and, according to the writer, Max himself carried away a golden cross.³¹⁵ The same incident is used for the same illustration by writers on Hungarian affairs.³¹⁶ Max gained a brief reputation for clemency and generosity when in Vienna in 1490 he persuaded the defeated Hungarian forces, by kindness and gold, to join him; "for Maximilian was not only the most humane," says a clerical chronicler of the period, "but also in liberality second to no king of his time."³¹⁷ Nevertheless, the same writer tells us that to get his soldiers together to fight the Hungarians in the first place, Max had to spread shrewd lies among them—for the Germans were accustomed to being beaten by the Hungarians.³¹⁸

Thus we see the image of Maximilian reflected in the words of different sorts and conditions of men, of various degrees and nationalities. At one end of the scale the scholar and poet sing the praises of their fellow author and patron; at the other the disgruntled diplomat of a foreign country sets forth a long list of

---

³¹³ "Extracts of Intelligence from Italy," *Letters and Papers*, II, Part 1, 531, no. 1854 (May 4, 1516).

³¹⁴ *Ibid.*, II, Part 1, 517, no. 1817. Pace to Burbank, April 3, 1516.

³¹⁵ *Io. Dubravii Olomvzensis Episcopi, Historica Bohemica* (Hanoviae, 1602), p. 257.

³¹⁶ Petrus Ranzanus, "Epitomes rervm Vngaricarvm," *Scriptores rervm Hvngaricarvm veteres, ac genvini*, cvra et stvdio Ioannis Georgii Schwandtneri (Vindobonensis, 1746), I, 408; and *Antonii Bonfinii rervm Vngaricarvm decades* (Basileae, 1568), p. 679.

³¹⁷ "Lvdovici Tvberonis, Dalmatae Abbatis, Commentariorvm de rebvs, svo tempore, nimirvm ab anno Christi MCCCCXC. vsque ad annvm Christi MDXXII," in Schwandtner, *op. cit.*, II, 156: "Vt erat Maximilianus, non modo humanissimus, verum et liberalitate nulli regum aetate sua secundus."

³¹⁸ *Ibid.*, p. 153.

defects and vices. In between we find all classes of opinion, each witness influenced, according to human nature, by his own experiences, his likes and dislikes, and especially by his own particular profit, hopes, or disappointments.

Such is the written testimony of Maximilian's contemporaries. What of the picture of the Kaiser as seen in the popular poems of the time, those sung to popular tunes, and those merely meant to be declaimed? We shall examine now the Kaiser's portrait in the contemporary *Volkslied* and *Spruch*.

III

MAXIMILIAN IN *VOLKSLIED* AND *SPRUCH*

A. The *Volkslied*

IN THE POPULAR SONGS of the latter Fifteenth and early Sixteenth Century Maximilian is a familiar figure. It has been said that a prince has seldom been the professed favorite of all parties without distinction in such degree as was Maximilian in the German folksong.[1] Nevertheless, mention of him is mostly of casual occurrence, as part of the general background. It is nearly always complimentary. It must also be taken into account, however, that such uncomplimentary songs as may have existed and which were probably few, would necessarily die out quickly, due to the censorship of local officialdom and to the lack of opportunity to sing them frequently. Thus we hear that a poem, "Wie Herzog Friedrich zu Würzburg Pfleger werden wollte," was being distributed on leaflets in Würzburg in the spring of 1493 by a girl from Bamberg.[2] In this poem little is said about Maximilian; but it is directed against the party to which he belonged and which had been worsted in the event described. Bishop Rudolf II von Scherenberg had the girl seized quickly and the copies of the poem burned, although he was of the successful party. Herzog Friedrich and Maximilian learned of the song, however, and demanded the punishment of the poet or at least of the printer.

Incidents such as this do not justify the inference that Maximilian was not a very popular figure in the current *Volkslieder* of his time. It is, indeed, safe to conclude that he was. Countless happenings affecting the empire and the imperial fortunes were

---

[1] Ludwig Geiger, *Renaissance und Humanismus in Italien und Deutschland*, p. 344. It should be noted here that in referring to the "historical" *Volkslied*, we have employed the terminology customarily used by such writers as, e.g., Liliencron in the work quoted below. These *historische Volkslieder* might more properly be termed "news letters" or "news songs"; strictly speaking, they are not folksongs in the popular sense.

[2] Rochus von Liliencron, *Die historischen Volkslieder der Deutschen vom 13. bis 16. Jahrhundert* (Leipzig, 1886), II, 329-332, no. 188.

commented on in song, and somewhere a reference to the Kaiser was usually brought in. Nevertheless, the incidental way in which mention is made of him is noteworthy. The poet is seldom an impartial observer of the event about which he sings. He writes under the impression of some particular occurrence and he is usually strongly for either one side or the other. The historical facts themselves are ordinarily taken for granted and used mostly as a background for the poem. In the foreground the folksong often develops into partisan poetry of a political or religious character, while the historical connections may become quite loose and the characters generalized. Events may even be displaced, so that a song written about one thing may be applied years later to a similar happening.[3]

Thus the term "historical folksong" is sometimes misleading. At first sight it gives an undue impression of authenticity in its account, as if "historical" were synonymous with "historically true." The fact that the poet was a contemporary of the historical event seems to lend his words authority.

A word should also be said about the melody and the form of the historical folksong, for these were of great importance for the effect produced on the contemporary listener.[4] Well-known songs gave a particular meaning to certain tunes, which might then be used later in a similar circumstance to achieve a similar effect. The first lines were very important, giving the theme of the verses to follow. Thus certain melodies became so familiar that no words at all were necessary to indicate their meaning. A good illustration is the story told of Maximilian and the imperial city of Regensburg. In 1486 the city had fallen away from the empire and accepted the protection of the Duke of Bavaria. Maximilian was deeply resentful, and refused to enter the city in 1490 as he sailed down the Danube. Instead, he took care that his feelings should become known to the crowd of Regensburg citizens who had gathered along the city walls to watch his ship go by. As he

---

[3] Cf. *Das deutsche Volkslied,* ausgewählt und erläutert von Julius Sahr. Neubearbeitet von Paul Sartori. "Sammlung Göschen," no. 25 (Berlin und Leipzig, 1924), I. Teil, p. 26.

[4] Liliencron, *op. cit.,* IV, 93f. ("Nachtrag").

came opposite them he had the royal musicians strike up the familiar tune: "O du armer Judas, was hast du getan!"[5]

The largest number of folksongs in which Maximilian is mentioned is the group which was written about his battles, and notably enough, about his successful battles. In a song of Flanders commemorating the battle of Blangy, the youthful engagement of Maximilian on the hills of Guinegate, where the French met defeat in 1479, we hear of Max as "ung jeune prince, humble et plein de vaillance."[6] In a Flemish song on the same event, we find again the account of the young archduke calling to his men to take courage before the battle; then, as the French soldiers approach, falling on his knees to pray and making the sign of a cross on the ground, which he kisses and bids his men do likewise:[7]

> Ons edel prynce Maximiliaen
> hy beete hem neder te voet
> ende hi viel over zijn knien,
> biddende gode met ootmoet:
> "kinderen, dus wil ick dat ghi allen doet
> ende ghi heeren van hooger weerde!"
> Met dien maecte hi een cruyce voor hem,
> hi custe die aerde,
> die tranen hem ontspronghen;
> sie riepen alle Flander de leeu
> met vlaemschen tonghen.

The insult given Maximilian by France, when in 1491 Charles VIII persuaded or forced the former's intended bride, Anne de Bretagne, to become queen of the French, was never fully avenged

---

[5] "Die XXVII. Maij. zu Mittag ist der König Maximilian zu Regenspurg durch die Bruckh gefaren, und zwischen den zwaien Prücken hat er den *armen Judas* pfeiffen und trumeten lassen. Er wolt auch in die Stat nit." From: "Anonymi Ratisbonensis Farrago historica rerum Ratisponensium ab anno Christi DVIII. usque ad annum Christi MDXIX," Oefelius, *Rer. Boic. Scrip.*, II, 519-a. Cf. accounts of the same event by Christophorus, *ibid.*, I, 565; and by Hochwart, *ibid.*, I, 224. For the first verses of the "Armer Judas" song, cf. Emil Weller, *Annalen der poetischen National-Literatur der Deutschen im XVI. und XVII. Jahrhundert* (Freiburg i. Br., 1862), II, 20 (no. 4), XII.

[6] Louis de Baecker, *Chants historiques de la Flandre. 400-1650* (Lille, 1855), p. 223.

[7] Liliencron, *op. cit.*, II, 160f., no. 158, Strophe 4. For the prose account of the same event, cf. Delepierre, *op. cit.*, pp. 126f.

in any important and decisive battle. There was no glorious victory to sing about; but the theme of a woman's broken heart and a forced parting inspired the song "Das Fräulein von Brittania," and this achieved added effect by being set to the music of a familiar lament on the separation of two lovers.[8] Here is no characterization of Maximilian, however, but the story of Anne de Bretagne, at least from the German viewpoint.

The unsuccessful outcome, too, of the engagements with the Swiss in 1499 gave no occasion for songs of praise on the German side. Rather there arose a flood of abusive and accusing songs on the side of the Swabian League, directed against the Swiss, who quickly answered with recriminations and derision. Many of these songs merely call upon Maximilian. A Swiss poet addresses "edler künig Maximilian" and "O römischer künig vil lobesam, aller genedigster herr!"[9] and tells him that if he had had Swiss soldiers he would have had an example of real loyalty. Another Swiss poet urges Max to stop fighting; he has been defeated and is now only wasting men.[10] Likewise "der alt gris," Peter Meiler or Müller von Raperswil,[11] expresses similar sentiments on the part of the *Eidgenossen*. The poets on Maximilian's own side confine themselves to such general laudatory statements as "Der romisch kunig ist aller eren voll,"[12] or encourage Max to rout "die grauwen puren."[13] Occasionally he even incurs a little criticism for his conduct of affairs. When Basel joined the Swiss Confederation in 1501, the poet, Caspar Jöppel, dared to sing:

> Das solt der römsch küng han besunnen,
> damit Basel nit von im wer komen,
> als sich das wol gezeme!
> der Österreicher spot was so groß,

---

[8] Liliencron, *op. cit.*, II, 292-300, no. 180-a; cf. a Flemish version in the *Antwerpener Liederbuch* of Hoffmann von Fallersleben (Hannover, 1885), pp. 174f., no. 115: "Van keyser Maximiliaen."

[9] Liliencron, *op. cit.*, II, 370-374, no. 197, strophes 28-29. "Ein new lied von den Schwizern und von dem schwebischen bund, hat gemacht bruoder Hans im finsteren tan."

[10] *Ibid.*, II, 397f., no. 205, "Von der Schlacht zu Glurns."

[11] *Ibid.*, II, 420-426, no. 210. This song given by Anshelm, *op. cit.*, II, 256-264.

[12] Liliencron, *op. cit.*, II, 386, no. 202, strophe 13: "Ein lied von dem schwebischen bund von den Schweizern."

[13] *Ibid.*, II, 379, no. 199, strophe 12: "Landsknechtlied von den Schweizern zu Feldkirch gesungen."

MAXIMILIAN IN *VOLKSLIED* AND *SPRUCH* 77

> das die von Basel gar übel verdroß;
> sie werden sich selbs lernen kennen.[14]

A more definite statement about the character of Max finally appears in a song on the Landshuter Krieg of 1504. On September 12 he gained a decisive victory over the Bohemian forces, which were supporting the Pfalzgraf near Regensburg. In the familiar *Landsknechtlied* of Hans Gern von Ems beginning:

> Es kumt noch wol ein gute zeit,
> daß man in fremden landen leit
> mit pfeifen und mit trummen . . .

we hear that

> Der römsch küng fürt der eren ein kron,
> in der schlacht was er davornen dran.[15]

This is, however, more detailed information than we are usually given. In "Ein hüpsch lied von dem Benzenouwer,"[16] which tells the story of the bombardment of the traitor Pienzenauer in the fortress Kufstein and his eventual execution with several of his followers in spite of Erich von Braunschweig's plea for mercy, it is not the Kaiser's bravery and military skill that stand out so much as the fact that he had sworn an oath to take vengeance on all the defenders and to slap the cheek of anyone who dared plead for them. This unfavorable picture may be explained in part by the last strophe, in which we learn something about the author:

> Der uns das lied von nûwem sang
> von nûwem gesungen hat,
> er darf sich ouch nit nemmen,
> von wägen siner stat;
> er ist darby gewesen,
> von adel ist er geborn,
> und wer er nit entrunnen,
> man hett im ouch geschorn!

---

[14] *Ibid.*, II, 458, no. 222, strophe 3: "Wie Basel ist schweizerisch worden."
[15] Strophe 8, "Die behemer Schlacht." *Liederbuch aus dem sechzehnten Jahrhundert*, von Karl Goedeke und Julius Tittmann (Leipzig, 1867), pp. 276ff., no. 10. Cf. Liliencron, *op. cit.*, II, 536-548, no. 241.
[16] Rochus von Liliencron, *Deutsches Leben im Volkslied um 1530*, "Deutsche National Literatur," XIII, 44-49, no. 11. Cf. Liliencron, *Die historischen Volkslieder der Deutschen*, II, 550-556, nos. 245, 246; and Aretin, *Beiträge zur Geschichte und Literatur*, IX (1807), 1286-1291, "Das Lied von dem Benzenauer."

Later investigation has also disclosed that the song presents Max in an unnecessarily harsh light.[17]

On the death of Maximilian's son, Philip, in Spain in 1506, a lament was written by Peter Frei.[18] The poet's praise of Maximilian is illustrative of the general way in which so much is said about the Kaiser in most of these historical folksongs and yet so little of a definite nature revealed:

> Der eren kron er billich trait
> ob allen andern künig gemait
> in kaiserlicher wirdigkait,
> darzů hat in got selber außerkoren
> zů künig und kaiser hie auf erd,
> daß er regnier das weltlich schwert,
> durch in das reich gemeret werd,
> dar zů ist er von edlem stamm geboren
> ain herzog und ain fürst aus Österreiche,
> auf erden lebet kaum der sein geleiche,
> darumb sond mir got täglich für in bitten;
> got im verleich weishait und kraft,
> sein grafen, freien, ritterschaft,
> durch das das übel werd gestraft
> umb gotes er, der für uns hat geliten!
>
> Das thů uns got der herr zů gůt!
> herr got hab uns fürbaß in hůt
> von Österreich das edel plůt,
> zů dem wir alle unser hoffnung setzen,
> zum künig Maximilian!
> sein lob ich nit aussprechen kan,
> got im groß wird und eren gan,
> got well den künig seines laids ergetzen!

In 1507 Maximilian's prospects of obtaining aid from the Estates seemed to be excellent, and everyone looked forward to his early departure for Rome to receive the imperial crown. From Flanders come promises of help with men and money, and one unknown Flemish poet describes "the bold eagle" as he first came from Austria to marry the Duchess of Burgundy:

---

[17] Cf. Oswald Redlich, "Zur Belagerung von Kufstein im Jahre 1504," *Mitteilungen des Instituts für österreichische Geschichtsforschung*, IX (1888), 104-113.

[18] Liliencron, *Die historischen Volkslieder der Deutschen*, III, 1-5, no. 251, strophes 12-13.

> Den Arent coen quam eerst wt Oostenrijck
> Met een leewinne was hi eerst ghepaert
> Een stout baroen, men vant niet zijns gelijc
> der leeuwen dieren heeft hi wel bewaert
> Sijn volc geschaert,
> stelde hi in ordinancien
> met wapenen ende lancien
> Hi en vant noeyt lien, die werc bien
> Si en mosten vlien Voor het wijse engien
> Ghemoet waren alle zijn cansen.[19]

It was about this time also that a German poem "Vom Romzug" was composed, beginning:

> Der römisch künig ist wol erkant,
> im dienen manche weite land,
> sein mächtigkait fürdrungen,
> ainer der ganzen cristenhait,
> sein lob von manchen zungen.

The song then goes on to tell of the various parties that will accompany the king on his trip to Rome and ends with best wishes for luck on the journey:

> Got helf dem künig auf diser fart,
> gelück werd an im nit gespart,
> daß er schaff seinen frummen!
> laß in mit kaiserlicher kron
> widerumb in teutsch land komen![20]

Maximilian was held back from his designs, however, by the refusal of the Venetians to allow him passage through their territory. Confidence in his ability to surmount these difficulties was expressed in a song written about 1508 by Hans Probst zu Schwaz, probably the Tirolese Schwaz below Innsbruck. The song was written to the tune of "Die Böhmenschlacht," in which the Kaiser's fame and success in arms had been celebrated shortly before. Since the melody, as we have pointed out above, was usually chosen to indicate an idea similar to that expressed in the original song, it was no doubt used here to signify the valor and might of the Roman King:

---

[19] *Antwerpener Liederbuch*, p. 162, no. 107, strophe 2.
[20] Liliencron, *Die historischen Volkslieder der Deutschen*, III, 15ff., no. 254, strophes 1 and 17.

> Der remisch kaiser ist tugend vol,
> er waiß wie er sich halten sol,
> das kan er wol erkennen;
> er waiß wer im trew oder untrew ist,
> noch praucht er frölichen klůgen list,
> daß er niemant tůt nennen.
>
> Der edel kaiser Maximilian
> stelt nach der kaiserlichen kron,
> die im got hat erkoren:
> das wolten geren understan
> vil böser Cristen mit falschem wan,
> den es auß neid tät zoren. . . .
>
> Ich traw dem edlen kaiser wol,
> er die recht als er pillich sol,
> lat sich dar an nit wenden;
> nun hat er doch ains heldes mût,
> er schafft und peut, was in tunkt gůt,
> bringt das zů gůtem ende.[21]

But Maximilian's progress toward Rome lagged, and it seems that even some of his admirers became a little impatient. A song of 1509, which has been ascribed to Pamphilus Gengenbach of Basel,[22] tells

> wie er mit clůgen sinnen
> sein feinde strafen kan;

and wishes him luck and victory in his expedition to Rome; but in his last strophe the author indicates that now it is time for Max to do something; he will not write about him again until he has finished the trip:

> Dar bei ichs nun laß bleiben,
> got geb ym glück und heil!
> von ym wil ich nit schreiben,
> biß er die fart verbring.

During Holy Week of the year 1512 Maximilian was in Trier when the Archbishop, Richard von Greiffenklau, removed from

---

[21] *Ibid.*, III, 26, 28, no. 257, strophes 4, 5, and 20: "Ain hipsches lied von dem Romzug."

[22] Cf. *Pamphilus Gengenbach. S R F.* Hrsg. von Karl Goedeke (Hanover, 1856), pp. 536-540; and Liliencron, *Die hist. Volkslieder der Deutschen*, III, 28-33, no. 258: "Ein news hüpsch lied von dem krieg zwischen dem bapst, keiser, künig von Frankreich und den Venedigern."

beneath the altar of St. Peter's Cathedral the relic supposed to be the seamless coat of Christ. The news of this event was at once spread abroad by numerous pamphlets, and resulted in the printing of the old minstrel poem of King Orendel by Froschauer in the same year. The contemporary accounts give all credit to Maximilian, not only for ordering this relic exposed to the public worship, but also for the discovery that it was there in the first place. A miraculous touch is given the incident in a song "Wie der heilige rock funden ward,"[23] which Liliencron believes was written in 1512. This relates how Max goes from the Netherlands to Cologne, where an angel tells him to proceed to Trier and see the coat of Christ. The pope accords his permission for the pilgrimage and the Kaiser goes to Trier. On the altar in the cathedral fifteen candles are seen mysteriously burning and no one knows whence they came. The altar is removed and the coat found beneath it, along with the dice with which the Jews had gambled for Jesus' clothes. The Kaiser also finds a book which no one except himself can read. He reads in it for three days and learns many divine things. Other miracles also happen, and everyone honors the pious King who has caused such wonderful things to come to pass.

> Du edler kaiser hochgeborn,
> got hat dir solich er erkorn,
> du erwirbst uns gottes hulde,
> die freid der ewigen seligkait,
> daß wir tailhaftig werden Jesus klaid,
> sprecht amen, das gescheche![24]

It was in the same year, 1512, that the citizens of Kaufbeuren complained to the Swabian League about the frequent depredations of a group of robber knights, whose headquarters were in the supposedly impregnable castle of Hohenkrähen in the Hegau. In November, supplied with arms by the Kaiser, the League sent an army of 8000 men under Paul von Lichtenstein and Georg von Frundsberg to take the fortress; and partly by good fortune, partly through accurate firing of their large guns, the besieging force took the castle within a few days. This quick action against

[23] Liliencron, *op. cit.*, III, 63-66, no. 266.
[24] *Ibid.*, III, 66, strophe 27.

a group which was fast becoming a major cause of resentment in the cities called forth much genuine rejoicing among the burghers. One singer, doubtless of Kaufbeuren, "ein kaufman . . . der ouch wirbt uf dem land," expresses forcefully the feeling of those who suffered most from the degenerating nobility:

> Maximilian, o keiser,
> du aller wirden ob,
> des unrechts ein zerzeiser,
> dir si ein ewig lob!
> hast Hohenkrän zerbrochen,
> gedemt ir dratzlich bochen,
> ich wolt er wurd erstochen
> der dirs zû argem mißt,
> kein frumkeit in im ist.[25]

Now it was hoped that the *Landfriede* was at last beginning to work, that the various factions of Germany were becoming unified into one whole and that the German eagle was recovering his lost glory. One singer, rejoicing in the signs of growing unity, compares what he thinks is about to be realized with conditions shortly before, when

> der adler hat schier verloren
> sein federn alle gar,
> die er in kurzen jaren
> uberkunt, solt nemen war![26]

Now even "Welschland" was becoming alarmed at the apparent unity of Germany, and the sad eagle, so long scorned, would again take his flight from one sea to the other.[27] Then, after foretelling the good order that will henceforth reign in the land, the poet goes on to the story of the taking of Hohenkrähen. The original poem ends with strophe 32, but an evidently later addition continues from strophe 33 to 38: "Ein beschluß und lobgesang zu eren dem durchleuchtigsten keiser Maximian":

---

[25] Liliencron, *Deutsches Leben im Volkslied um 1530*, pp. 372-376, no. 128: "Wider den Schenkenbach," strophes 12 and 10.

[26] Liliencron, *Die hist. Volkslieder der Deutschen*, III, 69, no. 267, strophe 5. This song by Hans Schneider was sung in 1513. The strophes 33-38 were evidently added sometime later, probably not very long afterward.

[27] *Ibid.*, III, 69, strophe 6.

33. Lob und dank so můß ich sagen
dem keiser Maximian.
er wil nit mer vertragen,
als er bißher hat gethan;
gar lang hat er geschwigen
und hat gewart der zeit,
mit kummer und mit leiden
ward es größlich vernůt.

34. Syn gleichen kan man nit finden
in der alt und nůwen ee
und auch im bůch der künigen,
daß ie kein keiser me
verachtung, schmoch hab gelitten,
als er dann hat gethon
mit gedult zů allen zeiten,
so ers möcht gerochen han.

35. Das wirt in got ergetzen
noch gar in kurzer zeit,
syn namen wirt er setzen
in manches land gar wyt,
dann man findt klarlich geschriben
in der gschrift, sag ich für war,
hoffart got nie ließ bleiben
und sazt demůt enbor.

36. Darumb bis wol gemůte,
edler keiser Maximian,
got hat dich in seiner hůte,
wil dich nit verlan
zů trost der christenheite
und auch der kurch zů Rom,
dann es ist an der zeite,
sie wurd sunst gar vergon.

37. Mit dir wirt got noch würken
vil gůts in diser zeit,
daß du der bösen Dürken
strafest iren großen nyd
und auch die christenheite
bringst auf ein rechten weg,
die iezund ist zerströute
recht als der kot am weg.

38.   Nit me so wil ich singen;
dich well behůten got,
biß du alls mögst verbringen,
das von dir geschriben stot!
Ich hoff dir soll nit schaden
das eclipsis diser sunn,
in hůt so well dich haben
Maria aller gnod ein brunn!

The relations between Germany and France had undergone several changes during these years. At first deadly enemies after the insult by Charles VIII, then unnatural allies in the League of Cambray in 1508-09, they finally had parted again in the confused jumble of shifting Italian intrigue. The accusations of desertion which the French showered upon Maximilian were answered, probably in 1510, in "Ain hüpsch lied vom römischen kaiser und den Franzosen,"[28] by an unknown poet who uses the familiar symbols of the lily and the peacock to represent respectively France and Austria. Sung to the "Fräulein von Brittania" melody to give a satirical touch to the parting of Germany from France, this song represents the lily reproaching the peacock for his breach of faith. The latter in reply reminds France of her long hypocrisy, recalls the incident of Anne de Bretagne, now the wife of Louis XII, and cites the broken French pledges in Gelderland. Another song, evidently written in 1513, since it celebrates the successful defense of Navarra by the Swiss against the French in June of that year, expresses hope that the Kaiser will do something decisive against France, and appeals to the Estates to stand by him in whatever he undertakes.[29] Then, when the combined forces of Maximilian and Henry VIII of England—but mostly of the latter—routed the French at Guinegate in the "Battle of the Spurs" in August of 1513, Gengenbach[30] sings of the skill of the Kaiser in the battle,

>   der aller förderst wolt er sein
>   mit synem eignem lybe.

---

[28] *Ibid.*, III, 87ff., no. 273.
[29] *Ibid.*, III, 90ff., no. 274.
[30] *Ibid.*, III, 101-104, no. 277, strophe 20. This battle is known as the *Sporenschlacht*, because of the wild flight of the French.

In this rout of the French, he says, the booty was great and Maximilian was highly praised by his English ally:

> 25. Groß lob und er, als ich verstand,
> hat gseit der küng von Engelland
> dem keiser Maximiane:
> spricht, er sei nit allein syn fründ,
> für ein vater wil er in hane.
>
> 26. Er hab für in gesezt lyb und gût;
> in lobt gar ser das edel blût,
> den prys thût er im geben,
> er meint daß in nöten syn gelych
> nie gewunnen hab das leben.

Then after warning Louis XII of his impending fall because of his pride, arrogance, disobedience, and selfishness, the song closes with a paean to Maximilian:

> 36. Do mit dis lied ein ende hat;
> got söllen wir loben frû und spat,
> das in so wol ist gelungen;
> dem edlen keiser Maximian,
> hab ichs zû eren gesungen.
>
> 37. Dann es im gat nach synem sinn,
> das ich im von ganzem herzen ginn,
> sein anschleg sind wunderlyche,
> darumb ich in genzlich verglych,
> Julio dem keiser ryche.

Another song of defiance against the French gives us the point of view of the *Landsknechte,* eager to fight under their leader. When in 1516 the agreement of Noyon between Francis I of France and Maximilian's grandson Karl appeared to have been broken by the former, it seemed to the Germans that a new outbreak of hostilities between the two nations must occur. Jörg Graff, the *Landsknecht*-singer who is responsible in part for the general recognition of Maximilian as originator of his order,[31]

---

[31] Cf. in Liliencron, *Deutsches Leben im Volkslied um 1530*, pp. 333-336, no. 117, the poem "Landsknechtorden" by Graff, which begins:

> Got gnad dem großmechtigen keiser frumme,
> Maximilian! bei dem ist auf kumme
> ein orden durchzeucht alle land
> mit pfeifen und mit trummen,
> landsknecht sind sie genant.

sings in 1517 of the power of the German eagle and prophesies that it will teach France more respect in the future.³² To the King of France he declares:

> 14. den kaiser mûst lernen kennen
>   den du lang hast veracht.

and asks him:

> 15. Was hilft dich dann dein großer gwalt?
>   wann dich der pfau will kriegen,
>   so bistu gar erkalt.

Still another poet, a Netherlander, showed his respect for the Kaiser by making the King of France appear afraid of the German arms. In "Van den hertogh van Gelder," probably written about 1517, Karl van Gelder asks the King of France for 20,000 soldiers; but Francis answers cautiously that he can not risk it, it might bring him

> in also groote ellende:
> de keyser dat isser so magtigen man,
> mocht tegen my nemen den oorlogh an,
> Bourgonje algemeyne,—groot en kleyne.³³

In the affair between Duke Ulrich of Wurttemberg and the Hutten family the Kaiser had acted very cautiously. When Ulrich fled to him in remorse after his bloody act, Maximilian was not unkind to him and took him along to Vienna to the meeting with the kings of Hungary and Poland. Ulrich was not without popular support at home, where the flight of the Duchess Sabina from the court had aroused a general sympathy for him. The Kaiser was impressed by the attitude of the people, and arranged a meeting between Ulrich and Matthäus Lang, the Kaiser's representative, on October 17, 1516, at Blaubeuren. Here an agreement was soon reached, and the duke again entered his lands. Immediately after the peace at Blaubeuren several songs were written in which little mention is made of Maximilian, although his figure is taken for granted in the background of the action. Thus one by Hans Umperlin expresses the hope that Maximilian will deal generously

---

³² Liliencron, *Die hist. Volkslieder der Deutschen*, III, 210f., no. 305.
³³ *Ibid.*, III, 205f., no. 303.

MAXIMILIAN IN *VOLKSLIED* AND *SPRUCH* 87

with the duke,[34] while others entreat the Kaiser not to give ear to Ulrich's slanderers and enemies.[35] Maximilian's disposition of the case could scarcely be anything but satisfactory to Ulrich's supporters, who were happy now to picture the friendly relations between the Kaiser and their duke, whom one poet describes as finally taking leave

> vom kaiser milt und zart,
> sein trůw er wol erkante.[36]

These appear to be but scanty notes, it is true; and as was brought out in the beginning of this chapter, the mention of Maximilian is really incidental to the main object of most of these songs. The absence of more abundant references to Maximilian in the contemporary historical folksong may have the following cause. With few exceptions the folksongs mention Max where it is possible to praise him, e.g., in his successful battles. When his praises are few in any period, it is probably because of the lack of suitable opportunities.

Max's death in 1519 gave occasion for several songs in which he is finally the main object of interest.[37] One was by Christoph Weyler of Vienna, the others by Georg Pleyer of Wels,[38] the town in which the Kaiser died. In the long accounts of Maximilian's pre-

---

[34] *Ibid.*, III, 195, no. 299, strophe 14. Hans' loyalty to his Duke appears realistically motivated in his concluding strophe:

> Der uns das liedlin newes singt,
> der nennt sich Hans Umperlin,
> er hat zwelf lebendige kind
> und seind die sibne klain,
> darzů hat er gar wenig korn;
> das liedlin will ich schenken
> meinem fürsten hochgeborn.   (Strophe 27, p. 196)

[35] *Ibid.*, III, 200f., no. 301, strophe 7; and 202, no. 302, strophe 3.

[36] *Ibid.*, III, 197, no. 300, strophe 2.

[37] For Weyler's song, cf. *ibid.*, III, 217-224, no. 307-a. For those of Pleyer, cf. *ibid.*, III, 217-224, no. 307-b, 225ff., no. 308; and Ernst von Frisch, "Jörg Pleyers Flugblatt von Kaiser Maximilians Abschied und Tod," *Gutenberg Jahrbuch 1935* (Mainz, 1935), pp. 150-153.

[38] Liliencron and v. Frisch, *loc. cit.*, have taken the great similarity of these laments as an indication that they all proceed from the same prose-report on the death of the Kaiser. It should be added that the resemblance of details in the songs to the account of Maximilian's death in Cuspinianus' *De Caesaribus* (pp. 609ff.) indicates some connection between the latter and the prose-report mentioned above.

science of his death, his last preparations, and partings, and finally the descriptions of the removal of the body and the burial, there are interwoven constant references to his humility, his piety, and his Christian spirit. We hear that he considered his body no better than those of other men and that therefore he would allow no gold or jewels to be buried with him. Instead he instructed that ashes and lime be strewn on his corpse to help atone for the sins of the body and that he be buried in a plain wooden casket well covered with lead.[39] Likewise his piety is praised,[40] and for this the finding of the coat of Christ at Trier is again brought forward as a Christian example.[41] His constant efforts to maintain peace during his life are mentioned repeatedly,[42] his justice toward poor and rich alike is praised,[43] and the sorrow of all at his death, especially of the poor, is described.[44] His desire to be buried near his mother in Neustadt instead of in Vienna is interpreted, not as a slight to Vienna, but as another evidence of his humility, for

> er wollt kein Hoffart treiben
> mit seinem Leichnam werth
> im Leben und nach seinem Tod.[45]

Christoph Weyler sings of the heavenly crown which is to recompense his virtues as a ruler:

> 2. Ein kaiser außerkoren,
> Ein kaiser erentreich,
> von edlem stamm geboren,
> wo findt man sein geleich
> von adel und von regiment,
> das er so wol hat gefürt
> biß an sein lezstes end?
>
> 6. Sein lob steet hoch zu preise
> fur ander fürsten all,
> der edel kaiser weise
> so gar mit reichem schall,

---

[39] Liliencron, *op. cit.*, III, no. 307-a, strophes 11-14, 25; and no. 307-b, strophe 5.
[40] *Ibid.*, III, no. 307-a, strophes 15-20.
[41] *Ibid.*, III, no. 307-a, strophes 3-5.
[42] *Ibid.*, III, no. 307-a, strophes 10, 38; no. 307-b, strophe 1: "sein Land hat er mit gutem Fried / regiret also schon."
[43] *Ibid.*, III, no. 307-a, strophe 6.
[44] *Ibid.*, III, no. 307-a, strophes 21-24, 33; no. 307-b, strophe 12.
[45] *Ibid.*, III, no. 307-b, strophe 25.

> geregiert hat sein grechtigkeit
> gegen armen und auch reichen,
> gegen got zu aller zeit.
>
> 7. Darumb hat sein begeret
> der ewig got so fron,
> dass er in selber eret
> wol in des hymels thron,
> daß er bald schied auß diser zeit,
> die ewig kron zu entpfahen,
> die er im hat bereit.

Whether or not one is inclined to describe Maximilian's reign as peaceful, it is true that during the unsettled period immediately after his death people looked with misgivings toward the coming election. The king of France had distributed large amounts of money among the electoral princes, and the fear of a foreign sovereign made the later years of Maximilian's rule seem a blessed period of quiet in comparison with what might come. Prayers for eternal rest for Max are mingled in a song by Gengenbach with apprehensions that the peace of the world is now gone.[46] In this state of the public mind, the rash step of Ulrich of Wurttemberg in seizing the imperial city of Reutlingen immediately after the Kaiser's death raised more laments for the absence of the restraining hand of Maximilian:

> Der fromm edel kaiser fûrte
> ein fridlichs regiment,
> so er iez ist gestorben,
> so hat es schier ein end,
> das trauret kind in mûter leib,
> got und der heilig sant Jacob
> die soln uns wonen bei![47]

What have we learned of Maximilian in the historical folksong? In general, nothing more than that he was a brave fighter in the front line of a couple of battles, that he was stern and unyielding in punishing a few offenders, that he was just in upholding the public peace, that he suffered insults with patience, and that during his last hours he turned his mind to thoughts of the Here-

---

[46] *Ibid.*, III, 234f., no. 311.
[47] *Ibid.*, III, 242, no. 315, strophe 3, "Ein newes lied von dem herzog von Wirtenberg."

after and strove to humiliate his body. Further, that he is always just about to take a terrible revenge upon the French, or preparing to march to Rome to receive the imperial crown, or on the point of crushing the Venetians and leading the Christian world against the Turks—all these hopes rise in eager sympathy to the lips of the poets.

Like other lyrical poems, the folksong does not primarily record information, but reflects the emotional experience of a popular group. We find abundant evidence of deep national agitation in these dealing with Maximilian. It appears in the fierce zeal with which the German poets attack the French and voice a romantic lament for Maximilian when Charles VIII seizes "das Fräulein von Brittania." The popular imagination loves to dwell on the sorrow of a gentle lady parting from her brave knight; and this is the sentimental picture which the folksinger develops in order to humanize his deep antipathy to the French, although he knew, perhaps, as well as we do, that there was no such emotion as love involved. With a mixture of hope, enthusiasm, and apprehension the German people looked to Max in the wars with the Swiss, the Italians, and the French. They wanted a strong and efficient leader and their singers pictured him as such. Even defeats could scarcely shake their confidence in this knightly figure. The glory of the imperial office still permitted an optimistic view of their hero, who represented the widespread longing for peace and unity within and national forces without. Or again, Max was the hope of pious souls who yearned for some great cleansing influence to sweep out the bad practices of the church and finally to unite all Christendom in a concerted drive against the Turks.

The Maximilian of the German *Volkslied* is thus a pious Christian, a gallant and a mighty leader, a just and peaceful ruler. And there is in addition something else less tangible: an atmosphere, a halo, compounded of expectant hope, romantic longing, and a deep-rooted awe of the name of "King" and "Emperor."

B. The *Spruch*

The *Sprüche* in which we are interested fall into two general classes. The first class are similar to the folksongs just considered in that they are expressions of the poets' personal feelings. The second stand under the direct influence of the Kaiser's political policies and are political propaganda. It must be admitted, of course, that the line between these two types is very difficult to draw. Even some of the folksongs staunchly support certain favorite plans of the emperor. But they are sincere and straightforward. The purpose of the authors may indeed coincide with the program of the Kaiser, yet they preserve an individual freedom in expressing it, and they seem usually to speak essentially for themselves.

This last is also true of the *Sprüche* with which Sebastian Brant repeatedly called upon Maximilian. He felt more keenly than the people of the eastern part of the empire that the Kaiser should have encouragement and support in avenging the insults of France. When, on November 7, 1492, a meteorite fell near Ensisheim, Brant interpreted it as a sign of divine interposition and a direct warning to Maximilian to prepare for defense:

> Nim war, der stain ist dir gesant,
> dich mant got in deim aigen land,
> daß du dich stellen solt zů wer.[48]

When, in the following January, the German forces achieved a signal victory over a French detachment near Salins, Brant saw in this fortunate beginning the fulfillments of his former prophecies and voiced anew the hope that finally the man and the time had arrived for making an end of the Turkish threat. Now he might live to see all his hopes realized and the king's honor restored; and he prayed that Maximilian's heroic deeds might continue to furnish him with material and themes for his pen,

> daß ich allzit din manheit groß
> und dugent schrib on underloß,
> als ich in gůter hoffnung bin.[49]

A *Spruch* on "Die behemsch schlacht" by another author furnishes us with a longer portrayal of the Kaiser than the majority of these poems. The unknown poet describes the battle near

[48] *Ibid.*, II, 308, no. 182, ll. 6off.
[49] *Ibid.*, II, 312, no. 183.

Regensburg in 1504, depicts Maximilian's personal bravery, then tells of his mercy to the Bohemians who fell on their knees before him, and prayerfully foresees his final conquest of the unbelieving Turks:[50]

> Kain herr von Österreich was nie,
> er wär ganz gůtig und auch mild;
> drumb fůrn sy weiß in rotem schild,
> ir rechter zorn in miltigkait
> die wirt ynen in ewigkait.
> Sechshundert hat er leben lan;
> sy můßten mir all har hon glan!
> Ach got, frist ym lang sein leben,
> biß er sich auch mag geben
> christenlichen glauben zů meren
> und das erst loch zerstören.
> Das gschicht wenn er wirt vertreiben
> den Türken und sich och schreiben
> zů Constantinopel kaiseer.
> O herr got, verleich ym die eer!

Maximilian's bravery is also mentioned cursorily in a poem by Heinz Gluf, written in 1488 to try to discourage Friedrich III from supporting the Swabian League. Graf Haug von Werdenberg, declares Gluf, is working to get control of the League, and after Friedrich's death he will turn against Maximilian,

> den edlen kunig kecken,
> der doch nit leicht ist zu erschrecken,

and try to wrest his inheritance from him.[51] Likewise an appeal is made to Maximilian by an anonymous *Spruchdichter* on the side of Duke Albrecht in the Landhut war of 1504. After bewailing the misery that has been caused by the conflict, the poet admonishes Max to punish those who have disregarded his decrees, and then proceeds to tell how Max took Kufstein:

> König Maximilian so groß
> mit macht und gwalt die stat beschoß.
> Kopfstain thet er so schnell zwingen;
> ir mußten über dklingen springen

---

[50] *Ibid.*, II, 540ff., no. 242.
[51] *Ibid.*, II, 268, no. 173.

> wol achtzehn die es ser beraw.
> Der erst was Hanns von Pienzenaw.[52]

It is noticeable that the deed is related here as an act of valor, and that the rest of the poem, calling upon Maximilian to make a speedy end of his enemies, shows the opposite viewpoint from that depicted by the poet of the folksong on the same event.[53]

An examination of further *Sprüche* yields little more in the portrayal of the Kaiser. Erasmus Amman of Augsburg wrote a poem on the entrance of Maximilian into Vienna in 1515, in which he gives us a picture of him as he relaxes in the pleasures of a dance:

> Darnach der kaiser holt vil frawen
> die waren lieblich anzûschawen,
> daß ichs nit gar ersagen kan;
> darmit so fieng der tanze an.[54]

Another poem, an Augsburg singer's first attempt, on the battle of Verona in 1516, praises Max for sending help to his besieged men.[55] We might also consider it a tribute to the Kaiser's racial tolerance when we read a poet's complaint that the Jews could not be driven out of Regensburg until after his death:

> Darumb kund es kein furgang han,
> byß da starb Maximilian.[56]

But unfortunately it was probably merely a financial consideration which prompted the Kaiser's generosity here, and the fact would be no secret to a contemporary. In 1522 another poet wishes that Max might return from death to lead a crusade against the Turks, and extolls his virtues as a ruler:

> Mecht man den herwider bringen,
> was wurd die welt iez gewinnen!
> streitbar, erfarn, gûtig, still
> ist er gewest; gnediger will
> allzeit bei im gewonet hat,

---

[52] *Ibid.*, II, 529-536, no. 240.
[53] Cf. above, p. 77.
[54] *Ibid.*, III, 169, no. 291.
[55] *Ibid.*, III, 187, no. 297.
[56] *Ibid.*, III, 322.

> summa aller tugend ain stat
> gar trefflich het er beschlossen.[57]

The other type of *Spruch* referred to above shows a strong tendency to promote the policies of Maximilian and say less about him than about his plans. Thus a long poem "Vom Fräulein von Britanien" by Hans Ortenstain in 1491 gives us again the German side of this incident, and ends with an impassioned appeal for action addressed to Kaiser Friedrich, the electoral princes, all other noble knights and lords, and finally for intercession by the Virgin Mary. To Friedrich he pleads:

> O kaiser Friderich, ich euch sag,
> hört dise jämerliche klag,
> es trift an euer flaisch und blût!
> Sparent nit euer zeitlich gût
> zů hilf dem durchleuchtigen künig Maximilian,
> der da ist euer geborner sun![58]

How effective his appeal was in forming public opinion may be indicated in some measure by the fact that Ortenstain's poem seems to have been the model for the historical prose-account of this affair in the *Chronicon Austriacum* of the Carinthian parish priest, Jacob Unrest.[59]

One of the most prolific writers of *Sprüche* designed to further the plans of the Kaiser is Hans Schneider of Augsburg, a poet by profession, who was intermittently in the service of Maximilian as "der küniglichen majestat sprecher."[60] In his first poem relating to the general political situation, he recommends Maximilian's plans against France in 1492 to the German nation and includes praise of the Kaiser in the usual strain:

> Maximilian du trewer held!
> Got hat dich außerwelt,
> daß du solt sein ein aufenthalt
> der cristenschar mit dem gewalt.
> Wiewol du verachtet pist,

---

[57] *Ibid.*, III, 414, no. 364.
[58] *Ibid.*, II, 299, no. 179.
[59] See Unrest's chronicle in S. Hahn's *Collectio Monumentorum* (Brunsvigae, 1724), I, 537-803. Cf. pp. 775-778. This is the opinion of Heinrich Ulmann, *Kaiser Maximilian I.* (Stuttgart, 1884-1891), I, 183.
[60] Liliencron, *Die hist. Volkslieder der Deutschen*, II, 302, no. 181.

> das wil dir got zu rechter frist
> sein hilf und gnad von himel senden,
> daß du die sachen magst volenden,
> daran der welt ligt schwer und kummer;
> das hofft meng herz auf disen sumer.
> Got wil dir selb tun hilf bekant,
> daß du der großen schmach und schand,
> die dir in Frankreich bescheen sind
> an deinem weib und deinem kind,
> daß du pald tust widergelt.[61]

Schneider then tries to stir up enthusiasm by citing the need to go against the Turks; but he suggests that the emperor "mach zwen haufen auß dem her," sending the one part against the heathen, and

> Den andern teil soltu senden
> in Frankreich an den ubelteter.[62]

In another poem, "Vom Haus Österreich," Hans Schneider borrows from an earlier *Spruch* by Ulrich Höpp, "Von Kaiser Friedrich,"[63] and changes it to fit Maximilian. After recounting the main outlines of events from Friedrich's marriage down to the death of Maximilian's son Philip, he voices the prayer that

> Got well Maximilian behüeten!
> Wer der nit, so müest wir uns nieten
> Mer dann ein abgejagter hund.

In conclusion he admonishes the cities:

> Darumb ir stet dürft euch nit schämen,
> habt acht wa ir ein zuflucht nemen
> und seind dem künig gehorsam gern,
> so träw ich wol dem frumen herrn,
> daß er euch treulich bei bestat.
> Also Hans Schneider gesprochen hat.[64]

In a similar manner Schneider continues to follow the Kaiser's fortunes. He praises Max' victories in the Netherlands.[65] In a

---

[61] *Ibid.*, II, 305, no. 181.
[62] *Ibid.*, II, 306.
[63] *Ibid.*, II, 3-8, no. 126.
[64] *Ibid.*, II, 568, no. 250.
[65] *Ibid.*, III, 17-21, no. 255.

poem on the disobedience of the Venetians he depicts the kings of England and France offering their aid "zu ern dem römischen konig dem frommen,"[66] an episode of very doubtful historicity. And in the same poem he ascribes Max' long delay in coming to Italy with an army to his magnanimity in postponing revenge rather than to the real cause, his helplessness. Finally, after the razing of Hohenkrähen in 1512, Schneider also wrote a couple of poems in which he tells how this action "zympt den frumen kaiser wol";[67] and he exhorts Maximilian to continue the example he has set in the destruction of the robbers' nest.[68]

Another example of a *Spruchdichter* in the service of the Kaiser is Martin (Maier) von Reutlingen. In May 1511 Maximilian used the news of Louis XII's success in Italy to try again to get money from the Estates for a six-months military expedition to Trent. For this purpose he sent a mandate to them, which this poet puts into rime in order to help form public opinion in its favor.[69] Still other examples could be cited where the official prose-account of an event is followed by a rimed version for more popular use.[70]

This leads us to a consideration of the influence of Maximilian himself on his reputation in the eyes of his contemporaries. Let us turn now to the literary works of the Kaiser.

[66] *Ibid.*, III, 33ff., no. 259.
[67] *Ibid.*, III, 78, no. 270.
[68] *Ibid.*, III, no. 271.
[69] *Ibid.*, III, 41-45, no. 262: "Vom Krieg in Italien."
[70] E.g., cf. Georg W. Panzer's *Zusätze zu den Annalen der älteren Deutschen Litteratur*, etc. (Leipzig, 1802), pp. 62f., nos. 259–c and 259–d, on the subject of Maximilian's captivity in Bruges.

IV

MAXIMILIAN'S SELF-PORTRAYAL

THE DESIRE to perpetuate one's memory after death is no doubt a human trait, but it has been regarded as an especially common characteristic of the men of the Renaissance.[1] Maximilian certainly shared this characteristic with his contemporaries. The list of works, pictorial and written, which he directed and partially wrote[2] bears eloquent testimony to this urge to transmit to posterity his picture as he himself conceived it. In the *Weisskunig* he expressed plainly enough his attitude toward kings who do not provide for their "remembrance." To a lord who reproaches him for the money he spends on his "gedachtnus" the young *Weisskunig* replies:

He who during his life provides no remembrance for himself, has no remembrance after his death and the same person is forgotten with the tolling of the bell, and therefore the money which I spend on remembrance is not lost; but the money which is spared on my remembrance, that is a suppression of my future remembrance, and what I do not accomplish during my life for my memory will not be made up for after my death, neither by thee nor by others.[3]

---
[1] Paul Van Dyke speaks of "that thirst for every and any sort of distinction, which was the dominant passion of the men of the Italian Renascence" (*Renascence Portraits*, New York, 1905, p. 269). Eduard Chmelarz refers to "dem Charakterzuge der Renaissanceperiode, dem Cultus der eigenen Persönlichkeit mit voller Geltung der Individualität" ("Die Ehrenpforte des Kaisers Maximilian I.," *Jahrb. k.-h. Samml.*, IV [Wien, 1886], 289). Cf. Max Jansen on the same question, *Kaiser Maximilian I.* (München, 1905), p. 134; Simon Laschitzer, "Die Genealogie des Kaisers Maximilian I.," *Jahrb. k.-h. Samml.*, VII (Wien, 1888), 7; and Georg Misch, "Die Stilisierung des eigenen Lebens in dem Ruhmeswerk Kaisers Maximilian, des letzten Ritters," *Nachrichten von der Gesellschaft der Wissenschaften zu Göttingen aus dem Jahre 1930, Phil.-Hist. Klasse* (Berlin, 1930), p. 440.

[2] Cf. "Gedenkbuch Kaiser Maximilians I.," *Jahrb. k.-h. Samml.*, V (Wien, 1887), Teil 2, p. xix, Regest no. 4023; Alvin Schultz' Einleitung to "Der Weisskunig," *Jahrb. k.-h. Samml.*, VI (1887), p. vii; Laschitzer, *op. cit.*, pp. 4f.; Theodor Gottlieb, *Büchersammlung Kaiser Maximilians I.* (Leipzig, 1900), p. 42; S. Steinherz, "Ein Bericht über die Werke Maximilians I.," *Mitteilungen des Instituts für österreichische Geschichtsforschung*, XXVII (Innsbruck, 1906), 152-155.

[3] "Der Weisskunig," *Jahrb. k.-h. Samml.*, VI (1887), 66, no. 24: "Wie der jung weiß kunig die alten gedachtnus insonders lieb het." "wer ime in seinem leben kain

Maximilian's ambition to write his own chapter in history is evident in nearly all of his public expressions. In his speeches to the Diets, in his mandates and proclamations, he showed his abilities as a purveyor of personal as well as political propaganda. In his writings he portrayed himself as he wished to appear in the eyes of posterity. In the *Freydal,* the *Teuerdank,* and the *Weisskunig* we see the knight in the tournament, the valiant youth of adventure, and the young king in battle against his enemies. The *Jagdbuch,*[4] a list of the Kaiser's various hunting preserves, their location and particular advantages, was compiled in 1500 by Maximilian's officers in charge of hunting and fishing, Carl von Spaur and Wolfgang Hohenleiter. With its colorful plates depicting Maximilian on different kinds of hunts it has added to his reputation as a great hunter. In the same manner the *Fischereibuch,*[5] a volume listing the royal fishing preserves, with notations concerning their nature and accompanied by illustrative plates, was prepared for Maximilian in 1504 by Hohenleiter and has helped to impress posterity with the Kaiser's skill as a fisherman. The *Zeugbücher*[6] reveal him as an inventor of armor and a soldier experienced in war and its machines. The *Genealogie* and the *Triumph* illustrate for us his glorious ancestry and his many mighty deeds. Finally, in the Hofkirche in Innsbruck stands the Kaiser's *Grabmal,* conceived and begun by himself about 1508 and finished by his grandson, Kaiser Ferdinand I, in 1566. The magnificent cenotaph is surrounded by bronze figures of famous

---

gedachtnus macht, der hat nach seinem tod kain gedächtnus und desselben menschen wird mit dem glockendon vergessen, und darumb so wird das gelt, so ich auf die gedechtnus ausgib, nit verloren, aber das gelt, das erspart wird in meiner gedächtnus, das ist ain undertruckung meiner kunftigen gedächtnus, und was ich in meinem leben in meiner gedächtnus nit volbring, das wird nach meinem tod weder durch dich oder ander nit erstat." Cf. the great similarity between this chapter and the words of Jacob Unrest, in Hahn, *op. cit.*, I, 781; also those of Georg Lauterbecken in his *Regentenbuch* (Wittemberg, 1581), pp. 183f.

[4] *Das Jagdbuch Kaiser Maximilians I.* In Verbindung mit Wm. A. Baillie-Grohman hrsg. von Dr. Michael Mayr (Innsbruck, 1901), cf. p. 1.

[5] *Das Fischereibuch Kaiser Maximilians I.* Unter Mitwirkung von Ludwig Freih. von Lazarini hrsg. von Dr. Michael Mayr, Innsbruck, 1901.

[6] "Die Zeugbücher des Kaisers Maximilian I.," beschrieben und erläutert von Wendelin Boeheim, *Jahrb. k.-h. Samml.*, XIII (1894), 94-201, and XV (1894), 295-391. This is a collection of pictures of many guns of various types with accompanying verses.

princes and ladies, kings and queens, as if to remind us of his eternal place among them after his death.

In the discussion of the *Spruch* we have noted the repeated use of this type of poem as propaganda for the imperial policies. It also appears that some of the writers of *Sprüche* were quite individualistic in expressing their approval of Maximilian's course, and that they and some of the folksingers voiced the policies of the Kaiser without necessarily being in his commission. This has been interpreted as a sign of the effectiveness of Max' journalism and his propaganda, which penetrated the innermost consciousness of the people.[7]

Seldom, indeed, did Maximilian lose an opportunity to work upon the popular mind. In 1492, when he was trying in all ways to induce the nation to go to war with France, a meteorite fell near Ensisheim and called forth the greatest excitement. It was considered a divine miracle in his favor and inspired Latin poems in his support. Yet in 1495, when politically all was quiet, a considerable fall of meteorites caused no excitement whatever, even though it was reported that crowned heads could be seen on the stones.[8] The later event, however, did not receive the notice from the Kaiser which the first meteorite had attracted. As late as 1503 Max was still referring to this stone as the first miracle by which the Lord expressed His approval of his policy.

The public inclination for pilgrimages and relics also provided Max with a chance to spread his fame. While his interest in the holy coat at Trier was probably mostly archaeological,[9] the incident nevertheless was interpreted by the people in quite a different light. As we have seen above (pp. 80f.), a popular legend ascribed the discovery to a divine vision accorded to Maximilian. Whether or not Max had anything to do with this interpretation is unknown, but it is safe to assume that it did not displease him. It will be remembered that when it was reported to Maximilian by Hans von Liebenfels in 1497 that a stag and a pheasant had appeared at

[7] Cf. Peter Diederichs, *Kaiser Maximilian I. als politischer Publizist* (Heidelberg, 1932), pp. 31f.
[8] Cf. Eberhard Gothein, *Politische und religiöse Volksbewegungen vor der Reformation* (Breslau, 1878), pp. 82f.
[9] *Ibid.*, p. 83.

a public oath of allegiance to him, he had written that the account gave him pleasure.[10]

An incident which Max did consciously use to influence the people, however, was the alleged miracle of the crosses which appeared on people's clothing in 1501. A letter of May 18 to the Kaiser from the Bishop of Liège gives a detailed description of these *Kreuzwunder* as they had supposedly occurred in his diocese. Maximilian had been unsuccessfully agitating for help in a campaign in Italy and against the Turks, and he saw in these miracles a welcome accident. The quick spreading of the Bishop's letter by means of *Flugblätter*, which some authorities consider almost the starting point of the epidemic of this type of publicity, was chiefly Maximilian's work.[11] He even heightened the effect by having people who were reputed to have been affected brought before him and by keeping a collection of the "crossed" objects to show his visitors. He went even farther than this. On the basis of material which he furnished, Pico della Mirandola, the Italian humanist, wrote for him his *Staurostichon,* in which the miraculous crosses were interpreted as divine admonitions to a war against the Turks.[12] By these methods not only the common people were to be reached, but the significance of the crosses was to be emphasized for the scholars of Humanism as well.[13]

It is hardly possible that Maximilian himself believed these stories. He seems to have been as rationalistic as any of the humanists of his age. He always kept well within the prescriptions and usages of the church, but he was not prevented by superstition or traditional inhibitions from criticizing the popes nor from asking questions concerning religion, such as those which he handed the Abbot Trithemius in 1508.[14]

---

[10] Letter of May 13, 1497, given by Joseph Chmel in *Urkunden, Briefe und Actenstücke zur Geschichte Maximilians I. und seiner Zeit,* "Stuttgarter Lit. Ver.," X (Stuttgart, 1845), 185ff., no. 163.

[11] Gothein, *op. cit.,* pp. 89, 96f.

[12] "Staurostichon Ioannis Francisci Pici Mirandulae Domini, et Concordiae Comitis, heroicum carmen de mysteriis Dominicae crucis nuper in Germaniam delapsis: ad Maximilianum Aug. Romanorum Regem," Freher-Struve, *Rerum Germanicarum scriptores* (Argentorati, 1717), II, 497-506.

[13] Gothein, *op. cit.,* pp. 98f.

[14] The questions run as follows:
1. Why does God want rather to be believed by mortals than recognized?

Other events and tendencies of the time were likewise used to good account by Maximilian in his efforts to build up public opinion in support of his plans against the Turks. The outbreak and alarming spread of syphilis, "die bösen Blattern," in Germany at the turn of the century was interpreted as a sign that the Lord was displeased with the prevalent luxury and godlessness, and it was believed that a crusade against the Turks might help atone for them.[15] Many cities made new regulations restricting luxury in dress; and at the Reichstag in Worms in 1495 a law was made punishing by fines swearing and drunkenness as well as excessive luxury in clothing.[16] The popular consciousness was thus kept alive to the need for moral reform, and the proposed plans of the Kaiser were always well in the foreground as the best means of accomplishing this reform.

Maximilian's speeches too were effective in spreading his reputation. When he could, he appeared in person at the Diets in order to influence important decisions with his oratory.[17] These speeches, either as heard or reported, played a considerable part in the impression made upon his contemporaries. Even Italian historians were influenced. Guicciardini, for instance, reports a part of Max' speech at the Diet of Constance in 1507, in which the Kaiser is anything but modest:

The king of France will give way to the bare name of our arms, for the

---

2. Can they, who by no fault of their own know nothing of the Christian religion, become blessed although without baptism and Christian belief, if they are faithful to the religion which they know?

3. Why are prophets of false religions also able to do wonders?

4. Why are the Holy Scriptures neither so clear nor so complete as they really ought to be? Why do they conceal so much and hide it in riddles? Why does one not find in them much which is also required for perfect belief?

5. How does it happen that magicians have power over evil spirits?

6. How can the doctrine of the righteousness of God be reconciled with the allowance of so much evil, often to the damage of good and pious people?

7. Is the special providence over the actions and destinies of men, and in general over everything that happens on earth, demonstrable from reason and documents?

Cf. Karl Klüpfel, *Kaiser Maximilian I.* (neue Ausg.; Berlin, 1870), pp. 179f.

[15] Cf. Gothein, *op. cit.*, p. 103; and Diederichs, *op. cit.*, p. 46. Throughout his book Diederichs gives many instances where Max, or his councillors under his direction, publicized these tendencies of the time.

[16] Cf. Karl Haltaus, *Geschichte des Kaisers Maximilian des Ersten* (Leipzig, 1850), p. 135.

[17] Diederichs, *op. cit.*, p. 9.

French have still fresh in their memories the battle of Guineguaste, in which I myself, though then but a youth, and scarce more than of boy's estate, by dint of true valor and greatness of mind, broke the army of King Louis; since which time the kings of France never durst venture to try the force of my arms, but had recourse to insidious arts and stratagems. . . . In me there shall be no want of fortitude of mind to expose myself to any danger, nor strength of body, hardened by continual exercise, to endure any fatigue. And as for counsel and skill in military affairs, my age and experience have so qualified me, that you need not want a leader worthy of that honor for such an enterprise. But the more authority you bestow on your king, and the greater the power and force with which he is invested, the more easy will you render the defense of the liberty of the Roman Church, our common mother; and, to your own exceeding glory, and that of the Germans, you will exalt to the highest degree the imperial dignity, whose greatness and splendor are communicated to every one here present, as well as to the whole body of this most powerful and warlike nation.[18]

Guicciardini then goes on to tell how the Italians began to fear the approaching German army; and here, in describing Maximilian, he echoes some of the very words used by the Kaiser:

For it was considered that the troops granted to Maximilian in the Diet, in conjunction with those which his own subjects were able to furnish, and those which he could raise at his own expense, would make a very powerful army, consisting all of fierce and resolute soldiers, expert in war, attended with an infinite train of artillery, and, what rendered it the more formidable, under the command of a general who, by his natural disposition, and long exercise in arms, was most expert in military discipline, and well qualified to undergo any fatigue of body, or anxiety of mind, that might be required for the most difficult enterprise, and therefore was in greater reputation than any emperor had been in these hundred years past.[19]

It was mainly through his own writings[20] and their illustrations,

---

[18] Guicciardini, *op. cit.*, IV, 90ff.

[19] *Ibid.*, IV, 120f.

[20] The problem of Maximilian's personal contribution as author to the works variously ascribed to him, especially to the *Freydal*, the *Teuerdank*, and the *Weisskunig*, has long been the object of literary investigation. It is now generally believed that Maximilian's personal activity in the first and last cases above consisted of a certain amount of dictation to his secretaries, who then worked out the final text with repeated personal criticism and correction by the Kaiser. The plates and woodcuts were likewise designed at his direction to illustrate his ideas and were then examined by him and accepted or rejected. We may, therefore, well speak of Maximilian as the author of these works, since not only the ideas of the whole,

however, that Maximilian sought to transmit his memory to posterity. First among these works in the chronology of the life they represent is the *Freydal*, which was meant as an introduction to the *Teuerdank*. It gives a picture of the Kaiser as a dashing young knight who rides from one court to another, meeting all comers in "rennen, stechen und kempfen."[21] His experiences are monotonously the same through some sixty-four courts as described in the text. More interesting than the text are the accompanying 255 plates showing Freydal in various types of combat with his knightly opponents. Published only in recent years, the *Freydal*

---

but the various steps in their organization and an indeterminate amount of the actual wording came from him. For discussions on Max' sources for the *Weisskunig*, see Georg Misch, "Die Stilisierung des eigenen Lebens in dem Ruhmeswerk Kaisers Maximilian, des letzten Ritters," *Nachrichten von der Gesellschaft der Wissenschaften zu Göttingen aus dem Jahre 1930*. Philologisch-Historische Klasse (Berlin, 1930), pp. 435-459; and Franz X. von Wegele, *Geschichte der deutschen Historiographie seit dem Auftreten des Humanismus* (München und Leipzig, 1885), p. 95.

Max' authorship in the case of *Teuerdank* was long considered the same as in *Freydal* and *Weisskunig*. Recently, however, evidence has been presented to show that Max owed more of the *Teuerdank* to outside help than was formerly supposed, Cf. Clemens Biener, "Die Fassungen des Teuerdank," *Zeitschrift für Deutsches Altertum und Deutsche Litteratur*, hrsg. von Edward Schröder, LXVII (Berlin, 1930), 177-196. (This author is in several works incorrectly cited as C. Breuer, e.g., in A. Taylor, *Problems in German Literary History of the Fifteenth and Sixteenth Centuries* [New York and London, 1939], note, p. 66.) Biener shows that the *Unfalo* of the "Silberkämmerer," Siegmund von Dietrichstein, served, with few changes, as the basis for some twenty-one adventures of the *Teuerdank*. Von Dietrichstein, Pfinzing, and other unknown helpers, Biener is convinced, used a certain amount of information heard either by them or others from the lips of the Kaiser and incorporated it then in their own way into the text. Otherwise, Biener believes, Max had no actual part in the writing of the *Teuerdank*, and the old story of Maximilian's poetic activity is thereby destroyed. For the best discussions of the subject see: Franz Redl, "Kaiser Maximilian I. von Habsburg in seinen Beziehungen zur Dichtkunst, Wissenschaft und Kunst," *Zeitschrift für die österreichischen Gymnasien*, 63. Jahrgang (1912), pp. 693-723, 873-892; S. Steinherz, "Ein Bericht über die Werke Maximilians I," *Mitteilungen des Instituts für österreichische Geschichtsforschung*, XXVII (1906), 152-155; Joseph Strobl, *Kaiser Maximilians I. Anteil am Teuerdank. Eine kritische Untersuchung*, Innsbruck, 1907; Otto Bürger, "Beiträge zur Kenntnis des Teuerdank," *Quellen und Forschungen zur Sprach- und Kulturgeschichte der germanischen Völker*, XCII (Strassburg, 1902), 92. Heft; *Der Weisskunig*, hrsg. von Alwin Schultz, in *Jahrb. k.-h. Samml.*, VI (Wien, 1887), vii-xxviii; *Einleitung* to the *Teuerdank*, by Simon Laschitzer, *Jahrb. k.-h. Samml.*, VIII, Wien, 1888; R. von Liliencron, "Der Weisskunig Kaiser Maximilians I.," *Historisches Taschenbuch*, 5. Folge, 3. Jahrgang (Leipzig, 1873), pp. 321-358; Paul Van Dyke, "Literary Activity of the Emperor Maximilian I," *American Historical Review*, XI (Oct. 1905), 16-28.

[21] *Freydal. Des Kaisers Maximilian I. Turniere und Mummereien.* Hrsg. von Quirin von Leitner. 3 Bde.; Nürnberg, 1880-1882. Cf. I, p. xvii.

could have had little influence on popular opinion in his day; but it indicates the Kaiser's desire to illustrate this side of his life.

A more vivid and a more lasting impression, however, may be ascribed definitely to that most popular of Maximilian's literary efforts, the metrical romance *Teuerdank*. First printed two years before his death, it continued to be popular throughout the Sixteenth and Seventeenth Centuries[22] and went through numerous editions.[23] It was never a secret that the hero Teuerdank was intended to be identical with Kaiser Maximilian; and whatever ignorance may have existed on this point was certainly dispelled by the broad hints of Pfintzing's *Clavis*. A few years later we find the romantic hero and the emperor openly identified in Sebastian Franck's *Chronica*[24] and his *Germania*.[25]

In Teuerdank's numerous adventures lies the starting point for many a story told about Maximilian down through the centuries. Not that these adventures are altogether lacking in a factual basis. During his long and active life Maximilian must have had many experiences and been exposed to many dangers similar to those narrated in *Teuerdank*.[26] Recent research has attempted to establish a historical basis for perhaps the best known of the Maximilian legends, that of the *Martinswand*,[27] which has as little claim to probability as any of the others. However slight the foundation of truth, the printing of the stories supplemented whatever may

---

[22] Cf. R. von Liliencron, "Der Weisskunig Kaiser Maximilians I.," p. 325, in *Historisches Taschenbuch*, hrsg. v. W. H. Riehl, 5. Folge, 3. Jahrg. (Leipzig, 1873), pp. 321-358.

[23] First printed by Hans Schönsperger in Nürnberg, 1517; a second edition by same printer in Augsburg, 1519; a third, by H. Stainer, Augsburg, 1537; then came a revision by Burckhard Waldis, Frankfurt a. M., 1553, followed by repetitions of the same, also in Frankfurt a. M., in 1563, 1589, and 1596, with slight variations only in the last two. Another edition, by Matthew Schultes in Ulm, 1679, was repeated with a new title in Augsburg, 1693. Later editions include that of Carl Haltaus, Quedlinburg and Leipzig, 1836; of Scheible in *Das Kloster* (Stuttgart, 1846), IV, 13. Zelle; also of Karl Goedeke, Leipzig, 1878; W. H. Rylands, London, 1884 (for the Holbein Society); and Simon Laschitzer, Wien, 1888, *Jahrb. k.-h. Samml.*, VIII.

[24] Sebastian Franck, *Chronica, Zeytbuch und Geschichtbibel* (without place, 1565), fo. 228-a. (First published 1531.)

[25] Sebastian Franck, *Germania* (Bern, 1539), fo. 281-aff.

[26] As Haltaus maintains in the introduction to his edition of *Teuerdank*, p. 101.

[27] Cf. M. Mayr, "Die geschichtliche Grundlage der Sage von Kaiser Max auf der Martinswand," *Forschungen und Mitteilungen zur Geschichte Tirols und Vorarlbergs*, 1. Jahrgang (Innsbruck, 1904), pp. 66-75.

have been alive in the way of an oral tradition and provided a fund of information for coming generations, as will be shown later.

It will be recalled that the hero Teuerdank, on his way to the Princess Ehrenreich, is led into a series of adventures by the allegorical figures Fürwittig, Unfalo, and Neidelhart. The character of these false guides is apparent in their names. The first figure represents the incautious forwardness of youth, the second symbolizes the pitfalls and accidents of fortune, while the third stands for the misfortunes instigated by the connivance of enviers and enemies. These are presented as captains of the Princess Ehrenreich and are delegated to meet and help Teuerdank on his way. They are actually in league with enemies of the prince at court, however, and under the guise of friendship expose him to every sort of danger. In every instance, of course, he escapes.

In order to establish an acquaintance with some of the Maximilian stories to which we shall have to recur, it seems worth while to give here a brief summary of the main adventures of the *Teuerdank,* omitting those which have been least persistent in the Maximilian legend, and putting together those which have the greatest similarity. The numbers refer to adventures or chapters; in the case of the first edition, they coincide with the numbers of the woodcuts.

There are fifteen adventures which occur while Teuerdank is hunting chamois and in which he is depicted as an intrepid climber and hunter, ever alert in the face of danger. The particular incidents which distinguish each adventure are as follows:

Nos. 15, 18, and 22. Teuerdank is endangered by being led into perilous places and left there.

No. 20. The chamois are chased to a sharp peak which no one has ever been able to reach, but Teuerdank manages it. He nearly falls, all but one of his shoe-spikes bend, but that one holds and he is saved. This episode is the one which is regarded by various commentators as the beginning of the legend of Max on the Martinswand.[28]

---

[28] Cf. Arnold Busson, "Die Sage von Max auf der Martinswand und ihre Entstehung," *Sitzungsberichte der kaiserlichen Akademie der Wissenschaften in Wien, Phil.-Historische Classe,* CXVI (Wien, 1888), 455-500. Cf. the review by S. M. Prem of K. Kirchlechner's "Über Maximilian als Jäger und im besonderen über das Abenteuer des Kaisers auf der Martinswand," *Mitteilungen des Instituts für österreichische Geschichtsforschung,* VII (Innsbruck, 1886), 194; and M. Mayr, *op. cit.*

No. 31. Teuerdank is told to pursue a chamois across a ravine. He is about to vault across with a pole when a hunter stops him from this exposure to certain death.

Nos. 37, 55, and 69. Peasants are hired to throw rocks down on Teuerdank, but he miraculously escapes being hit.

Nos. 49 and 53. Unfalo sends Teuerdank to hunt where loose stones fall about him.

No. 56. Teuerdank is sent to hunt when the wind is high, and it nearly blows him from the cliff.

No. 59. Teuerdank is directed to where the rocks are hollow beneath him. He falls but catches the bushes and is saved.

No. 62. A servant leads Teuerdank to where loose stones are covered by damp moss. He is saved by one shoe-spike.

No. 66. Teuerdank is lead by a hunter in winter over a crevasse. The hunter falls but Teuerdank avoids the danger.

No. 71. Unfalo encourages Teuerdank to shoot a chamois directly above him, in the hope that it will strike him in falling.

Eight chapters tell of adventures with wild pigs.

No. 17. Teuerdank is told to shoot at a pig to madden it, then to dismount and kill it.

No. 19. Teuerdank attacks a pig with a short dagger while on foot, but it runs away.

No. 35. Teuerdank's foot catches in the stirrup, nevertheless he manages to kill the pig. The hunters are ordered not to help him.

No. 38. Teuerdank is instructed to kill a wild pig while on foot. The hunters chase the pig to a slippery place, where Teuerdank falls and is almost pierced by his sword.

No. 41. Unfalo gives Teuerdank too small a horse and a pig bites its foot off.

No. 45. On a pig-hunt Teuerdank is led to a hidden ravine, into which he nearly falls with his horse.

No. 61. Another pig kills Teuerdank's horse and wounds the hero in the foot, but he kills it.

No. 68. Teuerdank is encouraged to chase pigs on thin ice; the ice breaks, he falls through and breaks his sword, but gets out safely.

Adventures nos. 41 and 61 above may be reminiscences of the incident reported by Maximilian to Sigmund Prüschenk from Antwerp, February 24, 1485. In this letter he tells how he has hunted and caught wild pigs, although they killed his dog and his horse.[29]

[29] "ich hab gejagt und wol gefangen mit meiner handt vorauß schwein aber sie haben mir mein hunt erschlagen und haben mir mein gut roß erschlagen und mir."

MAXIMILIAN'S SELF-PORTRAYAL

In five adventures (nos. 32, 43, 46, 64, and 72) Teuerdank is endangered on a ship during a bad storm. In no. 65 he is in a boat when a larger ship runs it down, but he seizes a rope and saves himself.

Five other adventures are encountered in hunting stags. In no. 13 a stag is chased into a narrow pass, where it must leap over Teuerdank, but the latter kills it as it passes over him. In no. 30 Teuerdank is urged to dismount and hold his crossbow ready; he catches his spurs in the brush, falls and discharges the bow, to his peril. Again, in no. 33, Unfalo tells Teuerdank to chase on horseback a stag which has run down a dangerous path; the horse makes a tremendous leap and lands safely. In no. 40 Teuerdank is given the lead-dog to hold in leash and it nearly pulls him over a steep precipice. Finally, in no. 44, Unfalo has Teuerdank ride with his weapon loaded before him. It goes off, but by leaning back Teuerdank escapes the shot.

Other adventures endanger the hero's life with weapons. In no. 34 a defective steel bow is given him, which breaks when shot. Once (no. 39) Unfalo directs him to inspect a loaded gun at night with a lighted torch. The gun explodes. Twice (nos. 50 and 57) he is told to fire guns which have been overloaded and which burst before him.

Horses are used three times to imperil him. In nos. 47, 51, and 54 he is given horses which shy easily or are inclined to run away. He is induced to ride over slippery ice to see some pretty girls, and his horse falls with him (no. 29). He has three adventures hunting wild bears (nos. 14, 27, and 48). Twice he has experiences with lions. In no. 16 he walks up to a lion and pulls out its tongue, to which the beast patiently submits. In no. 42 he enters the cage of two lions, having been told that they were tame. But they prove to be otherwise and he has to beat them off with a shovel. Twice too his life is in danger when servants nearly ignite large amounts of powder: no. 58 in Teuerdank's boat, no. 60 in his room. In no. 23 he is led over thin ice, which breaks. Another time (no. 26) he is directed to a broken stairway, which collapses. Again he tries to

---

Maximilians I. vertraulicher Briefwechsel mit Sigmund Prüschenk Freiherrn zu Stettenberg, hrsg. von Victor von Kraus (Innsbruck, 1875), pp. 47f.

prove that he can walk out on a high projecting beam without becoming dizzy, but the beam is rotten and breaks (no. 28). On two occasions during attacks of illness the doctors prescribe the wrong kind of medicine. Each time the hero secretly sends for his own prescription and recovers (nos. 67 and 70).

Then there is an adventure, no. 21, in which Teuerdank nearly catches his foot in a huge polishing wheel. At another time (no. 36) an avalanche is started above him while he is hunting. Once (no. 52) he is sent out during a storm and is almost struck by lightning. His enemy fails to persuade him to ride into an old well-hole (no. 63). His house is set afire while he is asleep (no. 73). Attempts are made to poison him (no. 96). In addition to all these perils, there are twenty occasions, from no. 76 on, when Neidelhart exposes Teuerdank to danger by urging him into previously arranged ambushes.

A work not published during the lifetime of Maximilian is his *Weisskunig*. When it finally was printed in 1775 the interest in the *Teuerdank* had already abated. An age which could no longer appreciate the metrical romance had still less interest in the prose account, and thus little notice was taken of its appearance.[30]

The *Weisskunig* is an expression of the urge of the man of the Renaissance to be best in all lines of endeavor. This is clearly set forth in a tentative preface to manuscript D of the *Weisskunig*:

> Größer gemyets nye kainer was, des wesen wunderlich, der tat unglaublich; sein leben ist nach gemayner sag alle menschen, die ye leben empfiengen, ubertreffen, umb des willen man in, der welt eröbert, von etlichen der sterkest gehaißen, von etlichen der freyest, nun der tewrest, nun der berumest und durchauß den namen seines vatern verdienet, deß geschicht furan ist klarlicher ze hören.[31]

Furthermore we can find in this work a definite tendency to portray in a good light those features which were criticized in Maximilian by his contemporaries, an attempt to soften the unattractive characteristics and to ignore those which are less easily defended.

---

[30] Cf. R. von Liliencron, *Der Weisskunig Kaiser Maximilians I*, pp. 325ff. The *Weisskunig* was first published in Wien, 1775.

[31] "Lesarten, Zusätze und Erklärungen" to *Der. Weisskunig*, hrsg. von Alwin Schultz, *Jahrb. k.-h. Samml.*, VI (Wien, 1887), 447.

We may pass over the first part of the book, which deals with the Old White King, Friedrich III, and begin with the second part. After describing the wonders that accompanied the birth of the son of the Old White King, the author begins at once to picture the boy as of superlative ability in every field he undertook. The children of the nobility who came to play with him were bested by him at every game.[32] In the account of his studies it is possible to see the reflection of a desire on Max' part to eradicate the memory of childhood difficulties in school. From Cuspinianus we remember to have heard that he could scarcely speak until he was nine years old and that his teacher often prompted his understanding by a liberal use of the rod.[33] The young prince in this story is quite different. He learned everything so readily that the teachers never had any reason to complain. He was so adept in the Scriptures that he asked his teachers questions which they could not answer. Therefore his father took him from his studies, since more learning would have only been a waste of time. At this time the son made a long speech to his father, asking and explaining riddles. The father, overjoyed, then gave him the name of "the Young White King."[34]

From now on the "Young White King" learned a variety of skills and learned them faster and more thoroughly than they had ever been learned before. First, he outdid his very best secretaries through the ease with which he learned to write.[35] Then he acquired "die siben freyen kunst" in a short time.[36] In this chapter we read that "he also permitted no robbery in his empire; on the contrary, it was safer to travel through his lands than anywhere else in the world." Now, too, he read many books until he learned how kings must rule the world, and took as his future motto the words: "Halt Maß!"[37]

When the young king studied astrology he soon learned not only all the doctors could teach him, but more.[38] Here we find a

[32] Schultz' edition of the *Weisskunig*, p. 54, no. 17.
[33] Cuspinianus, *De Caesaribus*, p. 602.
[34] *Weisskunig* (ed. Schultz), p. 56, no. 18.
[35] *Ibid.*, p. 58, no. 19.
[36] *Ibid.*, p. 58, no. 20.
[37] *Ibid.*, pp. 60ff., no. 21.
[38] *Ibid.*, p. 62, no. 22.

warning against doing things too quickly and rashly. One is supposed to wait for the most favorable time as foretold by the stars. Could this be a partial excuse for Maximilian's most besetting sin, his inconstancy, dilatoriness, and unreliability in action, of which the majority of his contemporaries accuse him?

The young king also learned magic, but only in order better to understand the meaning of the true belief.[39] In medicine he became so skillful that twice he saved his life by refusing the treatment of the physicians and prescribing for himself.[40] He learned the work of a secretary and personally supervised all letters. He could keep many secretaries busy; and was so diligent in dictating that he often had nine, ten, eleven, and even twelve secretaries taking dictation at one time and each on a different letter.[41]

It will be remembered that even Maximilian's enemies did not deny that he was generous. Their criticism was that he was too much so, that he was prodigal. This same reproach was made the young king by his father:

Thereupon the son gave his father this answer: "I shall not become a king of money, but I shall become a king of the people and of all those who have money; and every king attacks and makes war upon his enemies with the people and not with money, for where the treasure is, there is the heart, and the body remains with the treasure."[42]

Thus he grew up generous and remained so, especially to old servants and soldiers, helping out those who had formerly done evil to him. With an oft recurring exclamation the writer emphasizes this as an outstanding characteristic of the young king: "How great was his generosity! Where can one find such things written of another king?"[43]

The young hero learned to paint, for he heard a wise old man say that every good general should know this art. He then used

---

[39] *Ibid.*, p. 64, no. 23.
[40] *Ibid.*, p. 68, no. 25. This coincides with the two adventures which we saw in the *Teuerdank* (nos. 67 and 70).
[41] *Ibid.*, p. 70, no. 26.
[42] *Ibid.*, p. 70, no. 27. The lack of money caused most of Max' military failures and his experiences usually confirmed the words of Wimpfeling on this subject: "Die Kraftsehne des Krieges (das ist baar Geld). . . ." Cf. Wimpfeling's *Germania*, übersetzt und erläutert von Ernst Martin (Strassburg, 1885), p. 50.
[43] *Weisskunig* (ed. Schultz), p. 72, no. 27: "Wie groß ist sein miltigkait gewest! wo findt man sölichs von ainem andern kunig geschriben?"

his skill in several ways, but notably for the purpose of prolonging his memory: "He also maintained the great artists of painting and woodcutting and had many artistic works painted and cut, which will remain in the world in his memory, but with changed names."[44] Next he learned to build with stone and outdid all his masterworkmen in the building of fortifications for war.[45] In carpentry, too, he was clever and ingenious, and superior to everyone.[46] In music he took an example from King David and King Alexander, writing songs and inventing new instruments, so "that he excelled all kings and no one could equal him."[47] As he was superior to Alexander in music, so too he was better than Julius Caesar in war; for the latter had to fight only one land, while he had to fight many. Here the author appears to be a little concerned lest he may not be believed:

Some one may speak against this, my writing, but I know that no one will do so who is experienced and learned in writings and in the histories of the kings and who can weigh the manner of things; if one speaks against it then who is unlearned and inexperienced, he mocks himself.[48]

Although a short time before the young king had taken as his motto "Halt Maß!" he evidently did not consider it intemperate to set a fine table, for the *Weisskunig* tells us in a later chapter that he always had the most costly food and drink from many different kingdoms and lands and always according to their season.[49] With banquets and mummeries he became so well acquainted that he was soon the best in both.[50] He learned all there was to know about coinage[51] and mining,[52] and became expert in the use

[44] *Ibid.*, p. 74, no. 29: "Er hat auch die großen künstler der malerey und schnitzerey underhalten und vil kunstliche werch malen und sneiden lassen, die in der welt in seiner gedächtnus aber mit verkerten namen beleiben werden."
[45] *Ibid.*, p. 77, no. 30.
[46] *Ibid.*, p. 77, no. 31.
[47] *Ibid.*, p. 80, no. 32: "das er alle kunig ubertraf und ime nyemands geleihn mocht."
[48] *Ibid.*, p. 80, no. 32: "Es mocht ainer wider dise mein schrift reden, aber ich waiß, das sölichs kainer nit thuet, der in der geschrift und in der kunig geschichten erfaren und gelert ist und die gestalt der sachen erwegen kan; redt dann ainer dawider, der unerfaren und ungelert ist, der spot sein selber."
[49] *Ibid.*, p. 82, no. 33.
[50] *Ibid.*, p. 82, no. 34.
[51] *Ibid.*, p. 84, no. 35.
[52] *Ibid.*, p. 84, no. 36.

of all weapons.⁵³ When some one reproached him for spending so much time in hawking, the Young White King replied that this gave opportunities to many people to see him who otherwise would not be able to gain an audience⁵⁴—an idea repeated again in the *Jagdbuch* and depicted on the first plate of the *Fischereibuch*.⁵⁵ He was particularly enthusiastic about hunting deer, chamois, ibex, wild pigs, and bears,⁵⁶ as well as about fishing, in which he spared no cost.⁵⁷ He liked to hear the song of birds, and so he had a master of the birds who kept singing birds for him. Whenever he came into a city he had these birds carried into his bedchamber and other rooms, where they often set up such a noise that two people talking together could scarcely hear each other.⁵⁸

The Young White King could fight in every manner, in or out of armor and on foot or on horseback, either in the manner of the Germans or of other countries.⁵⁹ He knew all about horses and did not consider it beneath him to invent a new kind of bit for them. When told that he should let his master of the horse do such things, he quoted an old proverb about the nail holding the horseshoe, the shoe holding the horse, the horse the man, the man the castle, the castle the city, the city the land, and the land the kingdom.⁶⁰

He was ingenious in the matter of artillery, having invented new guns as well as carriages for them. He began boring guns from iron blocks instead of casting them. Also he invented a particular powder; and he was the best shot of all his men.⁶¹ The secret of making an especially hard armor had been in the possession of the "Treizsaurbeyn" family of Innsbruck, but they had died out and only a servant, Caspar Riedrer, knew the process. He told

---

⁵³ *Ibid.*, pp. 86-91, nos. 37-38.
⁵⁴ *Ibid.*, pp. 92ff., no. 39.
⁵⁵ At the end of *Das Jagdbuch Kaiser Maximilians I*. In Verbindung mit Wm. A. Baillie-Grohman hrsg. von Dr. Michael Mayr, Innsbruck, 1901. *Das Fischereibuch Kaiser Maximilians I*. Unter Mitwirkung von Ludwig Freih. von Lazarini hrsg. von Dr. Michael Mayr, Innsbruck, 1901.
⁵⁶ *Weisskunig*, pp. 94ff., no. 40.
⁵⁷ *Ibid.*, p. 97, no. 41.
⁵⁸ *Ibid.*, p. 97, no. 42.
⁵⁹ *Ibid.*, pp. 100-104, nos. 43, 44, 45, and 46.
⁶⁰ *Ibid.*, p. 106, no. 47.
⁶¹ *Ibid.*, p. 110, no. 49.

the Young White King about it, "whereupon the king pondered the same art with great diligence and invented it out of his own understanding."[62]

Little has been said up to now of the young king's personal appearance. Now we learn that when he went to the land of the "kunig vom fewreyßen" (i.e., Charles the Bold of Burgundy), the young queen's mother disguised herself in order to get an early glimpse of the Young White King and found him extremely handsome; "because of his beauty and good manners he was called the White King with the Kind Countenance."[63]

One of the most applauded abilities of Maximilian was, as we have seen, his knowledge of foreign languages, usually given as seven in number. In the *Weisskunig* we read how he acquired this skill, and we find some indication that his reputation as a linguist in the writings of contemporaries may have exceeded even his own description here. Thus we hear that he learned Wendish and Bohemian from a peasant who used to bring him rare fruits; "and although he used these languages very little, still he did not forget them, but when anyone spoke them, he understood them as much as necessary."[64] When he went to the land of his bride, he considered it essential that a ruler should understand the speech of his subjects,

and for this reason the young king applied particular diligence to the language of his spouse and learned the same language in a short time, and could speak, understand, and write it as if he had been born with this language.[65]

Likewise he learned Flemish, English, and Spanish.[66] He learned Italian also, "but since he could speak Latin well, that was a

[62] *Ibid.*, p. 108, no. 48: "Darauf hat der kunig derselben kunst mit großem vleiß nachgedacht und die aus seinem aigen verstand erfunden."
[63] *Ibid.*, p. 133, no. 61: "er wurde genennt von seiner schön und schicklichait wegen der weiß kunig mit dem guetigen angesicht."
[64] *Ibid.*, p. 74, no. 28: "und, wiewol er dieselb sprach gar wenig prauchet, so vergaß er doch der nit, sonder wann man dieselbn sprach redet, so verstund er die nach seiner notturft."
[65] *Ibid.*, p. 138, no. 64: "und aus sölicher ursach het der jung kunig zu seiner gemahl sprach sondern vleiß und lernet dieselb sprach in kurzer zeit und kunt dieselb sprach als wol reden, versteen und schreiben, als were er ain geborner von derselben sprach gewest."
[66] *Ibid.*, p. 140, nos. 65, 66, and 67 respectively.

great help to him in the Italian language."⁶⁷ This considerable knowledge made it possible for the young king to speak to his seven captains in seven different tongues.⁶⁸

In a note in the Kaiser's own handwriting to manuscript C of the *Weisskunig* we read further just where Maximilian professed to have acquired his linguistic knowledge:

> Note: the vii languages all together, how and from whom the w. k. learned them. First German as a child. Latin from the schoolmaster. Wendish and Bohemian from peasants. French from his wife. Flemish from the old women. Spanish from messages in letters. Lombardian from cuirassiers. English from archers.⁶⁹

After Maximilian had written these chapters on language, however, he evidently thought better of publishing what was doubtless an overdrawn account, so a marginal note to manuscript E, again in the Kaiser's hand, reads: "Note: this chapter is to be so fashioned as to show that the w.k. learned only to understand the English language and not to speak it."⁷⁰ It is not our purpose here to establish the linguistic ability of the Kaiser, although this information may throw some light upon it.⁷¹ Nevertheless, this in-

---

⁶⁷ *Ibid.*, p. 143, no. 68: "Aber nachdem er guet latein reden kunt, das was ime in der welschen sprach ain großer behilf."

⁶⁸ *Ibid.*, p. 145, no. 69.

⁶⁹ *Ibid.*, "Lesarten, Zusätze und Erklärungen" to the *Weisskunig*, p. 462: "Nota: die vij sprachen zumalen, wie der w. k. und von wem er die gelert het. Am ersten deu(t)sch von (knaben) kinderrweis. Latein vom Schulmaister. Windisch und behamsch von bauren, franzesisch von der frauen. Flamisch von den alten frauen. Yspanisch auß briefen in poten. Lombardisch (in) von kürisern. Englisch von bognern."

⁷⁰ *Ibid.*, "Lesarten, Zusätze und Erklärungen," *Weisskunig*, p. 463: "Nota: dys capitl sol gestelt werden, daz der w. ko. die englisch sprach allain gelernt hat zu verstan und nit zu reden."

⁷¹ Paul Van Dyke, *Renascence Portraits*, pp. 270f., comments on this subject: "But it was a time when a little knowledge of a foreign language went a long way, and Maximilian's linguistic accomplishments were perhaps as sound as those of most of the princely prodigies of the Sixteenth Century." It is interesting to compare Maximilian's attainments with those of Oswald von Wolkenstein, an imitator of the Minnesang in the Fifteenth Century, who wrote in awkward verse:

> Franzoisch, mörisch, katlonisch und kastilian,
> teutsch, latein, windisch, lampartisch, reuschisch und roman
> die zehen sprach hab ich gepraucht, wann mir zeran.

And, he adds: "Auch kund ich fidlen, trummen, paugken, pfeifen." Cf. *Oswald von Wolkensteins Gedichte* (Innsbruck bei Wagner), p. 22. Quoted by Ignaz Zingerle, *Tirols Antheil an der poetischen National-Literatur im Mittelalter* (Innsbruck, 1851), p. 11, notes 1 and 2.

tercalation does illustrate Maximilian's method of using every possible opportunity to improve his own picture for posterity; and it shows that in looking back over his work, even he occasionally found the features overdrawn.[72]

In connection with several familiar incidents it can also be seen that Maximilian intended to have his work show him in the very best light. For instance, when the Flemings had taken possession of Maximilian's son Philipp after the death of Mary of Burgundy in 1482, they gave as their excuse that Max was using up their money in warring and gambling and that his councillors and captains were thieves. This accusation is reproduced in the *Weisskunig* and the reply is not wanting: "That was all a falsehood, for in all his life he had never gambled away a thousand gulden; his councillors and captains were also pious and honorable, otherwise he would not have been able to carry on such great wars."[73]

Another complaint often made against the emperor was that he was so reticent and secretive about all his plans that it was difficult and often impossible to co-operate with him. It may be an indication of an unfinished attempt to deny this accusation that a woodcut shows the White King talking to his seven captains, and beneath in the Kaiser's handwriting the words: "How he always announced his plans to his captains."[74] The text for this woodcut, however, was never written.

It will be recalled that the outcome of the "Fräulein von Brittania" incident was anything but complimentary to Maximilian. Three woodcuts were made on this subject for the *Weisskunig*, which definitely connect the figure of the White King with the daughter of the "Ermine King" (Duke of Bretagne). The first one is entitled: "How the White King sends his messenger for

[72] Literary historians seldom omit mention of Maximilian's linguistic abilities. Victor von Kraus, in a discussion of the extent of the Kaiser's knowledge of French and Flemish (*Maximilians I. vertraulicher Briefwechsel mit Sigmund Prüschenk, Freiherrn zu Stettenberg* (Innsbruck, 1875), p. 10), declares: "Wie wichtig ist die Feststellung dieser kleinsten Tatsachen zur richtigen Würdigung von Maximilians Charakter und Entwicklungsgang."

[73] *Weisskunig*, p. 173, no. 85: "Das war alles die unwarheit, dann er het alle seine tag nye tausend guldein verspilt, es waren auch seine räte und hauptleut frum und erber, er het sonst so große kriege nit mugen furn."

[74] *Ibid.*, p. 212: "Wie er allezeit sein anschleg seinen hauptleuten hat anzeigt."

help to the Ermine King and asks him for his daughter."[75] The second shows "How the Ermine King gave the White King his daughter and married her by proxy."[76] The third refers to the King of France, the "Blue King": "How the Blue King abducted the Ermine King's daughter."[77] No text accompanies these woodcuts, and they were evidently included by mistake. After they were cut, probably it seemed to Maximilian too humiliating an experience to allow to happen to the White King, who should be able to overcome all obstacles. Therefore we read only that the daughter of this king, who is also called the "Black-white King," is promised, not to the White King but to "another king." Then after telling of the Blue King's perfidious behavior, the account ends laconically: "Concerning this matter much might be written."[78] Actually a fragmentary text was written on the incident which assigned the role to the Young White King, even calling him "kunig Maximilian" in one place; but the tone in which the young princess urges, half-reproachfully, the White King to hurry to her aid before it is too late can not have appeared sufficiently dignified or honorable with respect to the hero, and the passage was changed.[79]

The captivity of Maximilian at Bruges in Flanders in 1488 was terminated by his promise not to seek revenge when released. Now we hear of the Young White King in the same situation and of the mercy "which he promised them, and which he also kept and wanted to keep; but God would not let such a thing come to pass."[80] Although his cruel captors subsequently met due punish-

---

[75] *Ibid.*, p. 238: Wie d(er) w(eiß) k(unig) schickt sein potschaft umb hilf zu dem herml ku(nig) und bat ine umb sein tochter."

[76] Ibid., p. 239: "Wie der hermbl kunig sein tochter dem w(eißen) k(unig) gab und durch des w(eißen) k(unigs) potschaft vermehelt."

[77] *Ibid.*, p. 242: "Wie der plaw kunig des herml kunigs tochter weg fueret."

[78] *Ibid.*, p. 243, no. 123: "Von diser sach were vil zu schreiben."

[79] *Ibid.*, p. 509, "Lesarten, Zusätze und Erklärungen," manuscript E, fo. 273-a: "Indem kam im potschaft von der herzogin von Britani, die er zu ainer gemahl genomen het, und verkundet im, das er ir muesset persondlich zu hilf komen wider den k. v. Frankreich, (und wo ir der w. k. nit zueschrib das er ir) das wo er ir persondlich zu hilf kem (so mußt sy wider in klagen) dan sy müsset (sunst an irem land und leuten spot und schand leiden) sich den Franzosen ergeben und mocht solhen smerzen an iren land und leuten nit leiden," etc.

[80] *Weisskunig*, p. 261, no. 133: "auf gnad, die er inen dann versprach, auch inen hielt und halten wolt; aber got wolt solichs nit beschehen lassen."

ment, it is all represented as happening without the young king's knowledge or command.[81]

Other well-known events are similarly justified or commemorated. The transfer of the Tyrol to Maximilian from Duke Sigismund in 1490 may have involved some degree of good will on the part of the latter toward his successor. We know, however, that pressure from the province of Tyrol itself and from Friedrich III were the decisive factors.[82] Nevertheless, we read here that Sigismund, "an old weak man," gives his lands to the Young White King "of his own free will."[83] Then, too, the *Böhmenschlacht* has its parallel, in which the young king distinguishes himself by his valorous conduct;[84] and the taking of Kufstein and the fate of Pienzenauer are clearly seen in another chapter,[85] which coolly ends: "And he had the commander beheaded and all his aides who were seized with him."

A final incident, mentioned in manuscript D of the *Weisskunig*, is another lion-story. We are told that when the Young White King was a child of two-and-a-half years, a fierce, wild lion broke from its cage. Everyone fled, including the child's nurses, and left the young prince alone in the garden. When the lion approached him and he stretched out his arms for it, the lion lay down at his feet and let him climb upon its back, something which no one else, not even its master, could do.[86]

Numerous plans for other works occupied the Kaiser's later years and they were nearly all intended for the same purpose: a glorification of his person and his family. He had the intention of causing certain historical works to be written, and to this end

---

[81] *Ibid.*, p. 264, nos. 134 and 135.
[82] Cf. Albert Jäger, "Der Übergang Tirols und der österreichischen Vorlande von dem Erzherzoge Sigmund an den Röm. König Maximilian von 1478-1490," *Archiv für österreichische Geschichte*, LI (1873), 297-448.
[83] *Weisskunig*, p. 270, no. 144.
[84] *Ibid.*, p. 325, no. 193.
[85] *Ibid.*, p. 329, no. 194: "und ließ demselben phleger und allen seinen helfern, die mit ime begriffen wurden, die kopf abschlagn."
[86] *Ibid.*, "Lesarten, Zusätze und Erklärungen," p. 452: "so ist es nit ain klain anzaigen gewest seiner kounftigen maiestat, do der lew ausgebrochen, des ungestyem, wieten und grume yederman floche auch die amblen des kinds, drythalb jar alt, im garten der gepurge vergassen; aber do der lew zu dem kind nahet und sein das kind begert, sagt man, wie der lew vor im sich nidergelegt und gelitten auf in ze steygen, der kainen andern menschen noch seinen maister leyden mocht."

he supported two historians in particular, Ladislaus Sunthaim and Johann Cuspinianus. Although there is evidence that these men and others were supposed to collect materials for a history of the different parts of Germany,[87] it was specifically the history of the house of Hapsburg that interested Maximilian and it was that which received the most emphasis. As early as 1498 a Dr. Conrad Turst of Zürich received a gift from Max for a book "von den herrn von Habsburg."[88] About 1500 the painter Conrad Doll of Friedberg painted a genealogy of the Hapsburg house for the Kaiser.[89] The attempt to trace the genealogy of the Hapsburgs back to Noah intrigued Maximilian for a long time, although he was not willing to accept blindly the first artificially constructed pedigree handed to him, that compiled by Stabius.[90] With the Kaiser's encouragement and from the material collected by Sunthaim, together with other sources which he himself had investigated, the Freiburg professor, Jacob Mennl (Manlius), published a work entitled *Die fürstliche Chronik Kaiser Maximilians genannt Geburtspiegel*, a conglomeration of genealogies, Austrian history, and legends of local and other saints.[91]

Maximilian knew well the advantage of illustrations to a written text and therefore made plentiful use of woodcuts and pictures in all his works. Whereas the popes and princes of Italy glorified their names with the help of a Raphael, a Pinturicchio, or a Mantegna, Maximilian appreciated the attraction to the popular imagination of an art which was comparatively inexpensive and which could be multiplied rapidly and distributed easily in many places. The popularity of many a well-known work of the time was due as much to its pictures as to its text.[92] Thus it is that we

[87] Cf. Simon Laschitzer, "Die Genealogie des Kaisers Maximilian I.," *Jahrb. k.-h. Samml.*, VII (1888), 2ff.

[88] *Ibid.*, p. 10.

[89] *Ibid.*, p. 10.

[90] Cf. Joseph Aschbach, *Geschichte der Wiener Universität* (Wien, 1865), II, 369, who says that Max found Stabius' account of the descent of the Hapsburgs from Noah and Cham "ziemlich abenteuerlich," and therefore had it judged by the theological faculty of the University of Vienna.

[91] Cf. Laschitzer, *op. cit.*, pp. 12ff. And by the same author, "Die Heiligen aus der 'Sipp-, Mag- und Schwägerschaft' des Kaisers Maximilian I.," *Jahrb. k.-h. Samml.*, IV (1886), 70-289; V (1887), 117-262.

[92] E.g., this was the case with Schedel's *Weltchronik*, according to Wegele, *op. cit.*, pp. 55f.

MAXIMILIAN'S SELF-PORTRAYAL

find 255 plates in the *Freydal,* 118 woodcuts in the *Teuerdank,* about 250 more in the *Weisskunig,* and many more in the genealogical works.

The most monumental task which the Kaiser ever gave the woodcutters, however, was that involved in the so-called *Triumph* and the *Ehrenpforte.* The *Triumph,* also called the *Triumphwagen* and the *Triumphzug,* was an extremely ornate drawing, in which Maximilian is represented as riding in state in company with all the chief Virtues, preceded or followed in the procession by symbols of the things which he considered important in his life, all in the most confused order. For instance, there are representations of his favorite hunting sports, of his five royal officers, of his fondness for, and cultivation of, music, his court jesters, his tournaments, his Burgundian marriage, his various wars in Flanders, Germany, and Italy, and so on.[93]

Originally intended to accompany this as part of a whole was the *Porta Honoris* (*Ehrenpforte*), to which Stabius furnished appropriate verses.[94] Included in this imitation of a Roman triumphal arch are all of the ideas that had been carried out in all the other works of Maximilian, beginning with the *Freydal* and through *Teuerdank,* the *Weisskunig,* the *Triumphzug,* the *Genealogie,* right down to the reliefs on the Kaiser's *Grabmal* at Innsbruck.[95] The woodcuts which make up the *Ehrenpforte* show Max' genealogy, a series of historical events, scenes from his youth and private life, illustrations of his love of adventure and the hunt, and portrayals of dangers of all kinds. Some of the pictures bring out his personal qualities, his universal culture, his knowledge of languages, and his thorough education. Others commemorate his skill in war and in all its branches.

Opinions of the *Ehrenpforte* as a work of art vary. William B. Scott, in his Dürer biography, characterizes it somewhat flippantly as "an impossible structure, with portraits of all the ancestors of the emperor, and many other matters, in ninety-two large blocks,

[93] Cf. Franz Schestag, "Kaiser Maximilians I. Triumph," *Jahrb. k.-h. Samml.,* I (1883), 154-181.
[94] Cf. *Bilibaldi Pirckheimeri Opera* (Francoforti, 1610), pp. 183ff.
[95] Cf. Eduard Chmelarz, "Die Ehrenpforte des Kaisers Maximilian I.," *Jahrb. k.-h. Samml.,* IV (1886), 289-320.

which need never be put together."[96] Moritz Thausing on the other hand, also in a life of Dürer, praises it as "the most magnificent thing ever created for the woodcut."[97] Whatever the artistic value of the *Ehrenpforte* and *Triumph* may be, there is little doubt that Max intended them as important contributions to his self-aggrandizing program. It is a little-known fact that during Maximilian's lifetime 700 copies of the *Ehrenpforte* alone were printed.[98]

The foregoing shows how incessantly Maximilian was occupied, not only in extending his "remembrance," but in insuring that his memory among posterity should have a definite stamp and shape. Surely none of his various literary or artistic enterprises enjoyed a wider circulation or met with more interest among the people than did the *Teuerdank*. It was read, first of all, because it was about a well-known figure, and the reader was curious to be led behind the scenes, as it were, by the author, the Kaiser Maximilian himself. The many woodcuts also contributed greatly to the appeal of the book, sustaining interest where the text might fail. Even the general appearance of the large folio-volume made a favorable impression. The excellence of its type still makes it of interest to book lovers. Of all the mediums through which Maximilian sought to impress posterity, it is safe to say that this one volume has been the greatest single contributory influence.

Inseparably connected with the *Teuerdank* is the *Schlüssel*, or key, which Melchior Pfintzing, the Kaiser's chaplain who had helped most in the actual writing down of the text, appended in order to explain to the uninitiated the historical background of the various exploits described. The *Schlüssel* itself became a convenient way of making a résumé of the text. Its fate throughout the following years is enlightening for a study of the effect of Maximilian's propaganda in the Sixteenth Century.

[96] *Albert Durer: His Life and Works* (London, 1869), pp. 102f.
[97] *Dürer. Geschichte seines Lebens und seiner Kunst.* Zweite verbesserte Aufl. (Leipzig, 1884), II, 119.
[98] Cf. Karl Giehlow, "Dürers Entwürfe für das Triumphrelief Kaiser Maximilians I. im Louvre, eine Studie zur Entwicklungsgeschichte des Triumphzuges," *Jahrb. k.-h. Samml.*, XXIX (1910/1911), 14.

V

TEUERDANK AND THE MAXIMILIAN ANECDOTES IN THE SIXTEENTH CENTURY

A. *Teuerdank* IN THE SIXTEENTH CENTURY

SEBASTIAN FRANCK's *Germania* of 1538 gives us the first instance of the use of the *Teuerdank* in a historical work as a source for the history of Maximilian I.[1] Franck followed the *Schlüssel* which Pfintzing appended to the poem, but he also expanded it, drawing further information in many cases from the woodcuts or the poem itself and making some additions of his own. Arnold Busson, in his article on the origin of the legend of Max on the Martinswand, mentions Franck's use of the poem and points out how he amplified the adventures in *Teuerdank* and added certain features.[2] Busson was interested primarily in the development of one particular legend, and only hints that changes were made in other adventures as well. For our purpose it will be of interest to see just what was the extent of the alterations introduced by Franck.

The reader of the *Teuerdank* soon notices that small discrepancies exist between the text and the accompanying woodcuts. For example, in Adventure 16, where the verses tell of a lion in a cage, the illustration depicts the animal chained to a pillar out in the open. These differences are in themselves of minor importance, and are easily explained by the fact that several artists made the illustrations for the Kaiser and that the details of an adventure were sometimes changed after the picture was made. It is more important, however, to note that Pfintzing in his *Schlüssel* sometimes makes additions to the content of the text and sometimes contradicts it in minor details. These slight errors were then repeated or enlarged by Franck, who had nothing like the degree of familiarity with the material that Pfintzing had. A careful com-

[1] Cf. Wegele, *op. cit.*, p. 258.
[2] Arnold Busson, "Die Sage von Max auf der Martinswand und ihre Entstehung," *Sitzungsberichte der phil.-hist. Classe der kaiserlichen Akademie der Wissenschaften*, CXVI (Wien, 1888), 468-476.

parison of Franck's summary of the *Teuerdank* with the poem itself often reveals a very superficial reading, sometimes it appears that he could not have read the poem at all.[3] He leans heavily on Pfintzing's *Schlüssel*, and occasionally makes additions to it or changes it, usually with the evident purpose of giving a lively and dramatic tone to his account. At other times it is the woodcut which causes a wrong interpretation. When the text had been altered after the woodcut was made, Franck is more likely to follow the latter. Once,[4] at least, he mistakes another figure in the picture for that of Maximilian and interprets the adventure accordingly.

A few examples will illustrate the way in which the stories of the *Teuerdank* developed additional features through the *Schlüssel* of Pfintzing and then its imitation and amplification by Franck.

In Adventure 16 Teuerdank is induced by Fürwittig to enter a wooden cage in which lies a lion "extraordinarily large and terrible."[5] Teuerdank displays his courage by opening the lion's mouth and pulling out its tongue.

> Der stundt vor Im als ein zam hund
> Dann Er des Helds mandlich gemüet
> Erkannt/ darumb Er mit nicht wuet
> Gegen Im als Er vor het than.[6]

The *Schlüssel* now adds that this event took place in Bavaria, that the lion was six years old and tame, and that Teuerdank did this because he wished to emulate Samson.[7] Franck in turn follows the *Schlüssel*, but further localizes the action at Munich in Bavaria, and adds of the lion, "er aber wie ein lemblin regt sich nit."[8]

---

[3] Busson, *op. cit.*, p. 473, claims that Franck did not take the trouble to read the text at all. However, there are many places where Franck has more information than the *Schlüssel* contains, which he could have gotten only by reading the poem itself. E.g., Franck's *Germania. Von des gantzen Teütschlands/ aller Teutschen Völcker herkomen/ Namen/ Handlen*, etc. (Bern, 1539), fo. 282-a, nos. 11, 1, 2, 3, 4, 5, 7, 8, and 9; fo. 282-b, no. 10, and many others. Occasionally Franck uses the same wording as the chapter-heading of the poem, e.g., fo. 282-a, no. 6, and Adventure 31 of *Teuerdank* (ed. Laschitzer, *Jahrb. k.-h. Samml.*, VIII, Wien, 1888).

[4] *Germania*, fo. 281-b and 282-a.
[5] *Teuerdank* (ed. Laschitzer), p. 73.
[6] *Ibid.*, p. 75.
[7] *Ibid.*, p. 570. The *Schlüssel* attempts to assign a locality for many of these adventures.
[8] Franck, *Germania*, fo. 281-b, no. 4.

TEUERDANK AND MAXIMILIAN ANECDOTES

According to Adventure 19 Teuerdank was advised to creep through a thicket and attack a wild pig with a short sword. He starts to do it, but the dogs arouse the pig and it flees without giving the hero a chance to prove his valor.[9] The *Schlüssel* reports the adventure thus:

> Der Edel Ritter Tewrdannck vnderstundt sich aus frecher Jugend vor andern etwas sonnders zůthun/ nemlich ein groß hawendt Schwein mit einem degen in Osterreich in einer dicke das Er auf allen vieren geen můst zůstechen.[10]

Franck in his turn goes farther, assumes that the deed was accomplished, and ends his account: "vnnd erwürgt sie mit einem kurtzen degen."[11]

Adventure 20 has already been mentioned as the basis of the Martinswand legend. In this chapter Fürwittig arranges for a hunter to lead the hero to a very dangerous spot on a cliff while he is hunting chamois in view of onlookers below. After killing the chamois, Teuerdank's foot slips and all but one of his shoe-spikes give way, but after a moment of uncertainty he regains his balance and comes safely down.

> Tewerdannck wer khomen in groß schwer
> Het nichts gewisers gehabt dann den todt
> Aber Im hulff der ewig got
> Das Er mit dem ein fůß wider
> Hafftet/ da Er in setzt nider.[12]

Pfintzing's summary of this incident is brief and adds only that it took place "bey Innsprugk."[13] Franck's paragraph, however, reads as follows:

> Zum achten entgieng jm zu Ißbruck auff einem Gembsen geiåd/ auff einer hohen platten schafft/ vnd all zincken an sein fůßeisen/ daß man sich sein verwegt/ vnd jm das Sacrament zeygt/ noch halff jm Gott durch sein freydig gemůt vnd geschicklicheyt herab.[14]

---

[9] *Teuerdank*, p. 88.
[10] *Ibid.*, p. 571.
[11] *Germania*, fo. 281-b, no. 7.
[12] *Teuerdank*, p. 94.
[13] *Ibid.*, p. 571.
[14] *Germania*, fo. 281-b, no. 8.

The change from "bey Innsprugk" to "zu Ißbruck" may first be noted; then the addition of the sacrament, a characteristic feature of this Maximilian legend, which occurs for the first time here. It is possible that Franck was repeating the story as it had already developed in his day. It is more likely, however, that he was drawing upon fairly common knowledge of what had happened in similar cases.[15] We know from a report made by Antoine de Lalaing, Seigneur de Montigny, the companion of Philipp der Schöne of Austria on his first trip to the Tyrol in 1503, that it was the custom in Max' time to show the sacrament to hunters in such danger.[16]

Busson makes a good deal of the mention by Franck of the divine help given to Max in descending from the cliff. He even goes so far as to give Franck the credit for having brought the saving angel into the development of the legend, and points to Adventure 49 for his proof.[17] These two adventures, says Busson, later became merged in the one legend of Max on the Martinswand. In this chapter the hero is again on a chamois hunt and narrowly escapes death when a large stone rolls down and passes between his legs. Franck tells the story and adds that Teuerdank "solt von rechts wegen erfallen sein/ wann jn nit ein sonder von Gott zugeeygter Genius vnd Engel gefuret hett."[18] A closer examination of Franck's style, however, as well as of the *Teuerdank*, will disclose the fact that the mention of divine interference is no uncommon occurrence. In this same adventure Teuerdank himself says: "Aber got hat mich behüet wol."[19] Many other adventures of Teuerdank end with a remark about God having prevented evil from happening to the hero,[20] while angels not only appear as

---

[15] Busson, *op. cit.*, pp. 469ff.

[16] Antoine de Lalaing, Sr. de Montigny, "Voyage de Philippe le Beau en Espagne, en 1501" (Premier Voyage), *Collection des voyages des Pays-Bas*, publiée par M. Gachard (Bruxelles, 1876), I, 312 (1503. 16 septembre) : "Il advient aulcune fois que les chamois montent si très-hault, et les veneurs après, que quandt ils voelent descendre, ils ne scèvent trouver le chemin, et force leur est de demorer là. Et quandt on scèt cela, on faict venir ung prebstre qui leur monstre, du plus près qu'il puet, le corpz de Jhésucrist, adfin qu'il leur souviègne de leur salut et qu'ilz moerent en vraye foy catholicque; et n'y a aultre remède. Et est advenu ce cas pluseurs fois."

[17] Busson, *op. cit.*, pp. 486ff.

[18] *Germania*, fo. 283-a, no. 23.

[19] *Teuerdank*, p. 227.

[20] Cf. *ibid.*, pp. 72, 94, 121, 253, 321, 388, 404, 439, 559, etc.

characters in the poem but are actually pictured in the woodcuts.[21] From this it would seem that Busson has overemphasized the importance of Franck's addition to this particular adventure.

To Chapter 21, in which Teuerdank barely escapes injury when he puts his foot under a large polishing wheel,[22] Franck adds that the hero actually caught his shoe in the wheel and pulled it out with such force that he left the pointed toe behind under the wheel.[23]

Both the *Schlüssel* and Franck misinterpret Adventure 22 by mistaking the hunter in the woodcut for Teuerdank. They tell how the hero barely escapes disaster, whereas in the poem Teuerdank avoids the danger completely. They also say that the snow balled up under Teuerdank's shoes and caused him to fall, while snow is not mentioned at all in the poem.[24]

Franck adds to his account of Adventure 28, in which Teuerdank walks out on a rotten beam, "das hat er auch vff den vmbgengen der hohen thürn offt than."[25]

Likewise to Adventure 42, in which Teuerdank beats off two lions in their cage with a shovel, Franck adds the ordinary use of the shovel.[26]

Adventure 45 tells how Teuerdank pulls his horse back just in time to keep from riding into a hidden ravine.[27] Franck not only shows that he has read the poem here, but he adds something of his own to characterize Maximilian: "dañ an allen orten wolt er vorn dran sein."[28]

We read in Adventure 48 how Teuerdank rids the peasants of a local pest, a fierce bear, in spite of their warnings to him of the danger.[29] Franck makes the peasants' warning even more forceful, for they tell Maximilian "es hetten vor auch etlich an jm zu ritter werden wõllen/die sich zu todt gefallen vnnd erlegen weren."[30]

[21] Cf. *ibid.*, pp. 541ff., no. 115.
[22] *Ibid.*, pp. 96f.
[23] *Germania*, fo. 281-b, no. 9.
[24] *Teuerdank*, p. 571: *Germania*, fo. 281-b, f., no. 10.
[25] *Teuerdank*, pp. 127f.; *Germania*, fo. 282-a, no. 3.
[26] *Teuerdank*, pp. 190f.; *Germania*, fo. 282-b, no. 17.
[27] *Teuerdank*, pp. 205ff.
[28] *Germania*, fo. 283-a, no. 19.
[29] *Teuerdank*, pp. 220ff.
[30] *Germania*, fo. 283-a, no. 22.

A lightning bolt once makes a hole in the earth near Teuerdank, who is hurrying to get out of the storm.[31] Franck embellishes this incident by saying that the lightning was so terrible "daß ers bedehõrt/ sahe vnd entpfand/ eylend im schrecken beseits auß dem dampff/ schweb vnnd rauch reitten mũßt/ damit er nit erstickt."[32]

Again Franck seems to have interpreted the picture of a girl with outstretched arms who is watching another adventure of Teuerdank[33] as the representative of a group of onlookers, and adds of his own accord: "Die zũseher schrien schon/ helff Gott O Gott."[34]

In Adventure 60, where a fool is barely stopped from igniting a cask of powder in a room in the presence of Teuerdank,[35] Franck has strengthened the picture a little again by saying: "da erschrack Maximilian daß er schier erblindet."[36]

Another addition calculated to add vigor to the account was made by Franck to the 62nd adventure of Teuerdank, where the hero again falls and his shoe-spikes miraculously find a hold and support him.[37] Franck adds this embellishment: "daß man aber/ Gott helff dir/ zũschrie/ vnd die zũseher nahend vor leyd erblint waren."[38] A like addition is made to Adventure 63, when Franck declares that Maximilian "kam also schwerlich auß dem rachen deß todts von Gott gezuckt daruon."[39]

In the beginning of his account of Adventure 66 Franck digresses farther than usual:

> Zum 40. war Maximilian der art/ was er sah iemant wagen oder thũn das wolt er nachthũn/ vnd wañ man etwas wolt/ daß er thet/ so thet es nũn etwa ein verwegens kind vor/ so gedaucht es dißen helden ein schand seinn/ wann er inn einem ritterstuck es jm nit nach thon hett/ so es anders der vor jm mit eeren außfuret.[40]

---

[31] *Teuerdank*, pp. 236ff., no. 52.
[32] *Germania*, fo. 283-b, no. 26.
[33] *Teuerdank*, p. 245, no. 54.
[34] *Germania*, fo. 283-b, no. 28.
[35] *Teuerdank*, pp. 269ff.
[36] *Germania*, fo. 284-a, no. 34.
[37] *Teuerdank*, pp. 279ff.
[38] *Germania*, fo. 284-a, and -b, no. 36.
[39] *Teuerdank*, pp. 282ff.; *Germania*, fo. 284-b, no. 38.
[40] *Teuerdank*, pp. 293ff.; *Germania*, fo. 284-b, no. 40.

A still more important change and addition is made by Franck in reporting Chapter 87 of the *Teuerdank*.[41] In this adventure Teuerdank is making the rounds of the watch. Among the latter are several traitors who plan to shoot him down. Their behavior excites Teuerdank's suspicions, and he surprises them before they have a chance to carry out their designs. In the poem Neidelhart tells Teuerdank:[42]

> Ich will Sye straffen vmb die sach
> Vnnd sie martern lassen fürwar
> So lanng bis Ich von In erfar
> Warumb Sy solchs haben getan.

To this the hero offers no objections. Franck, however, makes much better use of this opportunity and paints the hero as forgiving, kind, and wise in seeking to make friends of enemies:[43]

vnd ob er wol wißt/ daß sie auff jn bestellt vnd besoldt/ gehalten hetten in willen jn zu entleiben/ wolt er sie doch lieber mit gůt dann mit Tyranney überwunden/ ließ jn hin gehen/ stellt sich als verstůndt ers nit/ vnnd überwann sich mit gůtte/ daß sie auß feinden freund worden.

Franck makes another addition in relating the contents of Teuerdank's Adventure 93:[44]

dann er ein sondern lust zu scharmützlen hett/ vnd sein man so wol dorfft bestehen vnd sehen/ als ein man so zu seiner zeit lebet/ wie wol er sunst ein friedliebender gůttiger fürst war/ der vngern kriegt dann den kriegsleuten lieb war/ vnd sagten er geb ein gůtten Bapst/ Julius ein gůtten Keyser/ iedoch durch vnbillicheyt auffgefordert/ dorfft man niemandt an sein statt stellen. In nôten hett er vier oder fünff in weittem feld nit geflohen/ vnd setzet es also hin/ daß er offt von den sein darumb ward angered/ daß er sein leben/ daran aller seins volcks sieg vnd wolfart stůndt/ offt so verwegen vnnd kůisch wie man spricht/ waget.

This comparison between Maximilian and Julius II was drawn more than once by Luther, and indeed, at about this same time.[45]

Finally, at the end of this summary of the *Teuerdank* by Franck

---

[41] *Teuerdank*, pp. 399ff.
[42] *Ibid.*, p. 403.
[43] *Germania*, fo. 286-b, no. 58.
[44] *Teuerdank*, pp. 430ff.; *Germania*, fo. 287-b, no. 64.
[45] Cf. Luther's *Tischreden* (Weimar, 1912-1921: *D. Martin Luthers Werke, kritische Gesamtausgabe*), III, 356f., no. 3492 (1536); IV, 265, no. 4369 (1539).

we find one of the first accounts of the antics of that famous character, Kunz von der Rosen, the court jester of Maximilian. This is not intended as an addition to *Teuerdank*, but as a number of stories related to Maximilian by way of his favorite jester. We read here of the great esteem in which he was held by the Kaiser and the wise counsel he gave under the guise of folly. We are told that his is the likeness of the thief hanging at the right of the image of Christ at St. Bastian's at Augsburg. Here too is related Kunz' prank at Augsburg, when he brought all the blind of the city together, tied a sow to a stake on the open square, and gave every blind man a club with the promise of the sow to whomever should succeed in killing it. Again at a time when the Kaiser was without money during a war Kunz advised him to become a secretary, by which Max understood that he was being informed of the greed, corruption, and wealth of his secretaries and councillors. On another occasion at Augsburg, Kunz caused general merriment when he fell purposely into a well and pulled in a number of other people with him.[46]

By these changes and additions Franck introduced a little more life and color into his account. He also enhanced the characteristics of courage and alertness which the original text ascribed to the hero by emphasizing further the dangers that beset him. Nevertheless, the changes are, generally speaking, rather few in number and not of great importance. More significant is the linking of the *Teuerdank* in a popular work with the historical figure of Maximilian. Here, now, was a precedent for taking the Kaiser's allegorical romance as autobiography. By the time of Matthew Schulte's edition of *Teuerdank* of 1679, more than a hundred years later, Frank's review had firmly intrenched itself as a summary and informative commentary to the *Teuerdank*. As such Schulte incorporated it into his *Clavis*, with further embellishments and additions of his own.[47]

Some of Schulte's additions were, to be sure, already well-estab-

---

[46] *Germania*, fo. 288-a.
[47] Cf. *Theuerdank*, Augspurg bey Matthåo Schultes (1679?). Also *Theuerdank*, hrsg. und mit einer historisch-kritischen Einleitung versehen von Dr. Carl Haltaus (Quedlinburg und Leipzig, 1836), pp. 127-136.

TEUERDANK AND MAXIMILIAN ANECDOTES

lished parts of the Maximilian tradition. One of the works from which he certainly borrowed much of his information was the *Ehrenspiegel* of Hans Jacob Fugger. Schulte probably did not know the original work of Fugger but the greatly enlarged and revised edition by Sigmund von Birken, who renewed the *Ehrenspiegel* for Kaiser Leopold I in the "löbliche fruchtbringende Gesellschaft" in 1668 in Nürnberg.[48]

Fugger-Birken's *Ehrenspiegel* is the most complete later source for information of an anecdotal nature about Maximilian. Here are collected the majority of things which his contemporaries had written about him, that is, the favorable accounts; for this work is devoted entirely to the praise of the Hapsburgs. The *Ehrenspiegel* of Birken draws some of the information for its history of Maximilian from the *Annales* of the Dutch Gerardus de Roo, who in his turn goes back to several of the men whom we have already discussed among the contemporaries of Maximilian: e.g., Joannes Aventinus, Joannes Cuspinianus, Henricus Glareanus, Joannes Dubravius, Wilibald Pirckheimer, Joannes Nauclerus, Joseph Grünpeck, Franciscus Guicciardini, etc.[49] Likewise Birken used the work of another Dutchman, Huyter, whose sources are similar to those of de Roo, containing most of those just mentioned.[50] Significant here, however, is the fact that the *Ehrenspiegel* includes, along with a great deal of other material about Maximilian, parts of the *Teuerdank*. And it is still more important that by this time the historical Maximilian and the poetic Teuerdank are quite completely blended.

---

[48] There are copies of the original Fugger manuscript only in Wien, München, and Dresden. Used here is *Spiegel der Ehren des höchstlöblichsten Kayser- und Königlichen Erzhauses Oesterreich. . . . Erstlich vor mehr als C Jahren verfasset/ Durch den Wohlgebornen Herrn Herrn Johann Jacob Fugger. . . . Aus dem Original neu-üblicher ümgesetzet. . . . Durch Sigmund von Birken. . . . Nürnberg, 1668.* Cf. Leopold von Ranke, *Sämmtliche Werke*, zweite Gesammtausgabe (Leipzig, 1873), I, 344-351 ("Beilage").

[49] *Annales rerum belli domique, ab Austriacis Habsburgicae gentis principibus, a Rudolpho I. usqve ad Carolum V. gestarum . . . per Gerardum de Roo* (Halae Magdeburgicae, 1709), p. 7. Gerard de Roo died in 1595. Cf. Wegele, *op. cit.*, p. 474.

[50] Ponti Hevteri, Delfii, Praepositi Arnhemensis, *Opera historica omnia: Bvrgvndica, Avstriaca, Belgica . . .* (Lovanii, 1643), p. II ("Avctorvm nomina"). Concerning Pontus Heuterus (1535-1602) cf. Fueter, *op. cit.*, p. 243.

Thus we find related in the *Ehrenspiegel* some seventy-two easily recognized adventures of *Teuerdank*.[51] These do not follow one another in their original order, but are arranged more or less according to subject, e.g., his adventures on the water, his adventures hunting chamois, etc. The first third of the adventures are told as if they were a part of the preceding history of Maximilian.[52] Then for the first time we are told about Pfintzing's relationship to Maximilian and to the *Teuerdank*, and that the following tales are from that poem.[53] In both cases, whether it attributes the adventure to the *Teuerdank* or tells it along with other stories about Maximilian, Fugger-Birken follows the details of the poem quite closely, although some variations can be found which indicate an acquaintance with the work of Franck.[54] On the other hand, there are two adventures in particular which have undergone considerable enlargement. The first is among those adventures not ascribed directly to the *Teuerdank*, but which can be easily identified with Chapter 77 of that work. This chapter of the *Teuerdank* tells how the hero fought and conquered a doughty knight "am Reinstram."[55] The *Ehrenspiegel* relates the encounter as between Maximilian and "Claudio von Batre" at the Worms Reichstag of 1495,[56] and it may have drawn its material from any of several contemporary sources which we have already investigated.[57] The other adventure enlarged by the *Ehrenspiegel* is ascribed to the *Teuerdank*, but is in reality the full-fledged legend of the Mar-

[51] *Ehrenspiegel*, pp. 1373-1383. Easily recognized are Adventures 13, 14, 16, 19-23, 32-65, 67, 68, 70, 72-74, 76-78, 26-30, 80-82, 84-96.
[52] *Ibid.*, pp. 1373-1377.
[53] *Ibid.*, p. 1377.
[54] E.g., in the story of Max losing the toe of his shoe in the polishing wheel, pp. 1381f., Adventure 21 of *Teuerdank* is seen with an addition by Franck, *op. cit.*, fo. 281-b, no. 9.
[55] *Teuerdank*, p. 576. Cf. pp. 348ff.
[56] *Ehrenspiegel*, pp. 1376f.
[57] E.g., in Cuspinianus, *De Caesaribus*, p. 606; "Wie Romisch kunikliche Majestat mit Cloi de Wadre zu Wurmbs in Frankreich kempft," in *Die Geschichten und Taten Wilwolts von Schaumburg*, "Stuttgart. Lit. Ver.," L, 156ff.; "Mémoires de Messire Olivier de la Marche," *Collection* of M. Petitot, Sér. I, X, 469; and Vinzenz Lang in a letter to Conrad Celtis of Nov./Dec. 1500 from Rome mentions a poem by Petrus Bonomus on the duel between Max and the Frenchman "Claudius Valdre" in Worms. Cf. *Der Briefwechsel des Konrad Celtis*, hrsg. v. Hans Rupprich (München, 1934), p. 442, no. 256.

tinswand.⁵⁸ Birken may have used the account alleged by Busson⁵⁹ to be the oldest version of the legend with all its characteristic features. This account occurs in a report on the journey of young Karl Friedrich von Cleve, which was published in 1587 by Stephan Winand Pighius under the title *Hercules Prodicius seu principis iuventutis vita et peregrinatio*.⁶⁰

One or two additions can be pointed out in the *Ehrenspiegel's* version of the *Teuerdank* which may be due to a careless reading of the latter or perhaps to supplementary information from other sources. For example, in Adventure 58 of *Teuerdank* a careless servant throws a lighted fuse on a sack of powder in a boat, but it is extinguished in time to prevent an accident.⁶¹ The *Ehrenspiegel*, however, says that the powder exploded with some injury to those standing about.⁶² Again in Adventure 22 of the *Teuerdank* it will be remembered that both Pfintzing and Franck misinterpreted the woodcut, with the result that they attributed to Maximilian the fall suffered by the hunter.⁶³ The *Ehrenspiegel* goes a step farther and says that Max held to a sharp stone to keep from falling until the blood came out of his nails, all of which the *Teuerdank* had distinctly ascribed to the hunter.⁶⁴

In connection with the story of Teuerdank's delight in standing on high towers to show his lack of dizziness, as in Adventure 28, the *Ehrenspiegel* adds that Maximilian did this, among other things, in 1492 at Ulm on the *Münster*, where on the north side toward the Haffengassen up on a cornice 350 steps high the following inscription in the stone still commemorates the date:⁶⁵

> Maximilianus Romanorum primus
> ac Hungariae &c. Rex, Archidux

---

⁵⁸ *Ehrenspiegel*, pp. 1379ff.
⁵⁹ Busson, *op. cit.*, p. 455.
⁶⁰ The Latin account of Pighius is quoted in full by Busson, *op. cit.*, pp. 456ff. The *Clavis* of Schulte's edition of the *Teuerdank* shows an even closer adherence to Pighius' version of this adventure. Cf. Haltaus' edition of *Teuerdank*, pp. 130f., no. 20.
⁶¹ *Teuerdank*, pp. 262ff.
⁶² *Ehrenspiegel*, p. 1375.
⁶³ *Teuerdank*, pp. 100, 571; *Germania*, fo. 281-b, no. 10.
⁶⁴ *Teuerdank*, p. 102; *Ehrenspiegel*, p. 1381.
⁶⁵ *Ehrenspiegel*, p. 1382.

Austriae, Burgundiae Dux, hoc opus
usque aedificatum visitavit Anno
Christi 1492.

We know that as late as 1787, on his visit to the *Münster,* the poet Friedrich Matthisson was shown the portrait of Kaiser Maximilian and at the same time heard the story of the latter's feat there.[66]

Another edition of the *Teuerdank* must be mentioned here, because it is undoubtedly of some importance in the further development of the connection between the Maximilian anecdotes and the *Teuerdank* in the Sixteenth Century. Unfortunately, this edition has not been available for the present work and thus its significance can only be appraised through other sources. The edition in question is that by Burckhard Waldis of 1553, republished in 1563, 1589, and 1596 (cf. above p. 104, note 23).

Fugger's *Ehrenspiegel* was probably written in 1555.[67] This was very shortly after the revision of *Teuerdank* by Waldis in 1553. The Waldis edition in turn was the result of the interest reawakened by the widowed Queen Marie of Hungary, granddaughter of Maximilian I. In 1550 she had commissioned Egenolf to print and to embellish with some sixteen woodcuts from the *Teuerdank* an account of tournaments arranged by her at Bruges and at Binche in the Hennegau in honor of her nephew, Prince Philip of Spain.[68] Egenolf had obtained possession of the Teuerdank woodcuts, and after having used them for the story of the tournaments, he conceived the idea of making still further use of

---

[66] "Tagebuch von 1777-1800," "Anhang" to *Friedrich Matthissons Gedichte,* hrsg. v. Gottfried Bölsing (Tübingen, 1913), II, 208. ("Stuttgart. Lit. Ver.," Bd. 261)

[67] Cf. Ranke, *Sämmtliche Werke* (Leipzig, 1873), I, 62f.

[68] Described by Joseph Strobl, *Kaiser Maximilians I. Anteil am Teuerdank; eine kritische Untersuchung* (Innsbruck, 1907), pp. 5f. It is a rare book and was used by Strobl at the university at Kreuzenstein. Its title is: *Thournier, Kampff vnnd// Ritterspiel. Inn Eroberunge aines Gefährlichenn//Thurns und Zauberer Schloss, Auch der Abentheurlichen In-//sell vnnd Güldinn Schwerdts. Zu Ehren dem Hochgebornen//Durchleuchtigen Fürsten vnnd Herrn, Herrn Philipsen, Princen auss Hispa-//nien U. Zu Bintz vnd Marienberg Ritterlich gehalten. // Sambt anderen wunderbarlichen Banketen, Lust und Freuden // Spielen, Köstlicher und Kurtzweillicher Herrlicheyten, Auss anschickung der // Hochgebornen Durchleuchtigen Fürstinn. Fraw Marien zu Ungern vnnd Behem Königinn, Wittib etc. // zugericht vnd volnbracht.* Franck. Chr. Egen. An 1550. Even Otto Bürger in *Beiträge zur Kenntnis des Teuerdank* (Strassburg, 1902), pp. 10 and 78, knows this work only by its content.

TEUERDANK AND MAXIMILIAN ANECDOTES

them for republishing *Teuerdank*. He gave the task of revision to Waldis.[69] In his revision Waldis expanded the original poem, adding several thousand verses and furnishing a text for the hitherto unwritten Chapter 117.[70] It seems likely that in all these verses he must have incorporated much from the best known Maximilian anecdotes and legends of his day. A single adventure, no. 60 in the original,[71] appears in the *Norica* (1829) of August Hagen.[72] It is possible that the adventure related here is from the Waldis edition; at least it would seem logical to suppose so. The adventure is longer than in the original and much different material has been added. A comparison of all the editions except those by Waldis has shown that it is from none of them. If our assumption is correct, the adventure should be examined briefly, and we may then regard our findings as an example of the Waldis edition.

In the original (p. 269) this adventure relates "Wie der Edel Tewrdanck durch einen Narren auß anweysung Vnfalo in einer Camer verbrendt solt sein mit pulfer." In Hagen's book the title shows careless copying by someone: "Wie der alte Teuerdank bald durch einen Narren in einer Kammer durch Pulver ums Leben gekommen wäre" (i.e. "alte" for "edel").

Hagen's text opens the story with details not found in *Teuerdank*. It begins by identifying the fool as Kunz von der Rosen, who is with Max on his way to Bruges. Kunz warns Max not to trust the city and refuses to enter with him. Max is imprisoned, Kunz attempts twice to rescue him, once by swimming the moat, which the swans prevent ("Ja gut französisch waren sie,"),[73] the second time by disguising himself as a monk who has come to offer his spiritual services. As in the anecdote in the form in which we have met it previously, Max refuses to flee from his prison in the monk's disguise and leave Kunz in his place to certain death. The author

---

[69] Strobl, *op. cit.*, pp. 5f.
[70] Cf. Haltaus' *Teuerdank* (Quedlinburg u. Leipzig, 1836), pp. 47-59; Waldis' Chapter 117, *ibid.*, pp. 50-56, his last chapter, pp. 56-59.
[71] Cf. *Teuerdank*, p. 269.
[72] *Norica, das sind Nürnbergische Novellen aus alter Zeit* (6. Aufl.; Leipzig, 1887), pp. 116-121.
[73] *Ibid.*, p. 117. This expression "gut französisch" in this connection is identical with the words of the *Ehrenspiegel*, pp. 995f.

of the *Norica* verses gives the most favorable interpretation to Max' reason for refusing Kunz' aid:

> Da spricht der Herr: nicht Kurzweil treibt
> Der Feind mit dir, gelingt der Plan.
> Zeuch hin und sei mein Freund fortan.[74]

The poem then continues, mentioning in two brief lines that Max was freed by the army. His love for hunting is cited, then the real subject of this adventure begins. It still varies from the original *Teuerdank,* however, in the manner of introducing the threatened disaster with the powder casks. Max and Kunz ride too far on a hunt and must seek shelter for the night in the woods. A light guides them to an old castle, where a solitary knight gives them food and lodging, but such plain food that Kunz resolves to seek better fare for his master after the others are asleep. Taking a lighted torch, he goes into a neighboring room and there to his joy sees some large casks, which he believes must contain wine. He hurries to them with his torch in his hand, when suddenly the door is thrown open and the voice of Teuerdank, who has awakened and become suspicious of thieves, commands him to take the light away from the powder. Kunz is severely frightened and begs to be punished for his carelessness, but Teuerdank answers kindly:

> Nein, guter Kunz, das thu ich nicht,
> Ich weiß, was Gutes du gethan,
> Zeuch hin und sei mein Freund fortan![75]

If, as we suppose, these verses are from the pen of Burckhard Waldis, then we can see that his conception of Maximilian was in the tradition of the kind, good prince.[76] It is interesting to conjecture just how much Fugger was indebted to Waldis for the material in the *Ehrenspiegel.* This, however, would necessitate a comparison of the Waldis work with the rare original Fugger manuscript.

[74] Hagen, *op. cit.,* p. 118.
[75] *Ibid.,* p. 121.
[76] Professor Archer Taylor has indicated the problem inherent in the attitude of Waldis here, i.e., that of an "outspoken Hessian Protestant of bourgeois origin" toward "an Austrian Catholic emperor." Cf. Archer Taylor, *Problems in German Literary History of the Fifteenth and Sixteenth Centuries* (New York and London, 1939), pp. 66f.

B. The Maximilian Anecdotes in the Sixteenth Century

Among sixteenth-century sources for anecdotes about Maximilian let us consider first the works of Martin Luther. The great reformer told many a tale about the colorful Kaiser, usually to illustrate some moral. These stories were no doubt current in his time.

We have already heard several of the stories about Kunz von der Rosen as related by Sebastian Franck. In Luther's *Tischreden* we read another anecdote of the Kaiser's jester. Kunz once met a poor priest who had a Bible under his arm. Kunz took the Bible from him, and when the priest asked for it back, Kunz promised to redeem it dearly if he would but follow him. Thereupon he led the priest to the Kaiser, who gave him ten gulden along with his book.[77]

Then there is the anecdote of the rime written by someone on a wall in Nuremberg, which challenged the reader to erase it if there were no prostitutes or knaves in his family. This rime was widely known, and when Max came to Nuremberg he had himself conducted to it. When he had read it, he smiled and said: "Nun, nun, der Reim soll von mir nit usthon werden."[78]

A couple of Luther's stories are about the Venetians and Maximilian. At one time when the Kaiser was fighting in Italy the Venetians surrounded the Germans in a valley and were so sure of their success that they invited the gentlemen and ladies of neighboring Padua to come and watch the fun of the slaughter. As the Germans fled, however, their powder-wagon broke, scattering a stream of powder behind them. They continued on, strewing their powder in their wake, until the Venetians had nearly caught up with them, whereupon they lighted the powder, the flames ran back and enveloped the enemy, and the Germans turned and killed all the Venetians and captured besides all the curiosity-

---

[77] *Tischreden*, VI (1921), 290, no. 6954.
[78] *Dr. Martin Luthers Briefwechsel*, hrsg. v. Enders, Kaweran, Flemming u. Albrecht, XI (Calw u. Stuttgart, 1907), 143, note 3. Cf. *Briefwechsel* (Luthers Werke; Weimar, 1937), VII, 611, no. 3115; and the *Werke,* L (1914), 396, LI (1914), 645, no. 12, 666, no. 12; also Ernst Thiele, *Luthers Sprichwörtersammlung* (Weimar, 1900), pp. 37ff., no. 12.

seekers who had come to watch the fun.⁷⁹ The other story about the Venetians relates that they presented Kaiser Friedrich III with a golden cradle for the infant Maximilian. The cautious emperor, to try out the gift, first laid a dog in the cradle, whereupon it burst into pieces.⁸⁰ Luther also told many times of the ridicule by the Venetians and the Florentines, who were fond of picturing Maximilian as a poor hunter with an empty purse.⁸¹

Maximilian's councillors were often made the subject of anecdotes. It had already been told of Friedrich III that in the illness preceding his death it had grown increasingly difficult to find pages to wait upon him, for the nature of his affliction had made him an unpopular patient. In order to keep servants about him Friedrich would hide gold pieces about the rooms and then let the pages secretly find and keep them, as if by accident.⁸² Possibly there is some connection in turn between this story and two others told by Franck.⁸³ Franck relates that the Kaiser, Maximilian's father, was extremely generous, and often saw that people were stealing from him, yet did not try to take revenge. Once he observed a certain person taking some of his silver and he only admonished him to go and never do it again; but he declared that had he done it to anyone else, he would have had him hanged. Again, Franck reports, one of the chamberlains, thinking that Friedrich was sleeping, seized three handfuls of gold from a pile lying on the table. When Friedrich pretended to awake from his nap, he went to the money, and to show the thief that he knew what had happened, took one handful of the gold and said: "That would have gone unnoticed." Then he took a second handful, saying: "That would have been enough." Finally he took a third handful and said firmly: "That is too much," whereupon the thief made a quick departure and was never heard of again.

Luther tells a story about Maximilian which bears a resemblance especially to the foregoing. Maximilian was once sitting and count-

---

⁷⁹ *Tischreden,* II (1913), 606ff., no. 2707 (1532). Also III (1914), 531-534, no. 3687 (1538).
⁸⁰ *Ibid.,* II (1913), 493, no. 2500-a and -b (1532).
⁸¹ *Ibid.,* II (1913), 609, no. 2709-b (1532); III (1914), 193, no. 3149-a, 194, no. 3149-b (1532), 559, no. 3717 (1538); V (1919), 160, no. 5449 (1542).
⁸² *Zimmerische Chronik,* I, 552 ("Stuttgart. Lit. Ver.," Bd. 91).
⁸³ Franck, *op. cit.,* fo. 255.

TEUERDANK AND MAXIMILIAN ANECDOTES

ing a pile of money, while one of his councillors stood beside him and watched for an opportunity to get some of it. Observing this, Max leaned back against the wall and shut his eyes as if he were sleeping. Soon he noticed the other come, take a handful of the money and put it in his pocket. The Kaiser remained silent, but soon he pretended to awaken, and then said: "My dear fellow, I see that this money pleases you exceedingly well. Let us see, take a handful and what you can hold, let that be yours!" The other did as he was bid. Then the Kaiser suggested: "Now count it so that we can see how much you can take at one time." The councillor counted it, whereupon the Kaiser commanded: "Now count the other also that you have in your pocket!" At that the thief had to take out what he had stolen at first; but the Kaiser let him keep both handfuls.[84] At another time Maximilian had a secretary who had stolen some three thousand gulden from him. Once when the secretary had come to him, the Kaiser asked: "What do you think a servant deserves who has stolen so and so much?" The secretary acted as if innocent and answered that such a one should be punished by hanging. "Oh, no," replied the Kaiser, clapping him on the shoulder, "we need you a little longer!"[85]

Luther speaks often in the *Tischreden* and *Briefe* of various sayings of Maximilian. To the king of England he is supposed to have remarked: "They call the king of France the most Christian, and do him wrong, for he has never done one Christian thing. They call me the most invincible and do me wrong too, for I have often been defeated. The pope they call the most holy, and are also unjust to him, for he is the greatest rogue who ever lived on earth. You they call the richest, and that is true."[86] On another occasion Maximilian declared that there were three kings in the world: he, the Kaiser, the king of France, and the king of England. He himself was a king of kings, for when he gave his princes something to do, they did it if it pleased them; otherwise they did not do it. The king of France was a king of asses, for everything that he ordered his subjects to do, they had to do like dumb beasts. The king of England, however, was a king of people, for

[84] *Tischreden*, VI (1921), 291, no. 6956.
[85] *Ibid.*, III, 236f., no. 3260 (1532).
[86] *Ibid.*, V, 131, no. 5416 (1542); II, 414, no. 2310 (1531).

what he asked them to do they did gladly and were fond of their master, like obedient subjects.[87]

In 1537 Luther wrote a letter to M. Ambrosius Bernd von Jüterbock, whose wife, children, and mother all had died within a week. In consolation Luther asked him to think of Maximilian's words of comfort to his son Philip over the loss of a faithful man in battle. "For thus he spoke to him: 'Dear Philip, you must get used to it. You will have to lose many more who are dear to you!'"[88]

In Luther's *Tischreden* for 1539 we read that Max once received a minister of the king of Denmark, and when the minister delivered his message without getting up, Max himself arose and listened standing until the minister was shamed into standing also.[89] In the same place we are told about Max' kindness in putting at ease a nervous petitioner who had forgotten his speech. Max began talking of familiar things until the man had time to regain his courage and was able to go on with his message. Finally a story told in other, later works[90] in connection with Kunz von der Rosen

---

[87] *Ibid.*, VI, 289f. no. 6953. Cf. *Die vier namhafften Königreich, nemlich des Königs der Teuffel, der Esel, der Menschen vnd der König. In ein kurtzen vnd scharpffen Hofspruch, von dem hochloblichen Helden Thewerdank fürgebildet* (Frankfort, 1538). Mentioned by Franz Redl, "Kaiser Maximilian I. von Habsburg in seinen Beziehungen zur Dichtkunst, Wissenschaft und Kunst," *Zeitschrift für die österreichischen Gymnasien* (Wien, 1912), Jahrgang 63, p. 706. Here is a case of the sayings of Maximilian being attributed back to the hero Teuerdank! The same story is told in slightly different form by Aventinus in 1529: "Was ungehorsam auch im reich sei under den fürsten und stenden des reichs, hat sich kaiser Maximilian in ainem büchlin, wider die stend des reichs außgangen, beklagt, Die fürsten wollen selbs herrn sein, mügen kain kaiser leiden. Darumb etwan kaiser Maximilian gesagt hat, der künig von Frankreich sei ain künig der esel; dan sein volk müß tragen, was er in auflegt, wie die mülesel. Der künig von England sei ain künig der deufel; die selben vertreibens und erschlagens. Der künig von Hispanien sei ain künig der menschen; die haltens mit ainander mittelmeßig. Aber er sei ain künig der künig: den die fürsten des reichs geben nichts umb den kaiser, wöllen selbs hern sein und in irem land ain jeglicher für sich selbs künig sein; dennoch sei er ir künig und kaiser. Das hat kaiser Maximilian von den fürsten des reichs gesagt." "Ursachen des Türkenkrieges," *Johannes Turmair's genannt Aventinus kleinere historische und philologische Schriften* (München, 1880-1881), I, 182.

[88] Letter of Nov., 1537. *Dr. Martins Briefe, Sendschreiben und Bedenken*, hrsg. v. Wilhelm Martin Leberecht de Wette (Berlin, 1825-1856), VI (1856), 191, no. 2465. Cf. *Tischreden*, II, 71f., no. 1361; and II, 486, no. 2491, where the date is given as 1532.

[89] *Tischreden*, IV (1916), 264, no. 4369.

[90] E.g., in Fugger's *Ehrenspiegel*, Wiener Handschrift, II, fo. 309, quoted by E Harzen, "Maximilian des Ersten Stammbaum und dessen 'Zotende Mendl,'" *Deutsches Kunstblatt*, V (6. Juli, 1854), 238.

TEUERDANK AND MAXIMILIAN ANECDOTES 139

is recounted here by Luther of "quidam mendicus importunus." This beggar asked the Kaiser for money and saluted him as a brother, since they both came from Adam, though Max was rich and he was poor. Max replied: "Here are two kreuzer. Go to all your other brothers and if they give you as much you will be richer than I."

Luther was fond of telling that once Maximilian was asked why he laughed and that he answered: He laughed to think that God had so well arranged the spiritual and temporal realms, the first under the rule of a drunken and dissolute pope, Julius II, the other under that of a chamois hunter.[91]

When Luther was once asked whether, when Samuel appeared to King Saul at the latter's request of the witch of Endor, it was the right prophet, Luther replied, no, it was only an evil spirit, proving that God forbids us to ask the truth from the dead. He continued:[92]

Just as a magician and necromancer, the abbot of Spanheim, brought it about that Kaiser Maximilian had seen all dead emperors and great heroes . . . walking one after the other in his room, and each figure clothed as he was when alive, among them the great Alexander, Julius Caesar, likewise Kaiser Maximilian's bride, whom the King of France, Carolus Gibbosus, took from him.

These stories show in what light Luther regarded the dead Kaiser Maximilian. Only once or twice do we read anything derogatory. One story, for example, runs as follows:[93]

The Emperor Maximilian in his campaigns was very superstitious. In times of danger he would make a vow to offer up as a sacrifice whatever should first meet him. One of his captains had taken captive a very fair virgin of an ancient family in Germany, and of the Protestant religion, and whom he loved exceedingly; but he was forced by the emperor to kill her with his own hands.

It seems probable that the Emperor Maximilian mentioned here is the Roman emperor and not our Maximilian, although there is

---

[91] *Tischreden*, III, 357, no. 3492 (1536); IV, 265, no. 4369 (1530).

[92] *Ibid.*, IV, 310, no. 4450 (1539). It is significant that elsewhere the first wife of Maximilian, Mary of Burgundy, is mentioned in this connection and not, as here, Anne de Bretagne.

[93] *The Table Talk of Martin Luther,* translated and edited by William Hazlitt, Esq. (London, 1857), p. 313. Cf. *Tischreden*, II, 634, no. 2753.

no indication that the two were confused. Another time Luther was telling how great lords should love their subjects and how some refused to take any chances if it should cost the life of a soldier. But Maximilian, he said, thought little of human life.[94] Except for these two asides, however, Maximilian seems to appear to Luther, as the genial ruler, clever, magnanimous, and sympathetic. He tells us how Maximilian applied his motto "Halt Maß!" to his treatment of the defeated Pfalzgraf after the Bavarian War in 1504, and praises him for his mildness and goodness in not imposing too difficult terms on the conquered.[95] He also quotes the words of the Elector Friedrich of Saxony, who said that he preferred Maximilian to all the princes he had ever seen and that he was at home in either jest or seriousness.[96]

From a few of Luther's utterances it appears that he would like to believe that Maximilian, had he lived long enough, would have been sympathetic to the Protestant cause. He likes to picture Pope Julius II lying defeated and humiliated at the Kaiser's feet—surely an impossible picture.[97] To Pfeffinger, the steward of Friedrich the Wise, Max is quoted as saying: "What is your monk doing? Assuredly his ideas are not to be despised!"[98] Another time Luther relates Max' words of sympathy for the martyred Huss: "Ay, indeed, they were unjust to the pious man!"[99]

Let us return now to the *Ehrenspiegel* and see what it has contributed in the way of Maximilian anecdotes. In addition to its confused mixture of history, legend, and poetry, the *Ehrenspiegel* introduces a number of stories about the Kaiser, some of which may have been related by Fugger, some added by Birken.[100] There

---

[94] *Tischreden*, V, 31, no. 5256 (1540).
[95] *Ibid.*, IV, 15, no. 3927 (1538).
[96] *Ibid.*, IV, 264f., no. 4369 (1539).
[97] *Ibid.*, II, 623, no. 2733: "Da er nu gedemüthiget war, also daß er Kaiser Maximiliano schier zu Füßen fiel und anbetet. . . ."
[98] *Ibid.*, V, 74, no. 5343 (1540): "Et Pfeffinger venit ad Maximilianum. Is vidit meas propositiones et interrogavit: Quid facit monachus vester? Certe non contemnendae sunt propositiones!"
[99] *Ibid.*, V, 262, no. 5583 (1543): "Ey, Ey, sie haben dem fromen man vnrecht gethan!"
[100] The numerous additions of Birken could be ascertained only by a careful comparison with the original manuscripts. Unfortunately they were not available for a comparison here. Some differences are cited by Ranke, *loc. cit.*, some also by

TEUERDANK AND MAXIMILIAN ANECDOTES 141

is the story of the boy Max being besieged with his parents in the Viennese fortress by his uncle until his complaints about the coarse fare and his tearful entreaties for dainty food move a tailor named Cronberger and his son to brave the besiegers and smuggle in fowl by way of the moat; for which Kaiser Friedrich and later Maximilian rewarded them most royally.[101] This story may have been borrowed by Birken from Gerhard de Roo, whom he mentions. It was probably known already to Fugger, however, through the riming chronicle of Michael Beheim, *Das Buch von den Wienern*.[102] Beheim was present at the siege, for he was serving at the time as a sort of court poet and general factotum to Friedrich III. His chronicle, which appeared a couple of years after the experience (1464), already exhibits most of the later characteristics of the story. The tale is also told by Cuspinianus and Sebastian Franck, from either of whom Fugger may have taken it.[103]

Again we read of the episode at Ensisheim in Alsace when Max wanted to get some papers from a locked chest, but he had no key. His councillors told him not to try to break the strong lock, but he seized it in anger and twisted it off with his bare hands, saying: "So you think that God and Nature have not given the kaisers and the kings strong fists too!"[104]

Toward the end of its account the *Ehrenspiegel* gives us a number of Maximilian's symbols and mottoes. Then follow a number of familiar anecdotes. There is, for example, the story of the scoffer who ridiculed Max' efforts to investigate his genealogy by writing on a wall the lines:

> Da Adam hackt und Eva spann/
> wer war damals der Edelmann?

to which Maximilian replied by writing underneath:

Aretin, "Nachricht von dem in der churfürstl. Bibliothek handschriftlich vorhandenen Fuggerischen Werke über die Österreichische Geschichte," *Beyträge zur Geschichte und Literatur* (München, 1803), I, 49-70.

[101] *Ehrenspiegel*, pp. 699f.
[102] Cf. in *Deutsche National-Literatur*, hrsg. v. Joseph Kürschner, X (Berlin u. Stuttgart, 1886), 283-386.
[103] Cuspinianus, *De Caesaribus*, p. 602; Franck, *op. cit.*, fo. 257-258.
[104] *Ehrenspiegel*, p. 1376.

142 TEUERDANK AND MAXIMILIAN ANECDOTES

> Ich bin ein Mañ wie ein ander Mann/
> nur daß mir GOtt die Ehre gann.[105]

We find too the story told by Luther about the haughty ambassador from Denmark whom Max shamed into standing in his presence. Then we are told of a very rich man who was of poor origin and who wanted Max to give him a patent of nobility. According to Fugger-Birken, Kaiser Sigmund had once been faced with a similar situation. We are not informed whether Max knew of this, but like Kaiser Sigmund, Max told the man: "I can indeed give you riches, but nobility I cannot give you. That you must attain through virtue." Also here is the account of the secretary who complained of a poet who was writing mocking songs about him and asked Max to forbid it in a proclamation. Max refused, saying that if he did so, the same writer would then start on him. He said that the secretary should not notice it, but let the songs come and go; for this sort of song would not last long, and he himself had had to endure many of the same kind. The songs of which the secretary complained, said Max, would not last as long as the song "Christ has arisen," of which a Jew complained that it had already lasted over 1500 years.[106]

When Maximilian was crowned at Aachen the Jews brought him as a present a golden basket full of golden eggs. Max, who liked a joke, had the Jews held. They became frightened and asked the reason for their detention. Thereupon Max replied that hens which laid such costly eggs should never be set free again.[107]

Another time when he came into a city, the citizens, who knew him to be a lover of art, brought him his picture done on wood with colors inlaid in metal and plaster of Paris and polished with wax. At first he liked it and praised it; but as each one of the many who had brought it began begging for payment and making a great fuss about it, Max became angry and exclaimed:

> Seht/ durch Gott/ wol fromme und gute Spiegelmacher gibt es in

---

[105] *Ibid.*, p. 1384. The same verses are found in Baudoin de Sebourc:
> Car trestous venons d'Eve, notre père fu Adans,
> Il n'est nul gentis, nul homme n'est vilains.

Cf. Kathleen T. Butler, *A History of French Literature* (London, 1923), I, 56.

[106] *Ibid.*, p. 1385.

[107] *Ibid.*, p. 1386.

dieser Stadt! Ein jeder/ der eine große Nase nachmachen kan/ der komt/ und will uns damit dienen.

At this he stopped the demonstration and would accept nothing more.[108]

The story once put into Latin verses by Hutten[109] is given about the same form by the *Ehrenspiegel*. In the presence of King Louis XI of France a councillor once called Maximilian scornfully the Bürgermeister of Augsburg. Instead of pleasing the king as he had hoped, he achieved the opposite effect, for Louis called him an ass and said that he should not thus speak of persons in high authority. "And believe me," added the king, "when this Bürgermeister rings the bells, then all Germany flies to arms and France begins to tremble."[110]

In the biography of Joseph Grünpeck,[111] and later in the works of Molinet,[112] de la Marche,[113] and Despars,[114] we read of the capture of the city of Tenremonde in December 1483.[115] Maximilian had two wagon-loads of men disguised as monks, nuns, and merchants approach the city from Malines under the leadership of Jacques de Fouquesolles, while Max and 800 knights stood by in ambush. When the unsuspecting guards had allowed the wagons to enter the city gates, the disguised soldiers jumped out and overpowered them, while the men in ambush rode up and entered and took the city. This historical anecdote is related often among the tales of Maximilian and finds a place also in the *Ehrenspiegel*.[116]

Finally the *Ehrenspiegel* has a number of anecdotes about Maximilian's jester, Kunz von der Rosen. There is the one, also told by Franck, in which Kunz advises Max to mend his fortunes by turning secretary or official.[117] The story is told of Kunz getting

---

[108] *Ibid.*, p. 1386.
[109] Ulrich von Hutten, *Schriften*, ed. Böcking, III, 211.
[110] *Ehrenspiegel*, p. 1386.
[111] Grünpeck, *op. cit.*, pp. 45f.
[112] Molinet, *op. cit.*, II, 412.
[113] de la Marche, *op. cit.*, p. 438.
[114] Despars, *op. cit.*, IV, 243.
[115] Molinet says it occurred December, 1483; Despars places it on November 26, 1484.
[116] *Ehrenspiegel*, p. 937.
[117] Franck, *op. cit.*, fo. 288-a; *Ehrenspiegel*, p. 1386.

his spurs tangled in the table cloth and breaking the costly crystal goblet that had been sent to Max by Venice. When the horrified Venetian ambassadors, who were present, ask him to punish Kunz, Max replies that if the present had been gold or silver, it still would be valuable, even though in pieces. As it is, it was only glass.[118] Another time when playing cards with Maximilian and some other princes, Kunz received two kings. Taking hold of Max who sat beside him, he said that he had won, for he now held three kings.[119] There is also the tale of the poor priest whose Bible Kunz took.[120] An anecdote which is here told of a cook of the Kaiser's is probably also related to the Kunz stories. This cook was present when some one was announced who promised to trace Max' ancestry back to Noah and the ark. The cook asked Maximilian not to let him do this. For, he said, till now he had adored Max as a god on earth, but if he found that he came from Noah they would be too closely related, since we all come from Noah.[121]

The *Ehrenspiegel* also tells the story about the attempts of Kunz to rescue Maximilian when he was being held a captive in Bruges in 1488. First, Kunz had two life-belts made and tried to swim across the castle moat to Max. The swans in the moat proved to be "gut Französisch," however, and attacked him so that he was glad to escape with his life. Another time Kunz learned how to cut a tonsure, had himself shorn and garbed like a monk, and gained access to Max in the guise of a confessor, intending to shave his master's head, exchange places with him, and let him

---

[118] *Ehrenspiegel*, p. 1385.
[119] *Ibid.*, p. 1386.
[120] *Ibid.*, p. 1386.
[121] *Ibid.*, p. 1386. E. Harzen, in "Maximilian des Ersten Stammbaum, und dessen 'Zotende Mendl,'" *Deutsches Kunstblatt*, V (6. Juli, 1854), 238, quotes at length from the Vienna manuscript of Fugger's *Ehrenspiegel*, II, fo. 309, the story of Kunz von der Rosen bringing an old beggar-man and "ain altes reisiges frechs veib" to where Max and Mennel were working on the *Genealogie* at Augsburg. Max gives them a small alms, but they ask for more, "because he is their brother." He tells them to go and get the same amount from all their brothers and then they will have a plenty; for if he gave the same amount to all his brothers, he would have nothing left for himself. With this he sends them away. Kunz then says that they cannot help bringing many fools and prostitutes into the genealogy if they continue. As he leaves, he asks that they give him a good place in the work when they come to him. This is, of course, the same story as that told by Luther, *Tischreden*, IV, 264, no. 4369.

TEUERDANK AND MAXIMILIAN ANECDOTES 145

escape in his disguise. When Max learned that a strong force was on the way to rescue him, and probably also because he felt it unbecoming his royal dignity to resort to such measures, he refused to take advantage of Kunz' services and sent him away disappointed and annoyed at his failure.[122]

In other works of the Sixteenth Century we meet again these stories about Kunz von der Rosen along with occasional different anecdotes. Indeed, the first information that we have about Kunz comes from Maximilian himself. The Kaiser had arranged a place for him in his plan for the *Triumph* under the heading "Schalcknarren";[123] and his connection, in general, with Maximilian would seem to justify some space here for a brief account of the tales told about this colorful figure.

The *Zimmerische Chronik* relates several stories about Kunz, among them the one we have just heard, of his using Maximilian as a "king" in a card game.[124] Then there comes the anecdote told often at table by Duke Ulrich of Wurttemberg, who was present at the time referred to. Herzog Reinhardt von Lothringen was in disgrace with Max because of his aid to France, and he decided to send a minister to ask pardon of the Kaiser. The minister, a doctor from Basel, was unable to get an audience with Maximilian; and yet he did not dare go home without having fulfilled his mission, for the duke had expressly forbidden his returning unsuccessful. Finally the doctor asked the help of Kunz. The latter bade him don a long coat and follow him into the presence of Max and the other princes, creeping on all fours. Although it was hard on his pride and self-respect, the poor doctor was desperate, and so he finally complied. When Max saw the two foolish figures, he

---

[122] *Ehrenspiegel*, pp. 995f. This story may be the result of an attempt to refute accounts by Flemish chroniclers to the effect that Maximilian repeatedly tried to escape, but without success. John Doran in *The History of Court Fools* (London, 1858), pp. 327f., quotes one of these: "Soo dat Maximiliaen, op verscheyde tyden, sig selven begonde te verkleeden in verscheyde verworpe kleedern, nu als eene vrouw, dan als een godsgewyde, weederom als een heerenknecht, om behendelyk zyne langdurige gevangenis te ontloopen; maer alles was te vergeefs. Hy was te well bekent, ende syne bewaerders hadden grooter sorge als hy meynde."

[123] "vnnd solicher solle der Connrat von der Rosen sein." Cf. Franz Schestag, "Kaiser Maximilians I. Triumph," *Jahrb. k.-h. Samml.*, I (1883), 160.

[124] *Zimmerische Chronik*, II, 262f., ("Stuttgart. Lit. Ver.," Bd. 92, Tübingen, 1869).

laughed heartily and asked the meaning of this peculiar conduct. Kunz replied: "He is the emissary of the Duke of Lothringen; and because you have not heard him, he now goes after you on all fours, and I with him. Dear Kaiser, hear him finally, and so we both need creep no more!" Max, much amused, then consented to hear what the minister had to say and sent him home satisfied. It was also thought by some that the whole scene had been prearranged by Max and Kunz as a means of ridiculing and humbling the duke.[125]

Still a third prank by Kunz recited by this source was played on an abbot of Fulda, who came to a Reichstag at Augsburg and wished to use Kunz to gain the ear of the Kaiser. He did not wish to give anything for the favor, however, and Kunz wanted remuneration. The jester, seeing the abbot's mantle of marten-fur lying on a table, picked it up, put it on, and went to the door. Here he stopped and said to the abbot: "Sir, if I am to accomplish anything with the Kaiser, I must be dressed accordingly, otherwise the Kaiser might consider me a fool in my clothes and perhaps give me a poor answer." The abbot never saw his mantle again, and he was persuaded not to attempt to recover it, since Kunz was well able to turn the Kaiser against him.[126]

We have already come across other anecdotes related in the *Zimmerische Chronik*. There was the story about Meister Albrecht, who stopped Max when fleeing from a battle. Another tale, which we have not previously encountered, illustrates Maximilian's amiability. A certain Butsch, a recorder in the chancellery at Innsbruck, was given the unpleasant task of handing the Kaiser the council's refusal to accept one of his propositions. Although Max was at first angry at the reply, the behavior of Butsch amused him so that he forgot his wrath and regained his natural good spirits.[127] Once again the Kaiser's anger at being kept waiting so

---

[125] *Ibid.*, II, 260ff.
[126] *Ibid.*, II, 262.
[127] *Ibid.*, IV, 354f. ("Stuttgart. Lit. Ver.," Bd. 94): "Uf ein zeit het der kaiser ein concept eins rathschlags der regierung überschickt und ires rathlichen bedenkens begert. Dieweil es aber ein sach, das der regierung des kaisers furnemen nit gefellig, do schluegen sie im solichs, gleichwol zum glimpfigisten ab, und seitmals zu erachten, das er ein sonders ungnedigs misfallen darab entphahen, do wolt kainer den hofdank verdienen und dem kaiser die antwurt bringen, allain der Putsch wardt darzu beredt, dann es war ein gueter fatzman, dessen sich der kaiser sonderlichen wol vermechte."

TEUERDANK AND MAXIMILIAN ANECDOTES

long by the council at Buchorn is dispelled by his amusement when he sees the councillors, hastily summoned from a lunch of curded milk, come running with traces of the meal still clinging to their beards.[128] There is the story of the good peasants of Vöcklipruck, who gave Maximilian what they considered a royal present, a rabbit in a sack. At the time of the donation they asked particularly that the sack be returned and said that it could be identified by a blue spot. Max was well pleased by the simple gift and took pains to see that the sack was returned. At the request of the citizens of Vöcklipruck he then gave them a coat-of-arms on which was painted a sack with a blue spot and a rabbit jumping from the sack.[129] Another anecdote is told of the many attempts to poison Max and of the faithful vigilance of his cook, Meister Hanns, who more than once saved his life by refusing to cook poisoned food.[130] We read too of a time when the Kaiser had only rabbit and lentils to eat in camp, while his officers were living in high style. He was urged to demand the better food from his officers, but refused, saying: "Be satisfied! Lentils are good food too."[131] There is a rather vulgar anecdote of a courtesan who stole Max' royal seal.[132] Finally there are related a couple of sayings attributed to the Kaiser. One was that no more courteous or subtle poison can be prepared for an old man than to get him to take a

---

Derselbig Butsch nam die sach an, gieng zum kaiser und überantwurt die schrift. Der kaiser standt an eim disch und las. Darab het er ein groß misfallen, beschaint sich an dem, das im die adern am hals ufliefen und groß warden, welches ain besonders gemerk, bei dem man aigentlichen abnemmen, das er zornig. Wie er nun ein passaige gelesen, sprach er: 'Butsch, die regierung ist ain narr.' Der Butsch buckt sich dief, sahe ernstlich und sprach: 'Allergnedigester kaiser, die regierung ist kain narr.' Der kaiser nam sich der antwurt nichs an, las fort. Über ein weil sprücht er wider zum Butschen: 'Wolan, Butsch, so bist du ain narr,' wolt in damit zu versteen geben, das es ain dorheit, seitmals niemandts sonst die antwurt bringen, das er darzu sich het bewegen lasen. Butsch wolt kain narr sein. . . . Darumb widersprach er dem kaiser und sagt: 'Allergnedigester kaiser, ich bin kain narr.' Der kaiser las fort und lechlet ab diser redt, und über ein kleins weile sprucht er: 'Wolan, Butsch, so bin aber ich ain narr.' Butsch sahe ganz ernsthaft darzu und lachet nit, bucket sich aber dief und sprach: 'Allergnedigester kaiser, das ist war, das ist war.' Dem kaiser vergieng aller zorn, mocht sein über die masen wol lachen. Es geriet diesem Butschen, dorft sonst wol zehen andern oder meren nit also hingangen sein."

[128] *Ibid.*, III, 433 ("Stuttgart. Lit. Ver.," Bd. 93).
[129] *Ibid.*, III, 434.
[130] *Ibid.*, IV, 149f.
[131] *Ibid.*, IV, 355.
[132] *Ibid.*, IV, 301f.

young wife.¹³³ The other, like that related by Luther, concerned the treatment of the defeated nobility, who Maximilian declared should be punished and humbled for their crimes, but who should be allowed finally to return to grace, else peace could never be restored.[134]

Among the *Colloquies* of Erasmus we come across a story about Maximilian in "The Fabulous Banquet."[135] Euglottus tells "of our Maximilian, who, as he was far from hiding his money in the ground, so he was very generous to those that had spent their estates, if they were nobly descended." To help one such young man, Max sent him to collect 100,000 florins from a certain city with the understanding that he might keep whatever he could collect over this amount. The young man collected 50,000 and handed Max only 30,000, which the latter was nevertheless glad to get. But Max' treasurers found out the truth, notified the Kaiser that there was a default, and called the young man up for questioning. The culprit readily admitted the fact and promised to give an accounting. The accounting failed to be made, however; and Max' officers continued to press the matter until the Kaiser finally ordered the defaulter to come and settle the affair in their presence. When he arrived, the young man asked to be allowed to examine the accounts of the treasurers first, since, he said, they were so skilled in matters of just that kind that they could serve as examples to him. Maximilian, but not the others, understood him and dismissed him. He had intimated that the treasurers were accustomed to hand in such accounts to Max, keeping most of the money for themselves.

The only tale among the *Facetien* of Heinrich Bebel (1508) important here is one with which we are already familiar. Maximilian is asked by a member of his chancellery to prohibit by edict the ridicule of a certain German rimester, to which Max replied by citing the complaint of the Jews to the "Christus surrexit" of the Christians.[136]

---

[133] *Ibid.*, I, 438; II, 130.
[134] *Ibid.*, IV, 10.
[135] *The Whole Familiar Colloquies of Desiderius Erasmus of Rotterdam*, translated from the Latin by Nathan Bailey (London, 1877), pp. 223f.
[136] *Heinrich Bebels Facetien*, hrsg. v. Gustav Bebermeyer ("Stuttgart. Lit. Ver.,"

TEUERDANK AND MAXIMILIAN ANECDOTES 149

Michael Lindener's *Katzipori* contributes to the anecdotes of Maximilian a story of a stupid man who asked the Kaiser for a doctorate and was given an answer similar to that given the rich man who requested a patent of nobility as told by Fugger-Birken.[137] Another story by Lindener is less about Maximilian than about the abbot of Fulda, whom Max instructed to answer in Latin the Latin speech of a papal legate. The abbot only pretended to know Latin and had to make an excuse to avoid exposing his ignorance.[138]

More numerous are the stories about Maximilian in the *Wendunmuth* (1565) of Hans Wilhelm Kirchhof. It does not take long to discover that Kirchhof took some of his tales directly from Luther. Inasmuch as Luther's *Tischreden* first began to be printed in 1566, it seems that Kirchhof must have seen one of the Luther manuscripts. There is no doubt about his dependence on Luther, since even the wording in some cases is, with very slight exceptions, the same.[139] As in Luther, we find the story of the robbery of Max by his servant while the Kaiser pretends to sleep;[140] the saying about the three kings;[141] the adventure of Kunz and the poor priest;[142] Maximilian's demonstration of politeness to the Danish minister and the bashful ambassador;[143] and the story of the thieving servant whom Max tricked into pronouncing his own sentence.[144] There are, in addition, other stories familiar to the reader of Franck and the *Ehrenspiegel:* the tale of Max' holding the Jews who brought the golden eggs;[145] of the secretary who

---

Bd. 276; Leipzig, 1931), "Liber Tertius et Novus," p. 136, no. 90. Cf. *Heinrich Bebels Schwänke*, hrsg. v. Albert Wesselski (München u. Leipzig, 1907), II, 40f., no. 90.

[137] *Michael Lindeners Rastbüchlein und Katzipori* (1558), (in "Stuttgart. Lit. Ver.," Bd. 163; Tübingen, 1883), pp. 72f. Cf. *Ehrenspiegel*, p. 1385.

[138] *Katzipori*, pp. 73f.

[139] Kirchhof's *Wendunmuth*, hrsg. v. Hermann Österley (Tübingen, 1869; "Stuttgart. Lit. Ver.," Bde. 95-97). E.g., *Wendunmuth*, II, 54f., no. 25; IV, 33ff., nos. 27-30, correspond respectively to *Tischreden*, VI, 291, no. 6956; IV, 265, no. 4369; VI, 289f., nos. 6953 and 6954; IV, 265, no. 4369.

[140] *Wendunmuth*, II, 54f., no. 25.

[141] *Ibid.*, IV, 33f., no. 28.

[142] *Ibid.*, IV, 34, no. 29.

[143] *Ibid.*, IV, 34f., nos. 30 and 31.

[144] *Ibid.*, IV, 35, no. 32.

[145] *Ibid.*, I, 51f., no. 42.

asked the Kaiser to suppress the rimes written against him;[146] the comparison of Max with Julius II;[147] and the incident of Kunz von der Rosen and the Venetian goblet.[148] There is repeated the story in the *Ehrenspiegel*[149] of the man who complained of the finery and other possessions of the *Landsknechte*. Max replied that they should be let alone, that this was all they had, and they did not have long to enjoy it anyway, since they were always in the front line of danger.[150] A new story is that of the peasant who had heard that no petition could gain the Kaiser's hearing, "sie were denn zuvor gespickt." He had his request written on a piece of paper, wrapped it around a half-thaler, and presented it to the Kaiser without bending his knee or bowing. The Kaiser received it graciously, and just then the money dropped out. When asked what was meant by this, the peasant replied that he had heard that no one got anything from the Kaiser unless his petition were "gespickt," but he was worried that the "Speck," of which he had but little anyway, might soil the petition, so he had put money in its place. If it was not enough, he would get more, although he did not have much. Then the Kaiser laughed, granted the petition, and returned the peasant's money. "Oh, go ahead," said the peasant. "Do not be ashamed to take it! Drink it up for all I care. I would have had to give it to some one else anyway and still have gotten nothing." This simplicity pleased the Kaiser, and he ordered a gift for the peasant in the bargain.[151]

One last story by Kirchhof is designed to illustrate Maximilian's dislike for pride, pomp, and false show. Once when he had encamped in a large city he wanted to go hunting,[152] whereupon all his court dressed up in their best satins and silks, while Max donned old clothes of poor cloth like that of his hunters. Before the hunt had ended, it rained hard and all the finery was spoiled. When the bedraggled wearers complained, Max told them that they should have known better and dressed as he had, for such

---

[146] *Ibid.*, I, 52f., no. 43.
[147] *Ibid.*, I, 2, p. 457, no. 13; and IV, 33, no. 27.
[148] *Ibid.*, II, 55f., no. 26.
[149] *Ehrenspiegel*, p. 1385.
[150] *Wendunmuth*, I, 53f., no. 44.
[151] *Ibid.*, III, 276f., no. 8. Cf. K. T. Butler, *op. cit.*, I, 61.
[152] "wie er denn ein guter weidmann und zum weidwerck großen lusten getragen."

TEUERDANK AND MAXIMILIAN ANECDOTES 151

clothes as theirs belonged in the ladies' rooms and at the dance, not on a hunt for wild animals.[153]

It would of course be strange if there were no mention of Maximilian in the wealth of material in the writings of Hans Sachs. In this Meistersinger's list of "All Roman Emperors in Order" we read under "Anno 1486":

> Nach dem zu kayser wart erwelt
> Maximilianus, der heldt,
> Ein dewrer fürst, streitbar, sieghafft,
> Großmütig, küner leybes-krafft,
> Gelert, mancherley zungen kündig,
> Inn allem ritterspiel außbündig.
> Regieret drey und dreißig jar.
> Von Flembling er gefangen war.
> Mit Venedig het er lang krieg.
> An welschem land erlangt er sieg.
> An Behamen er preiß erwarb.
> Zu Wels er seligklichen starb.[154]

Further than this, however, we do not hear much from Sachs about the Kaiser. There is a "Historia: Die geschickt keyser Maximiliani löblicher gedechtnuß mit dem alchamisten" (1568), the basis of which is an old legend of the Roman Morienes and the Sultan Kalid of Egypt;[155] the "Schwanck: Der blinden kampf mit der säw," which we have met before in the *Germania* of Sebastian Franck;[156] and finally the tale, also told by Luther, of Maximilian and the spirits of the dead who were raised to entertain him.[157]

Sachs' first *Historia* tells how an alchemist promised Maximilian that he would make gold from copper for him. At the end of the period specified by the magician, he runs away leaving a defiant message for Maximilian, who then perceives that the man was a Venetian and therefore an enemy.

---

[153] *Ibid.*, V, 430f., no. 155.
[154] Hans Sachs, "Historia. All römisch kayser nach ordnung, wie lang yeder geregiert hat, zu welcher zeit, was sitten der gehabt und was todtes er gestorben sey, von dem ersten an biß auf den yetzigen großmechtigsten kayser Carolum 5," "Stuttgart. Lit. Ver.," CIII (Tübingen, 1870), 371.
[155] "Stuttgart. Lit. Ver.," CLXXIX (Tübingen, 1886), 422-426; cf. note 1, p. 422.
[156] Cf. *Germania*, fo. 288-a. Sachs' poem was written in 1563.
[157] "Historia: Ein wunderbarlich gesicht keyser Maximiliani, löblicher gedechtnuß, von einem nigromanten" (1564), "Stuttgart. Lit. Ver.," CXCIII (Tübingen, 1892), 483-487.

The *Schwanck* mentioned above repeats the prank of Kunz von der Rosen, who collected twelve blind men, furnished them with old suits of armor, and had them compete in killing a sow. Sachs also wrote a *Meistergesang* on this same subject in 1550. It seems, indeed, that an older story must be the source of the anecdote, and that it was later attached to the name of Kunz von der Rosen; for there are references to similar events in *Fastnachtspiele* of the Fifteenth Century.[158]

In the third anecdote enumerated above Sachs declares that he heard at the royal court in Innsbruck in the year of Maximilian's death the story of a magician who produced for the Kaiser the shades of Hector and Helen of Troy and of Mary of Burgundy, Max's first wife. Luther, in his account, had said that the magician was the abbot of Sponheim, the well-known humanist Trithemius, and that among the dead raised for the Kaiser had been Alexander, Julius Caesar, and Anne de Bretagne. Sachs fills out the legend by telling how the Kaiser was warned to keep absolute silence during the apparition. When Max beheld the well-loved features of his first wife, Mary, however, he could not restrain himself and tried to embrace the shade, whereupon it disappeared with a frightful noise. The magician reproached the emperor, who replied:

> Die lieb ist gleich starck wie der tod,
> Sagt der keyser, die nött mich ie,
> Anzureden die liebst allhie,
> So ich ie het auff diser erd,
> Welche ist aller ehren werth.

Sachs mentions that Mary appears before the Kaiser in the blue dress that she was wearing when she was killed. This is not mentioned anywhere else, and this lends weight to the author's statement that he is telling the story according to oral tradition.

---

[158] Cf. "Stuttgart. Lit. Ver.," CLXXXI, 343, note: "Vgl. den Meistergesang im süeßen thon Harders: 'Die plinden mit der sew,' 'Ein bürger hies Kuncz von der Rosen,' 1550 Mai 10. . . . Es scheint eine alte erzählung zu grunde zu liegen, denn in den fastnachtspielen aus dem 15. jahrh. . . . heißt es: Als die sau, die di plinten haben erschlagen." For the Meistergesang by Sachs, cf. *Die Fabeln und Schwänke in den Meistergesangen*, hrsg. v. E. Goetze u. C. Drescher, "Neudrucke deutscher Litteraturwerke des xvi. und xvii. Jahrhunderts" (Halle a. S., 1904), CCVII-CCXI, 84f.

Furnished with the romantic figure of Mary of Burgundy by Sachs and with the magician Trithemius by Luther, this legend is now in its completed form. It makes its way in the society of the court as the counterpart to the stories of Faust, as they were told in academic circles, until finally all the elements of both forms are united in the *Faustbuch*.[159]

A rather isolated anecdote about Maximilian and the great Nuremberg artist Albrecht Dürer finds its way down through the writings connected with art. The Dutch painter and art historian of the second half of the Sixteenth Century, Karel van Mander,[160] tells us that Maximilian was once watching Dürer paint a mural when the artist began to encounter difficulty in reaching as high as he wished. Turning to a nobleman standing nearby, Maximilian asked him to hold the ladder upon which Dürer was standing. When the nobleman asked his servant to do it for him, objecting that such a task would be injurious to his honor as a nobleman, the emperor replied: "Albert is noble because of his art, and more than a nobleman; for I can easily make a nobleman of a peasant or of some insignificant person, but I cannot make such an artist of a nobleman." Straightway the Kaiser granted Dürer a noble coat-of-arms, three white or silver shields in a blue field, which he was thenceforth allowed to bear.[161]

We have now seen two distinct tendencies in the Maximilian tradition of the Sixteenth Century. One is the direct result of a conscious effort on the part of Maximilian himself to extend his memory and personality into the future in the form of his *Teuerdank*. The other is expressed in the group of anecdotes which arose in popular tradition, and eventually took written form in the stories of Luther, the *Ehrenspiegel,* and in collections of enter-

---

[159] Cf. Siegfried Robert Nagel, "Helena in der Faustsage," *Euphorion,* IX (1902), 65-69.

[160] Karel van Mander (1548-1608), *Het Leven der Schilders* (Amsterdam, 1764), I, 58 (first published in 1604). Cf. the account as repeated by Joachim von Sandrart (1606-1688) in his *L'Academia Todesca della Architectura, Scultura & Pittura: oder Teutsche Academie der Edlen Bau-, Bild- und Mahlerey-Künste* . . . (Nürnberg, 1675), I, 224.

[161] There is some resemblance between this story and the two stories told of the rich men, the one of which wanted Maximilian to give him a doctorate (*Katzipori,* pp. 72f.), the other who requested a patent of nobility (*Ehrenspiegel,* p. 1385).

taining stories and other literary works of the century. In some cases we have seen these two streams meet and merge.

The mass of legendary or anecdotal material told about Maximilian in the Sixteenth Century as we have reviewed it appears as a rather unwieldy body. It is difficult to force it into any kind of system, since it is a natural growth, largely founded on oral tradition and transmitted to us by men who lived at the same time or shortly after the emperor. The other branch, however, has the advantage of being fairly easily identified.

The sources of this anecdotal material are as numerous and obscure as those which go to make up the popular saga at any period. The tracing of some of the stories to their historical origin would be, indeed, a formidable task of research. Tales of late medieval magicians, narratives attached to other historical personages, humanistic material current during the Renaissance, proverbial wisdom—all join and embellish reports of actual incidents in the life of Max and weave a tangled mass of narrative about this popular figure. Like other folk-sagas, that of Maximilian is a mixture of history, literary reference, Märchen, folk-wisdom, and pure imagination. Its value lies in its manifest urge to adorn the person of the hero with characteristics of wide popular appeal.

These are in the main the same as those which we have observed in the reports of contemporary biographers and expressed or implied in the features of Max' self-portrait in the *Teuerdank*. In the anecdotal tradition we have examined Max appears in only a favorable light. He is a physically powerful man, a great hunter, whose feats on the chase surpass those of everyone else. In war he is clever in conceiving and executing stratagems, and is feared and respected, both in war and in peace, by contemporary foreign monarchs. In his dealings with his subjects he is kind, wise, and forgiving. His sense of humor is keen and he makes witty remarks which often become proverbial. Especially in his relations with the lower classes, his attitude is always one of kind condescension, gratitude, and appreciation for the homage of the people.

VI

MAXIMILIAN AND THE FAUST LEGEND

THE FOLKBOOKS of the Sixteenth and Seventeenth centuries had little room for a character so near in time and place as Maximilian. In the *Lalebuch* of 1597 there is introduced a colorless but amiable "König inn Vtopien,"[1] in whose relations with the Lalenbürger might be seen a resemblance to two incidents related of Maximilian. In the first of these the simple citizens of Lalenburg expend much mental energy trying to decide upon a fitting gift for the king, and they finally agree to give him a large dish of mustard (pp. 91ff.). The second occurrence during the visit of the king in Lalenburg concerns a meal of sour milk which is set before him.

The *Zimmerische Chronik* gives us accounts of other strange gifts which have been presented to Kaisers upon various visits;[2] we have already seen one of these accounts, in which the peasants of Vöcklipruck honored Maximilian with a rabbit in a sack.[3] That incident and the bearing of the Kaiser as related there show a faint resemblance to the Lalenburg story. In the second case the *Zimmerische Chronik* again furnishes us with a story of Max and his councillors of Buchorn, who come running at the Kaiser's call, the white curds of their disturbed meal still clinging to their beards.[4] These two incidents, however, provide all the connection which can be suspected between the *Lalebuch* and Maximilian.

The Sixteenth and Seventeenth centuries had another chapbook, however, which was much more popular and of far greater significance in the history of German literature than the *Lalebuch*, and in which the figure of Maximilian is definitely involved. This is the well-known *Faustbuch*.

---

[1] *Das Lalebuch (1597) mit den Abweichungen und Erweiterungen der Schiltbürger (1598) und des Grillenvertreibers (1603)*, herausgegeben von Karl von Bahder, "Neudrucke deutscher Litteraturwerke des xvi. und xvii. Jahrhunderts" (Halle a. S., 1014), CCXXXVI-CCXXXIX, 91.

[2] *Ibid.*, cf. note, p. 91.

[3] *Zimmerische Chronik*, III, 434 ("Stuttgart. Lit. Ver.," XCIII); cf. above, p. 147.

[4] *Zimmerische Chronik*, III, 433; cf. above, pp. 146f.

It seems certain that Maximilian's entrance into the Faust legend is by way of his connection with the scholar, Johann of Trittenheim, or Johannes Trithemius (1462-1516), the abbot of the Benedictine monastery of Sponheim near Kreuznach.[5] Maximilian consulted Trithemius in historical and genealogical matters and showed him various favors. We have already mentioned above the revealing questions on theology which he is supposed to have handed the abbot in 1508.[6]

Trithemius was a man of excessive energy and no mean talent. He had worked hard to obtain an education, was instructed in Greek and Hebrew by Reuchlin, and at the age of twenty entered the monastery of Sponheim as a novice. His tremendous zeal may be indicated by the fact that he was made abbot only fourteen months later. With boundless enthusiasm he collected manuscripts and works of all kinds until his library was one of the best in Germany. His own literary activity was great and his interests were varied, including such items as a *Steganographie,* a kind of shorthand, which gave him the reputation of being a magician and which later was actually put on the Index (1609). The new abbot's zeal brought about reforms in the monastery also, which although perhaps good for the inmates, were also felt as oppressive after the preceding freedom. Thus it happened that while Trithemius was absent in Berlin in 1505, the storm of opposition broke out against him and upon his return he found himself forced to resign his position. He considered a place at court unsuited to him and therefore declined offers from the Kurfürst of the Pfalz and from Kaiser Maximilian, finally becoming abbot of the Scottish monastery at Würzburg. His later life was filled with literary activity, chiefly historical. Unfortunately for his memory, it was discovered after his death that Trithemius had invented a good many supposed facts in his Frankish history. His reputation as the author of many books and as a scholar and master of ancient languages made him, like other scholars before and after him, the object of suspicion among those who could not understand him, and a

---

[5] For the life of Trithemius, cf. Wegele, *Gesch. der deutschen Historiographie,* pp. 69-83.

[6] Cf. Karl Klüpfel, *Kaiser Maximilian I.* (neue Ausg.; Berlin, 1870), pp. 179f.; and cf. above, p. 100f., note 14.

subject for the tales which were always being whispered about, ready to attach themselves to a prominent name. Trithemius died in 1516, and already in 1539 Martin Luther was describing to his table companions how Trithemius had produced for Maximilian the shades of Alexander, Julius Caesar, and Anne de Bretagne.[7]

Stories of magicians who conjure the spirits of the departed have, of course, been known since ancient times. Mention of royal personages in such stories is also no uncommon occurrence. The popular imagination needed little incentive to connect such stories with familiar names. Already during the lifetime of Maximilian's father, Friedrich III, the latter had attracted to himself the title of magician and companion of the devil, because of his habit of withdrawing from society and spending his nights observing the stars.[8] Maximilian acquired from his father a similar interest in the course of the stars and was fond of discoursing upon their properties.[9] The Young King of the *Weisskunig* was careful to learn the art of astrology and never to hasten any undertaking without consulting the heavenly bodies.[10] Grünpeck was often employed by Max to set up a prognostication from their courses.[11] Also in the *Weisskunig* we read of the evil spirit and that the Young King had learned the black art, but of course only that he might the better understand the meaning of the true faith.[12] In the *Teuerdank* the evil spirit appears in person to the hero and tries to bring him from the right path; but Teuerdank's true belief keeps him safe.[13]

Probably these few facts alone would have sufficed to draw Maximilian into a popular picture of medieval magic. In addition, however, Maximilian was known for his inquisitive spirit. His interests led him to delve into the past for old books, coins, or the history of his country; and likewise he liked to inform himself about the newest inventions which pointed toward the future. The success of his gunsmiths in turning out better cannon than ever

[7] *Tischreden*, III (Weimar, 1916), 319, no. 4450 (1539). See above, p. 139 and note 92.
[8] Grünpeck, *op. cit.*, p. 20.
[9] Pirckheimer's *Schweizerkrieg* (ed. Münch), p. 156; cf. above, p. 26.
[10] *Weisskunig*, Jahrb. k.-h. Samml., VI, 62, no. 22.
[11] Grünpeck, *op. cit.*, p. viii.
[12] *Weisskunig*, Jahrb. k.-h. Samml., VI, 64, no. 23.
[13] *Teuerdank*, ibid., VIII, 4a.

before, for which he received most of the credit, would alone have been enough to awaken among the people a superstition that he possessed supernatural powers.

Luther's account of Trithemius and Maximilian, ascribed to the year 1539, is the earliest such notice. Not until around the year 1564 do we find mention of the anecdote again. In the preceding year, 1563, a Dr. Johann Weyer (Johannes Wier or Wierus; 1515-1588), physician in ordinary to Herzog Wilhelm III von Jülich-Cleve-Berg, published his *De praestigiis daemonum*, the first forceful attack on the horror of the trials for witchcraft which had been rampant in Germany under the authority of the Church since 1484.[14] It seems likely that Weyer's book is definitely responsible for the reawakened interest in the tale of a magician performing his tricks before Maximilian. The *Historia* of Hans Sachs, mentioned above pp. 152f., falls in 1564, although he says he had heard the story from the court followers of Maximilian at Wels when he was there forty-six years before. The *Zimmerische Chronik*, which was probably written down between the years 1564 and 1566,[15] tells us that Maximilian's father practiced magic and left behind him at death a large number of works on the subject, mostly in Greek and Hungarian. These books Maximilian kept, but never used, knowing that no happiness could result. After Max' death, his grandson, Ferdinand, had these books burned.[16]

The account of Weyer is as follows: Once upon a time at the court of Maximilian I the conversation turned to the two heroes, Hector and Achilles. One of the councillors praised them so strongly, that Maximilian declared he wished he might see what they looked like. At that time, by good fortune, a necromancer happened to be at the court, and having heard the wish of the Kaiser, he offered to fulfill the latter's desire, only he stipulated

---

[14] Joh. Wier, *De praestigiis daemonum* (Basel, 1583), I, 13; cf. Carl Binz, *Doctor Johann Weyer, ein rheinischer Arzt, der erste Bekämpfer des Hexenwahns. Ein Beitrag zur Culturgeschichte des 16. Jahrhunderts*, Bonn, 1885; and by the same author, *Augustin Lercheimer und seine Schrift wider den Hexenwahn* (Strassburg, 1888), p. iii.

[15] Cf. Leo Lawrence Rockwell, *Zur Wortstellung in der Zimmerischen Chronik, mit besondrer Berücksichtigung des Satzanfangs* (Lancaster, 1938), p. 2.

[16] *Zimmerische Chronik*, II, 182.

that during the performance the audience must keep perfectly quiet. Thereupon the magician placed the Kaiser upon a seat inside a large circle, then read aloud mysterious things from a large book. Immediately Hector knocked at the door with such violence that the whole house shook. As soon as the door was opened, he entered, all in armor, with a shining iron spear, and flaming eyes, of fearful appearance. He was also larger and taller than men are now. After him came Achilles, also in stately dress and just as large. He looked at Hector and acted as if he were about to fall upon him. However, after they both had bowed before the Kaiser and walked back and forth three times, they disappeared. After these two the Prophet David appeared, adorned with his royal crown and carrying a harp, and of a pleasanter appearance than the other two. He walked three times past the Kaiser, but without bowing or any sign of reverence, then disappeared. When the Kaiser asked why David had failed to bow before him, the magician replied, it was because David's kingdom had exceeded all others on earth and because Christ was descended from the family of David.[17]

It was not until twenty years later that Weyer received support in his struggle against the trials for witchcraft. Then the Heidelberg professor of mathematics, Hermann Witekind, originally named Hermann Wilcken (1522-1603), wrote under the pseudonym of "Augustin Lercheimer aus Steinfelden" a *Christlich bedencken vnd erinnerung von Zauberey* which treated the subject clearly and thoroughly. Witekind's book appeared in Heidelberg in 1585, again in Strasbourg in 1586, and a third time in Speyer in 1597.[18]

Witekind gives a brief report of Johannes von Trittenheim, describing him as a learned man and wise, except in that he had devoted himself to the devil. The story of the abbot's relations with Maximilian he declares he has heard several times from re-

---

[17] Joh. Wier, *De praestigiis daemonum,* in the German version in J. Scheible's *Das Kloster* (Stuttgart, 1846), II, 188f.

[18] The second edition is a little larger than the first, while the third edition, the last one revised and essentially enlarged by the author, is nearly twice as large as the first. Cf. Carl Binz, *Augustin Lercheimer und seine Schrift wider den Hexenwahn* (Strassburg, 1888), pp. iii-xxvii.

spectable and authentic sources. The account is freely as follows: Maximilian I had lost his wife, Mary, daughter of Charles of Burgundy, and still grieved over her death. Knowing this, the abbot of Sponheim offered to bring her again before his eyes that he might once more enjoy the pleasure of her sight. Maximilian allowed himself to be persuaded, and they went together into a special room, taking one other person with them so that there would be three. Here the magician commanded that they speak no word so long as the apparition should last. Mary then appeared as had the dead Samuel to Saul, walked past them, smiled and bowed to the Kaiser, and was so identical with the living Mary that not the slightest thing could be found that was different. The Kaiser, remembering that his wife had had a black mole on the back of her neck, watched her as she passed him a second time and found that the spirit was similar also in this respect. Thus does the devil know how each of us is made and has such a good memory that he can copy us perfectly. Then the Kaiser was suddenly seized with fear, he motioned to the abbot to bid the spirit depart, and afterwards, in anger and trembling, he said to him that he should never perform such tricks again. He also confessed how difficult it had been for him to keep from speaking to the apparition. If that had happened, the evil spirit would have killed him. That was what the devil was after, but God had guarded him and warned him so that in the future he would avoid such things.[19]

It should be noticed here that we already have several distinct features of the legend, which in the following years will continue to be confused and blended:

(1) Luther had called the magician the abbot of Sponheim, Trithemius, and had said that he produced for Maximilian the shades of "all dead emperors and great heroes," among them Alexander, Julius Caesar, and the Kaiser's wife, Anne de Bretagne.

(2) Sachs ascribes the magic merely to "a necromancer" at the court of Max in Innsbruck, but adds that besides the spirits of Hector and Helena, the magician produced the shade of Mary of Burgundy. Sachs further says that Mary was wearing a blue dress, such as she was wearing when she died. The magician tells Maxi-

---

[19] *Ibid.*, pp. 36ff.

milian to sit still and speak no word. Maximilian disobeys by addressing Mary, whereupon she disappears in vapor with a loud and terrifying noise, and the magician rebukes the emperor for having endangered their lives.

(3) Weyer also speaks only of "a necromancer" at the court of Maximilian, who presents the phantoms of Hector and Achilles and who enjoins silence upon the spectators. He adds that the spectral heroes bow before the Kaiser, and that after them comes King David, who does not bow.

(4) Witekind's account, coming twenty years after the last two, like Luther's ascribes the conjuration to Trithemius and makes the subject again Mary of Burgundy at the court of Max. Witekind also mentions Samuel's appearance to Saul, as had Luther, and adds the feature that the Kaiser identified his wife by the black mole on her neck. Furthermore, in his account Maximilian is angered and forbids the abbot ever to repeat the performance; for if the Kaiser had spoken, the devil would have killed him.

In 1576 occurs the first mention which identified Faust as the magician who raises the shades of the Greek heroes. Here too the court circle with its magician begins to be displaced by the academic circle, although there are still reputed to be royal persons present. This account is the *Epitome Historiarum* of Wolffgang Bütner, who reports that he has heard that Faustus at Wittenberg showed the students "vnd einem hohen Mann N." the specters of Hector, Ulysses, Hercules, Aeneas, Samson, David, and others; and that "Fürstliche Personen" were also present and witnesses.[20]

Four years later, about 1580, Zacharias Hogel II in his *Chronica von Thüringen und der Stadt Erffurth* tells that about 1550 Faust at Erfurt showed the students of his course on Homer the shades of Priam, Hector, Ajax, Ulysses, Agamemnon, and others, last of all, however, that of the giant Polyphemus.[21]

In the first known printed *Volksbuch* of Faust, the Spiess *Faustbuch* of 1587, we now find a division made between the Faust of the court circle and the Faust of the academic world. In Part III

[20] (Weimar, 1576), Bl. 115a; cf. Alexander Tille, *Die Faustsplitter in der Literatur des sechzehnten bis achtzehnten Jahrhunderts nach den ältesten Quellen* (Berlin, 1900), no. 25, p. 48.
[21] *Euphorion*, II (1895), 54ff.; cf. Tille, *op. cit.*, no. 26, p. 49.

we read how Faust at the court in Innsbruck produces the ghosts of Alexander the Great and his wife.[22] But now it is not Maximilian, but his grandson, Karl V, at whose court the sorcery takes place. Now, too, various other elements are brought together here, only that the figures of Kaiser Maximilian and Mary of Burgundy are left out and what formerly was told of them is transferred to their successors in the tradition, Karl V and the wife of Alexander. Karl is asked to promise not to speak during the performance; new is the feature that he wishes to rise and receive Alexander when the latter bows before him, but Faust restrains him in time. Alexander's wife enters clad in a gown of blue velvet; this is the first time we have heard of the color of her gown and it must have come from the poem of Hans Sachs, since his is said to be the only earlier work which mentions it.[23] Karl remembers that she was supposed to have had a large wart on the back of her neck, looks, and finds that it is so. Here the conjuration of the dead Samuel is also mentioned.

Added here for the first time in connection with the Kaiser is the story of Faust conjuring horns on the head of a nobleman at the court of Karl, who then was highly amused at the knight's discomfiture. This is also an old story told of previous magicians, among others, one at the court of the Kaiser Friedrich III.[24]

Having thus disposed of the legend of the conjuration at the emperor's court, the Spiess *Faustbuch* proceeds to provide another such scene, with Faust among the students. On the Sunday after Easter they express a desire to see the beautiful Helen of Troy. Faust agrees to accommodate them, saying that he has already shown Karl V the shades of Alexander and his wife. After the performance the students wish to have Faust repeat it, so that they may have an artist come and paint Helen's likeness; but Faust declines, saying that he can not always awaken her spirit.[25]

---

[22] "Historia von D. Johann Fausten." Gedruckt zu Franckfurt am Mayn durch Johann Spiess, 1587. *Volksbücher des 16. Jahrhunderts,* hrsg. und erklärt von Felix Bobertag. "Deutsche National-Litteratur" (hrsg. v. Kürschner; Berlin u. Stuttgart), XXV, 239ff.

[23] Cf. Siegfried Robert Nagel, "Helena in der Faustsage," *Euphorion,* IX (1902), 68.

[24] Cf. "Historia von D. Johann Fausten," loc. cit., p. 241, note 19.

[25] *Ibid.,* pp. 256ff.

The Berlin edition of the *Faustbuch* of 1590 has a change in that in Chapter 53 Faust shows to the students at Erfurt not the beautiful Helen of Troy, but the heroes Menelaus, Achilles, Hector, Priam, Alexander, Ulysses, Ajax, Agamemnon, and others, finally, however, the horrible one-eyed giant, Polyphemus, who behaved so badly that all the students were thoroughly frightened and never again asked for such a demonstration.[26]

In 1599 the version of the Faust book edited by Georg Rudolf Widmann restored the figure of Maximilian in place of Karl V.[27] Widmann tells otherwise the same story as the Spiess book; but in an *Anmerckung* he adds the tale about Trithemius and ascribes it to Luther.[28] His account is exactly that of Witekind, and to this, without giving his source, he also appends the account of Luther that Trithemius showed Maximilian all dead Kaisers and other great pagans, among them Alexander, Julius Caesar, as well as his other bride and wife, "Fräulein Anna aus Britannien" (p. 434).

A new chapter was now brought into connection with Maximilian by Widmann. In addition, Faust, who wishes to show his gratitude for the presents Maximilian has recently given him, surprises the Kaiser by turning his bedroom into an enchanted paradise of flowers, trees, and singing birds. The Kaiser is very pleased and thanks Faust kindly.[29] The *Anmerckung* which follows (p. 439) informs us, however, that a similar story was currently told of Albertus Magnus, who in 1260 performed just such a feat for the pleasure of Kaiser Wilhelm, when the latter returned from his coronation in Aachen to Cologne.

Throughout the Seventeenth Century these connections between Maximilian or Karl V and the Faust legend continue to receive mention by various authors. The chapter on Kaiser Karl and Faust and the shades of Alexander and his wife is taken verbatim from the Spiess *Faustbuch* or one of its editions by Michael Sachse in his *Newe Keyser Chronica* of 1616.[30] In 1669 appears the *Titius Continuatus* of Daniel Schneider, who borrows directly from

[26] *Ibid.*, pp. 287f.
[27] Widmann's *Faust*, in J. Scheible's *Das Kloster*, II (Stuttgart, 1846), pp. 273-804.
[28] Scheible's *Kloster*, II, 600.
[29] *Ibid.*, pp. 437f.
[30] Magdeburg, 1606, pp. 303f., 279-a; cf. Tille, *op. cit.*, no. 60, pp. 115f.

Sachse and from the Faust book.[31] In 1674 Ch. Nikolaus Pfitzer revised Widmann's version of the Faust book and drew attention again to the figure of Maximilian in place of Karl. Pfitzer went even farther and extended the figure of Maximilian through four consecutive chapters (Part II, Chapters 10-13). Chapter 12 introduces a new story, in which Faust causes strange and beautiful clouds to form in Maximilian's banquet hall, thus entertaining the Kaiser and his guests. When some of the guests are so impolite as to remain at the table after the Kaiser has arisen, Faust makes the clouds shower rain upon them, whereupon they run away in great haste to the amusement of the Kaiser.[32]

The confusion that thus existed between the figures of Kaiser Maximilian and Kaiser Karl V in their connection with the Faust legend was attacked in 1676 by J. G. Schelhornius in the *Amoenitates Literariae*.[33] Schelhornius not only attempts to show that chronologically Faust was more likely to have been known to Kaiser Karl than to Maximilian, but he inveighs against those who would connect with Faust the mild and pious Kaiser Maximilian at all. He recalls the praise of Cuspinianus in his *De Caesaribus* for the upright emperor and asks if it is not reasonable to assume, if Faust had been at all known to Maximilian, that Cuspinianus would somewhere at least have made mention of it? These same sentiments are repeated a few years later by Johann Adam Osiander in his *Tractatus Theologicus*.[34] In the *Zeit-kürtzende Erbauliche Lust* of Kristian Frantz Paullini of 1697 all these stories told of Maximilian and his relations with Faust and Trithemius are scored as "ein leeres Gewäsch"[35] and "lauter Lügen."[36] ". . . Kai-

---

[31] Wittenberg, 1669, pp. 445f.; cf. Tille, *op. cit.*, no. 118, pp. 213f.

[32] *Das ärgerliche Leben und schreckliche Ende des vielberüchtigten Erz-Schwarzkünstlers Johannis Fausti. . . .* hrsg. v. Ch. Nikolaus Pfitzer, Med. D. Nürnb. A. 1674. Jetzo aber auf's Neue aufgelegt und mit 16 Holzschnitten verziert (Reutlingen, Druck und Verlag von B. G. Kurtz, 1834), pp. 149-157. See also hrsg. v. A. v. Keller in "Stuttgart. Lit. Ver.," CXLVI (1880), 431-439.

[33] (Francofurti et Lipsiae, 1726), V, 56-59, 66, 71-74; cf. Tille, *op. cit.*, no. 126, pp. 233f., 237, 240ff.

[34] Tubingae, 1687, p. 73; cf. Tille, *op. cit.*, no. 140, p. 277: . . . Fabulosum censetur a quibusdam, quod Maximiliano I. Alexandrum praesentavit Oeniponte, qui tamen Magiae non fuit Studiosus, sed verae virtutis custos rigidusque Satelles, fabulosum quod Rustico cuidam plaustrum foeni plenum soluto pretio devorarit, cum aperte constet haec de Monacho quodam referri in Colloquiis B. Lutheri.

[35] Franckfurt am Mayn, 1697, pp. 699f.; cf. Tille, *op. cit.*, no. 149, p. 302.

MAXIMILIAN AND THE FAUST LEGEND 165

ser Maximilian was a pious, devout man," declares Paullini, "an illustrious man of irreproachable piety and incomparable virtue, who concerned himself not at all with such trifles; neither has anyone who ever wrote of him mentioned anything of this. Read the entire (so-called) *Theur danck* and his deeds which an unknown person published at Ingolstadt in the year 1631;[37] there you will find all sorts of things about him, but not this nonsense."[38]

It is interesting to notice *Teuerdank* cited at this time as proof of Maximilian's character. The same arguments as Paullini's are repeated in 1704 by Herman Suden in *Der Gelehrte Criticus*[39] and the same mention of *Teuerdank* is made. Suden adds of Maximilian: "However, that he was very inquisitive in his youth, nearly all historians admit" (p. 377). Thus criticisms of the accounts linking Maximilian with Faust and Trithemius continue to occur throughout the Eighteenth Century.[40]

In spite of the criticism and ridicule aimed at disparaging such tales, the Faust stories of course continued throughout the Seventeenth and Eighteenth Centuries to furnish entertainment to eager readers. Jacob Daniel Ernst borrowed from Michael Sachse and retold the story of Karl V and Faust and Alexander.[41] In the same year (1685) Johann Georg Schiebel borrowed from Pfitzer's book and retold all its stories about Maximilian.[42] Then Jacob Daniel Ernst took from Schiebel a part of the same story and re-

---

[36] *Ibid.*, p. 306.
[37] Such an edition is unknown to me.
[38] *Ibid.*, p. 306.
[39] Leipzig, 1704, pp. 109ff.; cf. Tille, *op. cit.*, no. 164, pp. 376f.
[40] Such criticisms are found in the *Neu-eröffnetes Museum* (Leipzig, 1714), I, 280, cf. Tille, *op. cit.*, no. 184, p. 420; in the *Schrifft- und Vernunfft-mässige Gedancken* of Franciscus di Cordua (Hamburg, 1716, translated from the Latin), p. 108, cf. Tille, *op. cit.*, no. 193, pp. 462f.; in the *Physicalisch- und Historisch-Erörterte Curiositäten* of Johann Jacob Bräuner (Frankfurt a. M., 1737), pp. 752f. (cf. Tille, *op. cit.*, no. 239, pp. 554f.), who also mentions (p. 752) a writing with a similar purpose, the *Disputation de Fausto Praestigiatore* of Johann Georg Neumann; in Siegmund Freyherr von Bibra's *Journal von und für Deutschland*, IX (1792), 659a-661a, cf. Tille, *op. cit.*, no. 342, pp. 845-848; and in Christian August Behr's *Auswahl vorgeblicher Weissagungen* (Zeitz und Naumburg, 1794), p. 81, cf. Tille, *op. cit.*, no. 346, p. 884.
[41] *Neu auffgerichtetes Historisches Bilderhauss* (Altenburg, 1685), pp. 35ff.; cf. Tille, *op. cit.*, no. 137, pp. 269ff.
[42] *Neu-erbauetes Lust-Hauss* (Leipzig, 1685), pp. 265-268; cf. Tille, *op. cit.*, no. 138, pp. 273f.

lated it in a new work again about Maximilian.⁴³ Both of Ernst's works were in turn used by Misander (Adami) and both the story of Maximilian and Trithemius and of Karl and Faust are related in the *Deliciae Biblicae* in 1692.⁴⁴

In this way the Maximilian-Karl-Trithemius-Faust tales continued into the Eighteenth Century. In 1693 Nicolaus Remigius again told of the magic room prepared for Maximilian by Faust, making use of the words by Schiebel.⁴⁵ Christoph Zeisseler in 1695 tells both of Trithemius and Max and of Karl and Faust in his *Neu-eröffneter Historischer Schauplatz*.⁴⁶ Peter Goldschmidt in his *Verworffener Hexen- und Zauberer-Advokat* of 1705 gives us again the stories of Sachse.⁴⁷ In 1715 Simon Henrich Reuter's *Reich des Teufels* repeated the words of Pfitzer, and added the stories of Witekind and Luther, prefacing both with the criticism of their credibility, probably taken from Bräuner's account.⁴⁸ Finally the two tales were taken again from Ernst's *Bilder-Hauss* by Samuel Friedrich Lauterbach in 1727 for his *Pohlnische Chronicke*.⁴⁹

From here on throughout the Eighteenth Century the mention made of Maximilian in connection with Faust becomes more and more rare, while that of Maximilian and Trithemius or Mary of Burgundy practically ceases.⁵⁰ The abbreviated version of the

---

⁴³ *Ehrenholds Reifflich-betrachtete Eitelkeit* (Altenburg 1688), pp. 215ff.; cf. Tille, *op. cit.*, no. 142, pp. 289f.

⁴⁴ Dresden und Leipzig, 1692, XVII, 387-390; cf. Tille, *op. cit.*, no. 144, pp. 293ff.

⁴⁵ *Daemonolatria* (Hamburg, 1693), Theil II, pp. 509f.; cf. Tille, *op. cit.*, no. 145, pp. 296f.

⁴⁶ Leipzig, 1695, pp. 147f.; cf. Tille, *op. cit.*, no. 146, pp. 298ff.

⁴⁷ Hamburg, 1705, p. 496; cf. Tille, *op. cit.*, no. 165, pp. 382f.

⁴⁸ Lemgo, 1715, pp. 264, 676f.; cf. Tille, *op. cit.*, no. 366, pp. 949-952.

⁴⁹ Frankfurt u. Leipzig, 1727, pp. 10f.; cf. Tille, *op. cit.*, no. 219, pp. 522f.

⁵⁰ Mention of Faust at the court of Maximilian at Innsbruck is still made in occasional works, e.g., in the *Allgemeines Historisches Lexikon* (Leipzig, 1722), II, Sp. 232, cf. Tille, *op. cit.*, no. 367, p. 963; in the *Neu-vermehrtes Historisch- und Geographisches Allgemeines Lexicon* (Basel, 1729), pp. 277f., cf. Tille, *op. cit.*, no. 224, p. 531; in the *Grosses Vollständiges Universal Lexicon* (Halle u. Leipzig, 1735), IX, Sp. 340-341, cf. Tille, *op. cit.*, no. 236, pp. 550f.; in Fassmann's *Gespräche in dem Reiche derer Todten* (Leipzig, 1738), XV (232. Entrevue.), 511, cf. Tille, *op. cit.*, no. 240, pp. 568f.; and in Louis Moreri's *Grand dictionnaire historique* (Amsterdam, 1740), IV, 36a, cf. Tille, *op. cit.*, no. 243, p. 578.

MAXIMILIAN AND THE FAUST LEGEND 167

Faustbuch made by the "Christlich Meynende" in 1728 briefly mentions the stories of Pfitzer's version, and that is all.[51]

The reasons why the figure of Maximilian gradually dropped out of the Faust tradition in the later plays of the Eighteenth and Nineteenth Centuries may be fairly obvious. First, as time passes there is a popular tendency to transfer to some more recent and better-known figure those attributes or those tales which formerly were ascribed to another. Secondly, it is sometimes expedient for political reasons to keep all mention of royalty far from home whenever it might give any cause for offense. In the case of Maximilian and Karl·V we can see both of these causes in effect: Karl was the more recent Kaiser and the seat of his government was farther away. Still later the conjuring was made to take place at foreign courts. A French adaptation of the Faust legend of about 1700 places Faust at the English court of Queen Elizabeth.[52] In the Ulm puppet play of Dr. Faustus of about 1770, the magician performs his feats at the court of the King of Bohemia in Prague.[53] In another puppet play the court chosen is that of the Duke and Duchess of Parma.[54] The Faust of Maler Müller (1776) takes his sorcery to the court at Madrid.[55]

Having traced Maximilian's course through the *Faustbuch* thus far, a logical conclusion to this chapter of the legend would seem to be the treatment of the Kaiser in the *Faust* of Goethe. Let us first see if there is any proof that Goethe had Maximilian in mind when he created the emperor of the Second Part of *Faust*.

Goethe was indeed aware of the connection between Maximilian and the conjuration scenes of the Faust books. He had read Hans

---

[51] Cf. *Des Christlich Meynenden Geschichte Fausts*, in Scheible's *Das Kloster*, II, 93; cf. in *Bibliothek der Romane*, I (Berlin, 1778), ii. "Volks Romane," 91f.; cf. Tille, *op. cit.*, no. 310, p. 731.

[52] Comte Antoine Hamilton, "L'Enchanteur Faustus," *Oeuvres*, Septième Partie (1777), pp. 162-204; cf. Tille, *op. cit.*, no. 156, pp. 325-344.

[53] Cf. "The Ulm Puppetplay," Philip Mason Palmer and Robert Pattison More, *The Sources of the Faust Tradition from Simon Magus to Lessing* (New York, 1936), pp. 251-269; and in Scheible's *Kloster*, V, 783-805.

[54] *The Life and Death of Dr. Johannes Faustus*, translated from German into English, London, 1893.

[55] *Fausts Leben*, vom Maler Müller. "Deutsche Litteraturdenkmale des 18. Jahrhunderts." In Neudrucken herausgegeben von Bernhard Seuffert (Stuttgart, 1881), III, 113f.

Sachs' poem, described above, in 1773.[56] In addition to this he was probably familiar with the story from acquaintance with Faustbooks. Moreover, Goethe knew some of the literature concerning Max from the Sixteenth Century. In 1771 he had read the *Teuerdank* (Ulm edition of 1679)[57] and in 1773 the *Germaniae Chronicon* of Sebastian Franck (Augsburg, 1538), in which the Teuerdank adventures and the descriptions of the Kaiser are expanded more fully.[58]

However, it is not necessary to establish this fact to find that Goethe was thinking of Maximilian at one time in the development of his *Faust*, for in the Paralipomena we can read one of the earliest outlines of a scene with Maximilian as a prominent actor.[59] In this scene Mephistopheles describes to Faust the Reichstag at Augsburg, which Kaiser Maximilian has called, and persuades Faust to go there with him on his cloak. The Kaiser is just arising from the table and walks to the window, wishing that he might have Faust's cloak so that he could go hunting in the Tyrol and be back in the morning for the meeting. Max greets Faust cordially and asks for a demonstration of spirits, and this is promised to him. In the evening a magical theater is built, and there appear on the stage, first, the figure of Helen of Troy, then that of Paris. No agreement can be reached regarding the third figure to be conjured, the spirits on the stage become uneasy, things become increasingly strange, finally the theater and the spirits disappear.

This was Goethe's early conception of the emperor in *Faust*. Later changes, however, brought with them a change in his conception of the emperor's part in the tragedy. Some characteristics belonging peculiarly to Max remained in his picture. The whole concept of the emperor, however, was broadened to meet the demands of the play. "In the emperor," said Goethe to Eckermann on October 1, 1827, "I have endeavored to represent a prince

---

[56] Cf. Karl F. König, *A Record of Goethe's Belesenheit in the Pre-Weimar Period of His Life* (Yale Diss., 1935; unpublished), II, 423.
[57] *Ibid.*, II, 321.
[58] *Ibid.*, II, 400.
[59] Goethes *Werke*, hrsg. im Auftrage der Grossherzogin Sophie von Sachsen (Weimar, 1888), XV², 174f.

who has all the necessary qualities for losing his land, and at last succeeds in so doing."[60] Obviously, when a poet sets out with so clear an intention as this, it would be unfair to attempt to identify his character with any particular person. It might be said that Maximilian possessed a goodly number of the qualities of Goethe's emperor. But it would be stretching a point unnecessarily far to try to identify with Maximilian his every characteristic.

Let us consider briefly just what they have in common. In the first act of the second part of *Faust* (Kaiserliche Pfalz, Saal des Thrones), we see an emperor who prefers playing to holding a council (ll. 4761-4771), we hear how the state is in an uproar, how injustice is rife, the judges corrupt (ll. 4772-4811). The lack of money forms the chief complaint (ll. 4852-4875), and we see the emperor becoming impatient to get hold of the money which the astrologer tells him is his. In the meantime he decides to enjoy himself until the proper time draws near for removing the money (ll. 5057-5060).

We have learned that Maximilian always lacked money, that he put much faith in astrologers, and that justice was not always administered as well as it could have been in his lands. It may be that some of these features suggested the more exaggerated picture drawn of Goethe's emperor here. But still we can only surmise.

In the long mummery and carnival masquerade which follows the first scene (ll. 5066-5986) may be seen what is more likely a picture of our Kaiser. Maximilian was inordinately fond of just such functions as this, as we can remember from the *Freydal* alone. In the description of the procession here one can almost see before his mind's eye some such grand spectacle as was planned in the *Triumphwagen* or the *Triumphzug*.

In the next scene (ll. 5987-6172) the Kaiser enjoys the "jugglery of flame"; and when he hears of the financial relief, he gives gifts to all his court. We remember that Maximilian was fond of anything new or unusual; and that he was always praised for his generosity.

[60] *Conversations of Goethe with Eckermann and Soret*. Translated from the German by John Oxenford (New Edition; London, 1879), p. 286.

In Scene V (ll. 6183-6186) the emperor demands a magic show, in which he wishes to see the specters of Helen of Troy and Paris. In Scene VII (ll. 6377-6565) the show takes place, but it is disrupted by Faust's passion. Here the only thing in common with the Maximilian-Faust legend is that the two shades are raised for the Kaiser.

In the succeeding scenes it is even more difficult to establish any connection between Maximilian and Goethe's emperor. That his kingdom has revolted and is trying to depose him might conceivably have its parallel in the trying circumstances in which Maximilian found himself in 1507, when there were murmurs to the same effect. Also his pleasure-loving nature is again emphasized: he wishes it might be possible both to rule and to enjoy at the same time (ll. 10242-10251). Faust's sympathetic remark characterizes the Kaiser as kind and amiable: "Er jammert mich, er war so gut und offen" (Line 10291). Ll. 10407-10422 show us the emperor eager for battle, but unlike Maximilian, this emperor has no experience in fighting. The help of Mephistopheles in winning the ensuing fray reminds us of the Faust of 1563, who declared that he had been responsible for the victories of the Kaiser in Italy.[61]

Again, the emperor shows his generosity in rewarding his officers after the battle has been won (ll. 10783-11042). He is also generous to the Church. A last little touch, however, forces us to think once more of Maximilian and his careful audacity in his relations with the Church. At the end of this scene the bishop, after having had one request for land granted, presses the emperor to give also to the Church that waste land under the sea which has been promised to Faust. The emperor is vexed and declares that the land does not even exist. The bishop replies that whoever is patient enough will make it exist. The emperor, however, ends the scene and the act by remarking, that he might just as well cede over the entire empire to the Church!

We can see, then, that Goethe's emperor, although at first

---

[61] Cf. Johannes Manlius, *Locorum Communium Collectanea* (Basileae, 1563), p. 44, cf. Tille, *op. cit.*, no. 12, p. 16; and Joh. Huldr. Ragor, *Gattierung* (Manlius Loc. Com. Deutsch) (Frankfurt a. M., 1566), p. 90, cf. Tille, *op. cit.*, no. 14, p. 19.

MAXIMILIAN AND THE FAUST LEGEND

identified with Maximilian, later came to be something quite different from the Maximilian we know. It is possible to draw certain parallels. Their value, however, is questionable. Thus it will always be when we attempt to dissect and to analyze a character created with genuine imagination.

VII

THE MAXIMILIAN LEGEND BECOMES LITERATURE

AT THE THRESHOLD of the Seventeenth Century, the popular conception of Maximilian's character was virtually complete. In the period that follows, the great figures of the Sixteenth Century faded in popular consciousness and lost their power to stimulate the expansion of anecdote and legend. The early stirrings of national patriotism which had gilded the figure of Maximilian as a German leader now gave place to a narrower adherence to the territorial states and dynasties and popular interest focused on courtly or military heroes. From now on, we may find evidence of the persistence of the Max legend and of its reflection in imaginative literature, but hardly any new developments. The present study is mainly concerned with the formulation of the legend of Max: to trace the appearance of the great Renaissance Kaiser and the anecdotes concerning him through the three centuries after 1600 would be indeed a tremendous task, involving an exhaustive investigation of the entire body of German lyrical, dramatic, and novelistic literature, and would be impossible within the limitations imposed by American libraries. Furthermore, such evidence as has been found makes it highly doubtful whether the Maximilian legend underwent any noteworthy changes after 1600, when it appears fully equipped with the features that we have shown in the foregoing pages. It will, however, throw some light on the attitude of later generations of German writers toward Max and his deeds if we examine a few of the more important authors who introduced the Kaiser into the historical scene as a hero or a subsidiary figure.

There is some indication that the interest in the great Hapsburg emperor as a legendary figure still retained life in the Seventeenth Century. This was at least sufficient to call forth a new edition of the *Teuerdank*. In 1679 this underwent another revision, which was published in Ulm in that year and republished in Augsburg in 1693. The author of this was Matthäus Schultes. His work was perhaps suggested by the revision and republication in 1668 of Fugger's *Ehrenspiegel* by Sigmund von Birken in Nuremberg. Schultes says in his preface that the *Teuerdank* had been neglected for a hundred and sixty-two years, i.e., since 1517. He must therefore have been unfamiliar with the editions of Waldis. This is borne out by the fact that Schultes' *Schlüssel*, which appears in each adventure immediately below the individual woodcuts instead of at the end of the book as is the case with Pfinzing's Key, follows in some of its deviations from the original the work of Sebastian Franck,[1] in others the *Ehrenspiegel*,[2] while in at least one adventure (no. xxiix, i.e., no. 28) both Franck and the *Ehrenspiegel* are drawn upon.[3] For his Martinswand chapter (no. 20) the author may also have used the Latin account of Stephen Winand Pighius (1587), for it reads like a translation of the latter.[4] In addition to these borrowings, Schultes has added verses for some six extra woodcuts which, he says, have been found. The content of these adventures is as follows:

No. 118. Max enters a competition at crossbow-shooting in Augsburg in 1518.

No. 119. Max goes to Flanders and is nearly captured by Louis XI.

No. 120. Max tilts with the Kurfürst Friedrich von Sachsen in Augsburg in 1510.

No. 121. In Utrecht in 1483 Max forces his soldiers to keep his promise to the inhabitants.

No. 122. Max assists Henry IV [!] of England against Louis XII at Terouan in 1513.

No. 123. Max exhibits his bravery in the *Böhmenschlacht* of 1504 and Erich von Braunschweig saves his life.

---

[1] This can be seen by comparing Schultes' Ulm, 1670, edition, under chapters no. xvi, xlii, liv, lxvi, lxxxi, and lxxxvii respectively with Franck's *Germania*, fo. 218-b, no. 4; 282-b, no. 17; 283-b, no. 28; 284-b, no. 40; 286-a, no. 53; and 286-b, no. 58. In all these cases Schultes' chapter numbers correspond to those of the original edition of the *Teuerdank*.

[2] E.g., in chapters no. xx (the Martinswand legend), lxxvii, xcv, and xcvi, which correspond respectively to the *Ehrenspiegel*'s accounts, pp. 1379-1381, 1376-1377, 980-997, and 1383.

[3] Franck's *Germania*, fo. 282-a, no. 3, and *Ehrenspiegel*, p. 1382.

[4] Cf. Arnold Busson, "Die Sage von Max auf der Martinswand und ihre Entstehung," *Sitzungsberichte der kaiserlichen Akademie der Wissenschaften in Wien, Phil.-historische Classe*, CXVI (Wien, 1888), 456ff.

In addition to these six extra adventures, the material for which may have been obtained either from Franck's *Germania* or from Birken's *Ehrenspiegel,* there is appended to Schultes' *Teuerdank* a fifty-eight-page "Kurtze Geburts- Lebens- und Todtes-Beschreibung Dess Allerdurchleuchtigsten Ritters Maximiliani, etc." The author of this biographical sketch is unnamed, but he may have well been Schultes himself. The information it contains could also have been found in the works of Franck and of Birken.

Schultes also attempted to clothe the verses of the *Teuerdank* in a more modern garb; and at the same time he condensed the poem into fewer verses. However, his changes can not be said to have enhanced the original.[5]

Schultes' edition of 1693 remained the last one for many years. Not until 1836 was a new edition undertaken, this time with a scholarly attitude, by Carl Haltaus. It is possible that this attempt to make *Teuerdank* available for historical and literary study was suggested by the appearance of a work six years earlier, in which Maximilian is presented as the last hero of the chivalric age. This was *Der letzte Ritter* by Anastasius Grün (Anton Alexander, Graf von Auersperg), written 1827 to 1829. It will be examined below.

The revival of the legend of Max in *Der letzte Ritter* belongs to the romantic cult of the past, which developed later in Austria than in the German lands of the West. In Strasbourg and Frankfort, amid a generation that looked upon the Middle Ages as a period of barbarism, young Goethe had found his way back to the Sixteenth Century and discovered Maximilian among its interesting figures. His picture of the Kaiser in *Götz von Berlichingen,* incomplete though it is, is the only one attempted by German writers in the period of Classicism. Herder knew of the *Teuerdank* and the *Weisskunig,* to be sure, and called them "famous products of our language, concerning a royal Majesty," but he confessed that he had never found time to read them.[6] In the previous chapter we have discussed Maximilian's relation to Goethe's *Faust.* In *Dichtung und Wahrheit* Goethe tells us that as a boy he was familiar

---

[5] Carl Haltaus, *Teuerdank* (Quedlinburg u. Leipzig, 1836), p. 60.
[6] From Herder's essay, "Andenken an einige ältere deutsche Dichter." In "Zerstreute Blätter," *Werke* (Berlin, Hempel'sche Ausgabe), XV, 317.

with the features of Kaiser Max, for his likeness hung in the Frankfort Rathaus along with those of other Kaisers; and he remembers that Max was praised as a friend of the people and of the burghers.[7] *Dichtung und Wahrheit* brings also other evidence that the Max legend was still alive in the old coronation city on the Main. Goethe's father referred to Max in connection with drawing; he said that everyone should learn to draw, and that Kaiser Max had recommended it.[8] In a *Colloquium*,[9] a boyhood work, Goethe mentions the adventure of Max on the Martinswand, and that "an angel in the form of an old man" is supposed to have rescued him. This shows Goethe's early acquaintance with the figure of Max in the most widely known episode in the *Teuerdank*. Later in life, when he visited the scene of the supposed adventure, Goethe declared that he would not have been afraid to walk back and forth there without an angel, although it might indeed be a foolhardy undertaking![10]

The only work of Goethe in which Maximilian plays any part of importance is *Götz von Berlichingen*. There is a reference to Maximilian's capture in Bruges in 1488 in *Egmont*,[11] but this is incidental. In *Götz* Maximilian appears on the scene and has something to say. A careful comparison of *Götz* with the *Lebens-Beschreibung Herrn Gözens von Berlichingen* in the edition of 1731[12] reveals, however, that some of what Maximilian says was supplied by Götz. Goethe had read this edition in 1771 and had turned to it again in 1773.[13] The only scene in which Maximilian appears[14] shows us two Nuremberg merchants begging the Kaiser for aid against Götz and Hans von Selbitz. The Kaiser exclaims:

Heiliger Gott! Heiliger Gott! Was ist das? Der eine hat nur *eine* Hand, der andere nur *ein* Bein; wenn sie denn erst zwei Hände hätten, und zwei Beine, was wolltet ihr dann tun?

[7] Goethe's *Werke* (Sophienausgabe), XXVI, 27.
[8] *Ibid.*, XXVI, 186.
[9] "Labores juveniles," *ibid.*, XXXVIII, 211-212.
[10] *Italienische Reise* ("Auf dem Brenner, den 8. September abends." 1786). *Ibid.*, XXX, 16.
[11] *Ibid.*, VIII, 207. (Speech by Vansen, 2. Aufzug.)
[12] "erläutert, etc. . . ." von Verono Franck von Steigerwald, Nürnberg, 1731.
[13] Cf. Karl F. König, *A Record of Goethe's Belesenheit in the Pre-Weimar Period of His Life*, II, 293, 400.
[14] III. Akt. Augsburg. Ein Garten.

And as the merchants press their petition, he continues:

> Wie geht's zu! Wenn ein Kaufmann einen Pfeffersack verliert, soll man das ganze Reich aufmahnen; und wenn Händel vorhanden sind, daran Kaiserlicher Majestät und dem Reich viel gelegen ist, daß es Königreich, Fürstentum, Herzogtum und anders betrifft, so kann euch kein Mensch zusammenbringen.

These two speeches of the Kaiser's are found, nearly verbatim, in the 1731-edition of Götz' autobiography (pp. 130f.). At the end of the same scene, Maximilian, in conversation with Weislingen, regrets that he must use force against the brave knights. Only the urgent advice of the other convinces him that he must resort to action, but still he insists that no harm must come to them.

Altogether, the picture of Maximilian in *Götz* is of a mild, temperate man, admiring the last of the independent knights and admired in turn by them, but disliked for the same reasons by the clerics. The only faults of his which are brought out are his habit of making plans faster than it is possible to execute them, and his tendency to take bad counsel.

It has been pointed out[15] that the patriotic-popular tendency, which is first seen in the *Bardentum, Ritterdrama*, and *Ritterroman* of the *Sturm und Drang* as a purely aesthetic countermovement against French taste, developed in the Napoleonic period into a national movement against the oppressive political ascendancy of the French. August Wilhelm Schlegel in his Vienna lectures designated historical tragedy as the most deserving genre of the Romantic School and pointed to the periods of the Hohenstaufen and the Hapsburgs as rich in material for historical pictures. An Austrian, Hormayr, had already turned to this field, and his *Archiv, Taschenbuch*, and his *Österreichischer Plutarch*[16] became important sources for those who were now beginning to search for material. Historical subjects were used by such painters as Russ, Perger, Petter, and Krafft; and especially the national-historical pictures of the first-named artist, which were displayed in 1822, awakened new interest in the nation's past.

[15] By Eduard Castle, ed. of Grün's *Der letzte Ritter—Romanzenkranz*, in Grün's *Werke* (Berlin, 1909), I, 3ff.
[16] Hormayr's *Österreichischer Plutarch* (Wien, 1807) was mentioned in Chapter I, p. 13, above. Maximilian is the subject of no. 10, V, 86-186.

It was to be expected that the legend of Maximilian should retain its vitality longest in Austrian lands. An early follower of Hormayr was the Viennese dramatist and critic, Heinrich Joseph von Collin, a friend of Schlegel. Collin wrote a poem, "Kaiser Max auf der Martinswand in Tyrol. 1493,"[17] which consists of twenty-six strophes in ballad style on the familiar adventure and includes all the regular features of the legend. It begins with Max in full chase after the agile chamois:

> "Hinauf! hinauf!
> In Sprung und Lauf!
> Wo die Luft so leicht, wo die Sonne so klar,
> Nur die Gemse springt, nur horstet der Aar,
> Wo das Menschengewühl zu Füßen mir rollt,
> Wo das Donnergebrüll tief unten grollt:
> Das ist der Ort, wo die Majestät
> Sich herrlich den Herrscherthron erhöht!
> Die steile Bahn
> Hinan! hinan!
> Dort pfeifet die Gemse! Ha, springe nur vor;
> Nachsetzt der Jäger, und fliegt empor!
>
> Gähnt auch die Kluft,
> Schwarz wie die Gruft;
> Nur hinüber, hinüber im leichten Schwung!
> Wer setzet mir nach? 's War ein *Kaiser*-Sprung!
> Klimm, Gemse, nur auf die Felsenwand!
> In die luftige Höh', an des Abgrunds Rand,
> Mach ich mit Eisen mir *doch* die Bahn.
> Nur muthig hinauf, und muthig hinan!
> Jetzt ohne Rast
> Den Strauch erfaßt!
> Wenn tückisch der Zweig vom Gesteine läßt,
> So hält mich im Fall' die Klippe noch fest."
>
> Der Stein nicht hält;
> Der Kaiser fällt
> In die Tiefen hinab zwey Klafter lang;
> Da ward Herrn *Maxen* doch gleichsam bang. . . .

In this way is introduced Max' perilous situation on the Martins-

---

[17] Heinrich J. von Collin, *Sämtliche Werke* (Wien, 1813), IV, 80-93. Collin died in 1811; this poem was probably written shortly before his death.

wand. From here on the story follows the regular pattern of the legend, ending with the rescue of the Kaiser by an angel in the form of a peasant lad.

Collin's patriotic lyrics are Austrian and dynastic in their loyalty. When he appeals to the great spirits of the past, it is not Maximilian but Rudolf von Habsburg that he addresses.[18] However, another poet, this time an East Prussian, the *Freiheitsdichter* Max von Schenkendorf, in a poem of July 1813, "Die Deutschen an ihren Kaiser," cites Maximilian among the glorious spirits of Germany's past:[19]

> Preis dem wackren Gemsenjäger
> Ruhm in Fehden, Ruhm in Frieden,
> In Gedichten Ruhm beschieden
> Dir, o ritterlicher Max.

Schenkendorf, like Collin, thought first of Max as the hunter and knight. Perhaps we might have expected something more from a patriotic poet, calling in a dark moment of the country's history for help from her former emperors. According to the Maximilian tradition, however, this characterization of the Kaiser, though brief, is quite in keeping with the pattern.

Among German Romanticists it was Achim von Arnim who revived the legend of Max and sought to recreate the figure of the Kaiser on the background of his age. This he does in his novel *Die Kronenwächter*, or *Bertholds erstes und zweites Leben* (1817),[20] a work which has often been cited as the first German historical novel deserving that designation. Arnim's main source was the *Waiblinger Chronik* of Wolfgang Zacher,[21] but undoubtedly he

---

[18]
>   "Ruft Rudolf von des Himmels Höhen
>   Zu Franz herab: Es wird bestehen,
>   Weil Östreich will,
>   Hoch Österreich!"

From "Österreich über alles" (1808). *Deutsche Literatur. Politische Dichtung*, II, 59.

[19] Max von Schenkendorf, *Sämtliche Gedichte* (Berlin, 1837), pp. 123ff. Cf. strophe 6, p. 124.

[20] "Deutsche National-Litteratur," hrsg. von Max Koch, CXLVI, 2. Teil.

[21] Cf. Alfred Schier's introduction to *Die Kronenwächter* (Bibl. Inst.; Leipzig, 1911), I, 3. He calls it the *Chronicon Weiblingense* (1666), Manuskript der Stuttgarter Bibliothek, Cod. hist. fol. 109. Zacher's work was not available for reference here.

was familiar also with the popular *Ehrenspiegel*.[22] Another source, used in Arnim's portrayal of the marriage festivities of Markgraf Kasimer and the Kaiser's niece, Susanne von Bayern,[23] can be found in the contemporary description, dated October 26, 1518, by Johann Haselberg, "Buchfurer auß d' Reichenau Constentzer bistumbs."[24] Arnim has woven into his novel many of the familiar details of Maximilian's life and character, his faults as well as his virtues. To Berthold he is "der ehrwürdige, ritterliche, in allen Kunsten versuchte Kaiser Maximilian."[25] Berthold also remarks how much milder the Kaiser appears in real life than in his pictures (p. 117). With Marx von Treitzsauerwein, Berthold discusses Max' faults: how he has given so much time to hunting, fishing, and other pleasures, that more important things have been neglected. Berthold notices that everyone likes Max. They speak of the Kaiser's habit of too great plans, too varied activities and skills, of his intention to make himself the head of the Church (pp. 131ff.).

Arnim also incorporates the popular tale about Max' jester, Kunz von der Rosen, in which Kunz amuses the crowd by tripping the monks into a well at Augsburg (p. 133), and the one in which Kunz breaks the goblet presented by the city of Venice (p. 134). Max' popularity among the citizens is also shown in a scene depicting Maximilian as taking part in the pleasures of a dance (pp. 144f.).

By far the most original treatment yet given the adventure which supposedly befell Maximilian on the Martinswand is that which Arnim weaves into the Kronenwächter legend. From Marx Treitzsauerwein, Berthold hears how Max once lost his way while hunting chamois, and, as he was wandering about, suddenly caught sight of a mysterious castle stretching its towers above the clouds. Its walls seemed to be made of transparent glass. When the Kaiser

---

[22] E.g., the words of Max upon taking farewell of Augsburg, written to Berthold by Treitzsauerwein ("Deutsche National-Litteratur," CXLVI, 2. Teil, 180), are identical with those of the *Ehrenspiegel*, p. 1362. For other comparisons see Wilhelm Hans, "Die Quellen und historischen Grundlagen von Arnims Kronenwächtern," *Euphorion*, X (1903), 153-159.
[23] "Deutsche National-Litteratur," CXLVI, 2. Teil, 116ff.
[24] Hutten's *Schriften*, ed. Böcking, V, 283-299.
[25] "Deutsche National-Litteratur," CXLVI, 2. Teil, 115.

tried to go toward it, it disappeared in the clouds, and Max found himself unable to go farther in any direction. Then he felt that his last hour had come, and he knelt to pray. He felt a hand on his shoulder, and turning about, he saw a smiling blond boy whom he took for an angel. But the boy took his hand with a physically firm pressure and led him to a sure path down the mountain, telling the Kaiser to say nothing of his rescue if he valued his life; for he had been sent to plunge Max to his death and was now risking his own life, unless he brought back with him Max' sword as a sign that he had fulfilled his mission. Max then gave him his sword, saying that it had been Charlemagne's. He asked about the castle he had seen, but the boy had already taken the sword and disappeared. A few days later the Kaiser met mountaineers, who led him to his followers. He kept silence about his experience, said he had lost his sword in climbing, and secretly had another made just like it. For many years he had remained silent about his adventure, but now, feeling death near, he had confided in Marx, for he had confirmed the legend of the descendants of the Hohenstaufen and he feared for his "son" and the great plans of his life (pp. 152f.).

When later Anton tells Anna of his childhood and past, he discloses that he was the blond youth who had saved the emperor's life. Anton says that in order to make him willing to commit the bloody deed, he had been told that the Kaiser was a terrible person. When he found Max kneeling in prayer, however, mild of face and full of trust in Heaven, Anton was unable to withstand such a friendly prince:

> Solch einem Antlitz widerstehe, wer aus Felsen gehauen; ich beschloß, den Kaiser zu retten, führte ihn zu einem Wege, den ich beim Jagen kennen gelernt hatte, und erbat mir zur Belohnung sein Schwert. Er streichelte mich mit der Hand, küßte das Schwert und gab es mir (pp. 260f.).

While Arnim's rendering of the Martinswand legend thus sounds more plausible than the old versions, it is at the same time the most imaginative treatment we know. Other than this, Max appears in the *Kronenwächter* only in the usual ways. Various well-known facts are included in describing him. We hear that he always carried his coffin about with him (p. 180). We see him joining the peasants in their procession to the church of St. Leonhard in Göggingen (p. 156) just as it was pictured in the *Ehrenspiegel* (p. 1274). Max' enlightened attitude toward Rome and the pope is not only brought to our attention (p. 155), but we see an invention of Arnim's in the plan by which Max secretly aids Luther to escape from Augsburg (pp. 146f.). Also an invention of Arnim's are Max' plans, revealed by Treitzsauerwein, to elevate the citizen-class, because the nobility is a couple of centuries behind the times (p. 132).

The work of this century which occupied itself most exclusively with the figure of Maximilian was *Der letzte Ritter*, already referred to, a *Romanzenkranz* by Anton Alexander, Graf von Auersperg, best known under the pseudonym Anastasius Grün. Auersperg sprang from an ancient noble family of Carniola and was to become an early advocate of liberal ideas in Austria in his *Spaziergänge eines Wiener Poeten* (1831), and after the Revolution of 1848, a leader in the struggle for constitutional government. *Der letzte Ritter*, written when he was only twenty-three years old, was the product of a youthful romantic enthusiasm for Austria's past. It is significant that he chose for his hero, not Rudolph von Habsburg, the favorite of the lyrical poets who had preceded him, but the popular figure of the Hapsburg dynasty, Kaiser Max. In over 3,000 verses he celebrates the most outstanding events in the Kaiser's life, or those events which best lend themselves to the plan he has in mind, the glorification of the whole character of Max. From the cradle to the grave, Grün follows the emperor's fortunes in some fifty poems. Many well-known tales and events from the Kaiser's experiences are lacking in Grün's work, since the poet treated those subjects which he thought best suited for his poetic purpose.

Grün received much of his inspiration and his material for the work from Hormayr, whom we have mentioned above.[26] In addition he was familiar with the *Ehrenspiegel*; and among Max' works he knew both the *Teuerdank* and the *Weisskunig*.[27] In his

---

[26] Cf. introduction by Eduard Castle to *Der letzte Ritter* (Berlin, 1909), I, 3ff.
[27] Quotations from the last two works preface the cycle.

dedication "to his friend, Joseph Fellner," he describes how he has read eagerly in all manner of chronicles and pig-skin volumes, including the *Teuerdank*. Besides these stimuli, the nationalistic paintings of Russ fired his enthusiasm and made his lively historical sense receptive for a national subject.[28]

The cycle of poems begins with the carpenter who fashions Maximilian's cradle, and it ends with the same man at work on Max' coffin. Within these limits, the principal subjects treated include: Max' childhood; his education under the harsh teacher; his engagement to Mary of Burgundy; Kunz von der Rosen; Max' battle with the French; his meeting with a Frankish challenger and the latter's defeat; Max' victory at Guinegate; Mary's death; the capture of Dendermonde; Max' coronation; Max, warned by Kunz, nevertheless rides into the captivity at Bruges; his refusal to be rescued by Kunz; his mercy when liberated, forbidding revenge; the Martinswand legend; Max' capture of Vienna; his conquest of Claude de Barre at Worms; his defeat by the Swiss; his philosophic calm; the Bavarian War; the *Böhmenschlacht;* Max joins the procession to the church of St. Alban near Terouanne; he grants protection to the gypsy girls entering Augsburg; Dürer makes the last painting of Max, who jokes about his big nose; the women of Augsburg hide Max' boots and hat to make him stay longer; Max parts from Augsburg; his last illness; he always carried his coffin about with him; his last directions for his burial; his death.

Romanticist though he was, Grün nevertheless gave evidence that he belonged to an era when even a poet must keep the reader aware that the author is conscientious about historical sources. He furnished his poem with numerous notes, and in some of them his source is directly mentioned. For example, in the poem *Vermählung,* which describes the marriage of Max and Mary (lines 457-500), a note informs us that the poet was thinking principally of the series of woodcuts for Maximilian's *Triumphzug*. When dealing with the capture of Dendermonde by soldiers disguised as monks and nuns (lines 861-932), he cites Joseph Grünpeck as his authority. A note to the poem *Zwei Tage* (lines 1677-1784),

---

[28] Cf. Eduard Castle, *loc. cit.*

concerning the war with the Swiss, refers the reader to J. v. Müller's *Geschichten schweizerischer Eidgenossenschaft*, 2. Buch.

It cannot be said that Grün deviated from the established tradition in his treatment of Maximilian. He went to greater lengths than anyone else had done to clothe his exploits in poetic garb and the result is at times a somewhat inflated imagery. The figure of Maximilian in his poems remains, however, substantially the traditional one. He inclines, if anything, toward the more romantically exaggerated picture given us by Grünpeck. Indeed, he makes a definite effort to emphasize Max' mildness, his forgiving spirit, and his generosity, even where his sources may not have been so kind. Thus we read in *Max vor Dendermonde* (lines 861-932) that after the Kaiser had taken the city by cunning, he showed forgiveness and mercy to the captives (lines 913-932). After his release from Bruges, he forbids any act of revenge on the city (*Willkomm und Abschied;* lines 1237-1264). Finally, as a last example, the poem on *Max vor Kufstein* (lines 1985-2084) follows tradition in that Maximilian is angry and swears that he will not spare Pienzenauer and his helpers; but although he carries out his bloody vengeance, he is really sorry, says Grün's poem; and while Erich von Braunschweig still is made to plead on their behalf, the mention of Max giving Erich a slap on the cheek has been softened. Moreover, it is said that later Max is seen kneeling in prayer before the grave of these victims of his own justice. In these ways the harsh features are carefully eliminated from the figure of the Kaiser and the total impression left by the poem is entirely in the old adulatory tradition.

In traversing the literature of the century since Anastasius Grün's *Romanzen* we can point to only a few works in which the figure of Max appears. Individual anecdotes concerning Max find treatment occasionally in the German ballad. About 1850 a minor German poet of the Rhine country, Wolfgang Müller von Königswinter, wrote twelve four-verse strophes on "Kaiser Max und Albrecht Dürer," in which we have a retelling of the story from Karel van Mander's *Het Leven der Schilders* (1604),[29] that Maximilian once asked a nobleman to hold a ladder for Dürer, and

---

[29] See above, p. 153.

when this was refused, Max performed the task himself.[30] Many years later, before 1913, the Austrian poet Ernst Rauscher (1834-1919) goes back to the Max legend for a ballad of twelve strophes, "Der Backenstreich." This is fashioned on the old *Pienzenauer Lied* and has the same content.[31]

In the field of the drama Max has fared very poorly. Perhaps we may explain this by saying that the legendary figure of Max is essentially an epic figure, full of action and color, but not involved in stirring conflicts or tragic crises. There is a "Lustspiel in fünf Acten" by Gustav Freytag (1841), *Die Brautfahrt oder Kunz von der Rosen,*[32] in which the Kaiser is portrayed as a bold hunter and fearless knight, a gentle prince to the young Matthäus, a kind and true master to Kunz, a brave and tender suitor to Mary of Burgundy. The comedy has as its subject the coming of Maximilian to Burgundy to press his suit for the hand of Mary. The incident mentioned in the woodcut and Chapter no. 119, which were added in Schultes' *Teuerdank,* where Max comes to Flanders and narrowly escapes capture by Louis XI, forms the plot of Freytag's play. Interwoven into the plot are various Maximilian anecdotes, sometimes with variations from the source. For example, in Act III, Scenes 1 and 3, the legendary duel between Max and Claude de Barre is represented as taking place between Max and the French knight, Raoul von Monrepas, who, like Claude, had hung his shield outside the inn as a challange (pp. 50-57, 63-66). In Act IV, Scene 2, Max takes part in a competition at crossbow-shooting, and, as usual, wins (pp. 85f.). In the same scene Kunz plays cards with Ravenstein and claims that he has received four kings, producing Max as the fourth king (p. 88). When Max comes to the Burgundian court, Mary's step-mother, Margaret of York, cannot wait to get a look at the young prince, whom the French have declared to be deformed; and she goes in disguise to watch Maximilian as he comes from his apartment (Act V, Scene 2; pp. 95f., 104-107). Through these adventures and

[30] In *Lieder- und Ependichter der Neuzeit*, 2 Theil, "Bibliothek der Deutschen Klassiker" (Hildburghausen; Bibl. Inst., 1863), XXI, 484f.
[31] In *Die österreichischen Alpenländer im Spiegel deutscher Dichtung*, von E. G. Ricek (Wien, 1913), 2. Teil, pp. 5f.
[32] *Dramatische Werke von Gustav Freytag* (5. Aufl.; Leipzig, 1890), I, 1-112.

many incidents true to the history of the period Maximilian goes in disguise as "Herr Teuerdank," until, disclosed as the young prince by Kunz' card game, he appears at the court of Mary to receive her hand in marriage.

In the extensive field of the historical novel Max probably appears many times. This genre, however, is extremely difficult to survey thoroughly, because of the inaccessibility of so many works.[33] August Hagen's *Norica* (1829) professed to be the sixteenth-century manuscript of one Jacob Heller, a friend and intimate of many Nuremberg artists and notables; and Hagen does capture to a remarkable degree the spirit and flavor of the period which he depicts. We have already mentioned the *Norica* above (pp. 133f.) in connection with an adventure from the *Teuerdank*. In another place in Hagen's work Maximilian is described as a friend and patron of art, simple, dignified, generous. In the same passage we find his remark to his father when reproached for giving away so much of his money, which we have already seen quoted in the *Weisskunig*.[34] We witness Maximilian giving directions to Dürer for the execution of some murals, and in his zeal trying to draw the sketch himself; but Dürer must help him out (pp. 217f.). Again, we watch while Max puts the poets' crown on the head of the humanist Pirckheimer (pp. 292-299). And finally we have given here an entire adventure from the *Teuerdank*, as we have seen.

Later historical novels which have been examined add nothing more to the Maximilian legend.[35] Indeed, what we have seen of

[33] E.g., Felix Salten's *Kaiser Max, der letzte Ritter*, mentioned by Hermann Bock and Karl Weitzel in *Der historische Roman als Begleiter der Weltgeschichte* (Leipzig, 1921), p. 148, where it is said to present an idealized personality of the Kaiser; and A. Achleitner, *In Treue fest, ibid.*, p. 148, a treatment of the Pienzenauer incident at Kufstein in 1504. Both volumes were unavailable for this work.

[34] *Weisskunig*, Chapter no. 27: "Von des jungen weyßen kunigs miltigkait." *Jahrb. k.-h. Samml.*, VI, 70ff.; and Hagen, *op. cit.*, p. 212.

[35] E.g., Henry Thode, *Der Ring des Frangipani* (Frankfurt a. M., 1895), unfolds an interesting and plausible conjecture concerning Maximilian's relations to Apollonia Lang. Wilhelm Jensen, *Auf der Ganerbenburg* (Weimar, 1896), in a brief comment, indicates a kindly attitude toward Max, but no respect for his political accomplishments (cf. pp. 24f.); the legendary figure does not come into consideration here. Julius Wilhelm Otto Richter, *Hans Holbein der Jüngere* (Berlin, 1900), gives us in a didactic tone a short glimpse of Maximilian's arrival in Augsburg in 1504 and his reception by Juliane, the four-year-old daughter of

the figure of Maximilian in literature after the beginning of the Seventeenth Century has contributed little to its development. As stated above, the legend was then complete, and what was written about Max after that time is a re-stating of older material, a re-working of older legends and anecdotes. Maximilian and the legends clustering about him are seldom brought into an imaginative setting, as was done in Arnim's *Kronenwächter*. Ordinarily the plain telling of the story is made to suffice, and the tale can be traced back to its origin with a fair amount of ease.

Konrad Peutinger. An English authoress, Anna Coleman Ladd, wrote in 1912 a book, *Hieronymus Rides. Episodes in the Life of a Knight and Jester at the Court of Maximilian, King of the Romans* (London, 1912), wherein is related a romantic tale of doubtful value; some few facts of Max' life are used: his great activity, his meeting with Mary of Burgundy, an early love affair (extended beyond fact), the story of Max and his coffin, the singing birds he used to carry about with him, and the dishonesty of his councillors. Artur Maximilian Miller's *Herr Jörg von Frundsberg* (Freiburg i. Br., 1933), incorporates in his narrative information about Max' organization of the *Landsknechte*, his capture in Bruges, his plain dress in camp (just as Götz von Berlichingen describes him in his autobiography; and Götz is also mentioned here); Max is said to have taken advantage of the Bavarian War; we are told of his bravery in the *Böhmenschlacht* and his rescue by Erich von Braunschweig; his knowledge of heavy ordnance; his just anger, once aroused, shows no mercy; at Verona in 1516 his dream warns him to leave Italy; Karl V is referred to as Max' "nephew."

VIII
CONCLUSION

IT HAS BEEN USUAL to refer to Faust as the youngest of German sagas. Here, the Renaissance took mythological elements from the Middle Ages, *Märchen* and anecdotes of its own time, attached them to a contemporary personality, and wove all into a fabric which is as much a composite of the grandiose and the bizarre as the German *Weltbild* of the Sixteenth Century was. A similar mixture of history and of popular fancy was also put into the legend of Maximilian, but the results were altogether different. Although the saga of Max does not lack supernatural elements, it had no root in popular mythology and raised no profound questions of man's relation to the Infinite. The hero could not escape the light which beats so fiercely on the throne and makes so difficult the full idealization of a historic personality. Nevertheless, it did place something approaching a hero's crown on the Kaiser and handed down the knightly and glorified figure to succeeding generations. The beginnings of the yearning for German national greatness which came to humanists like Celtis and Hutten and was not altogether absent from others like Wimpfeling and Peutinger, and was even faintly observable in more popular writers and publicists, created a situation favorable for depicting a shining figure in the Hapsburg emperor, whose eagerness to extend and consolidate dynastic interests was, to be sure, all too clear, but whose enthusiasms led him to attempt to recreate the chivalric past. The effect was to decorate the wearer of the imperial crown with brilliant personal qualities, among which shone a genial and popular temper.

As was pointed out early in this work, the contemporary attitude toward Max was from the beginning unfavorable as well as favorable. Nevertheless, the latter feeling far outweighed the former. It was chiefly the humanists who sought to establish that tradition. Their praise was, as we have seen, extravagant and for the most part consisted of glittering generalities, so that the halo which they placed about the head of their royal friend and patron is difficult to grasp. Their dependence on the Kaiser was too evident. Futhermore, their general use of Latin could not give their eulogies a popular appeal. Their idealization of Max is not convincing to posterity, and their contribution to his popularity among contemporaries could not have been great. Foreign observers, chiefly English and Italian, viewed his character with rather unfavorable eyes, although, as has been pointed out, certain Italian statesmen and writers dwelt on his attractive traits of personality. Perhaps more damaging to the legend in Germany were the criticisms of reformatory patriots and disappointed self-seekers among his subjects, but their number was not large, and the burghers of the cities, in spite of their independent attitude toward the imperial office, cherished many stories of Maximilian that lit up popular traits in his character. It was due to these and to the material, chiefly anecdotal, contributed by the lesser nobility, that the emperor found an important place in the entertainment literature of the century.

In the enhancement of Max as a popular figure, the *Volkslied* undoubtedly played a significant role. It added to the anecdotal literature and threw a light on many interesting aspects of his life and character, striking in the main a note of authenticity through its timeliness and giving the impression of personal observation. It tended to glorify his figure and placed him in the atmosphere of romance which is characteristic of the *Volkslied* as a genre. The *Spruch* came for the most part under the influence of Maximilian's own publicistic activity and was thus less important in its effect on the popular mind.

It has been shown that Maximilian's contribution through his autobiographical works contributed the largest share toward the perpetuation of his personality in the literature of the Sixteenth Century and later. The effect of the *Teuerdank* and the *Weisskunig* was to increase and consolidate material already in existence concerning his life and character. The popular narratives which had passed from mouth to mouth or found their way into the folksong and collections of anecdotes were gradually united with the material in the autobiographical allegories; and each successive editor of the *Teuerdank* incorporated into his work some

CONCLUSION

traditions with which he was familiar concerning Maximilian, and added stories of other origin which he identified with the Kaiser. It has been noted above that at the same time a similar process was under way among the writers on the history of Maximilian, who incorporated into their supposedly historical accounts poetic images from the *Teuerdank* and other works inspired by Maximilian. Thus the initial purpose of the emperor—to provide for his remembrance among posterity—was attained. His personality projects itself forcibly into the history-writing of his time. Thus, finally, an admixture of truth and poetry is woven together into a legend that presents the romantic and attractive picture which the German people came to regard as the real Maximilian. In its formation, as it appears in the development which we have followed, Maximilian himself played the most important part. In Chapter 24 of the *Weisskunig*, the young White King declares: "Was ich in meinem leben in meiner gedächnus nit volbring, das wird nach meinem tod weder durch dich oder ander nit erstat." In the light of what we have learned, this prediction appears somewhat inadequate, for other elements from contemporaries enlarged the picture drawn by the poets and scribes who worked under the Kaiser's eye and still others joined the popular elements of tradition with the figure of Max common to his various works. Nevertheless, it was he who furnished the stimulus for the works which were to perpetuate his personality and he who saw to their execution.

When the generation that followed Kaiser Max passed from the scene, his figure had taken form. That it continued to live in popular interest to the end of the Seventeenth Century is evidenced by the later editions of the *Teuerdank*. Some evidence has also been adduced from Goethe to show that the knightly personality of the Kaiser was still alive among German burghers at the height of the *Aufklärung*. Goethe lifts the curtain from it in *Götz* and Arnim gives it full space on the historical scene in his great novel of the Reformation Age. It was left to the young Austrian heir of Romanticism, Anastasius Grün, to revive the knightly figure in all the trappings of the Indian summer of chivalry.

In the last chapter we stated our belief that the legend of Maximilian was complete in its essential features at the end of the Sixteenth Century. Further study in the literature after 1600 may bring to light new information on the occurrence and the treatment of the Kaiser's romantic figure. Perhaps in the popular *Räuberromane* and *Ritterdramen* which were initiated by Goethe's *Götz* and Schiller's *Räuber,* or, it may be, in the moral weeklies of the Eighteenth Century, or in the popular histories of that period, there may be found material which will illustrate our legend from a new side. In the field of the historical novel, especially, future investigation may provide interest and profit for the further course of the Maximilian legend.

BIBLIOGRAPHY

Abbreviations: Jahrb. k.-h. Samml. = *Jahrbücher der kunsthistorischen Sammlungen des allerhöchsten Kaiserhauses in Wien;* "Stuttgart. Lit. Ver." = "Bibliothek des litterarischen Vereins in Stuttgart."

1. General Historical Works

Andreas, Willy. Deutschland vor der Reformation. Eine Zeitwende. Stuttgart und Berlin, 1932.
Below, Georg von. Die Ursachen der Reformation. Mit einer Beilage: Die Reformation und der Beginn der Neuzeit. "Historische Bibliothek," XXXVIII. München und Berlin, 1917.
Bernheim, Ernst. Einleitung in die Geschichtswissenschaft. "Sammlung Göschen," nr. 270. Berlin und Leipzig, 1926.
Bezold, Friedrich von. Geschichte der deutschen Reformation. "Allgemeine Geschichte in Einzeldarstellungen," 3. Hauptabt., Teil 1, hrsg. von Wilhelm Oncken. Berlin, 1886.
Burckhardt, Jacob. Die Kultur der Renaissance in Italien. Ein Versuch. 9. Aufl., von L. Geiger. Leipzig, 1904.
Coxe, William. History of the House of Austria. Vol. 3. London, 1847.
Droysen, Joh. Gustav. Geschichte der preussischen Politik. Bd. 2. 2. Aufl., Leipzig, 1868.
Fueter, Eduard. Geschichte der neueren Historiographie. 3. Aufl., München und Berlin, 1936.
Geiger, Ludwig. Renaissance und Humanismus in Italien und Deutschland. Berlin, 1882.
Gothein, Eberhard. "Die Lage des Bauernstandes am Ende des Mittelalters, vornehmlich in Südwestdeutschland." *Westdeutsche Zeitschrift,* IV (1885), 1-22.
Gothein, Eberhard. Politische und religiöse Volksbewegungen vor der Reformation. Breslau, 1878.
Heuterus, Pontus. Opera Historica Omnia: Bvrgvndica, Avstriaca, Belgica, etc. Lovanii, 1643.
Hormayr, Joseph Freiherr von. Wiens Geschichte und seine Denkwürdigkeiten. Bde. 3-4. Wien, 1823-1825.
Huber, Alfons. Geschichte Österreichs. Geschichte der europäischen Staaten, III. Gotha, 1888.
Hume, David. The History of England. A New Edition. Vols. 3-4. London, 1802.
Janssen, Johannes. Geschichte des deutschen Volkes seit dem Ausgang des Mittelalters. Bd. 1. 17. und 18. Aufl., Freiburg i. B., 1897.

Janssen, Johannes. History of the German People at the Close of the Middle Ages. Second English edition, revised. Vols. 1-2. London, 1905.
Kaser, Kurt. Deutsche Geschichte zur Zeit Maximilians I. (1486-1519). Deutsche Geschichte im Ausgange des Mittelalters (1438-1519), II. Stuttgart und Berlin, 1912.
Lamprecht, Karl. Deutsche Geschichte. 5. Bd., 1. Hälfte. Berlin, 1894.
Lanz, Karl. Geschichtliche Einleitung zur zweiten Abtheilung der Monumenta Habsburgica. Das Zeitalter Kaiser Karl's V. und seines Sohnes König Philipp II. "Monumenta Habsburgica," I, 2. Abt. Wien, 1857.
Lettenhove, Kervyn de. Histoire de Flandre. Tome Cinquième: "Ducs de Bourgogne." Bruxelles, 1850.
Münch, Ernst. Die Fürstinnen des Hauses Burgund-Österreich in den Niederlanden. Bd. 1. Leipzig, 1832.
Muther, Theodor. Aus dem Universitäts- und Gelehrtenleben im Zeitalter der Reformation. Erlangen, 1866.
Nagl, Johann Willibald. Deutsch-Österreichische Literaturgeschichte. Bde. 1, 4. Wien, 1899, 1937.
Ochs, Peter. Geschichte der Stadt und Landschaft Basel. Bde. 4-5. Basel, 1819-1821.
Pastor, Ludwig. Geschichte der Päpste seit dem Ausgang des Mittelalters. Bd. 3. Freiburg i. B., 1895.
Ranke, Leopold von. Deutsche Geschichte im Zeitalter der Reformation. Gesamt-Ausgabe der Deutschen Akademie, I. München, 1925.
Ranke, Leopold von. Geschichte der romanischen und germanischen Völker von 1494 bis 1514. Sämmtliche Werke, XXX. 2. Aufl. Leipzig: Verlag von Duncker und Humblot, 1874.
Robertson, William. The History of the Reign of the Emperor Charles V. A New Edition. Vol. 2. London, 1774.
Roo, Gerard de. Annales Rerum Belli Domique, ab Austriacis Habsburgicae Gentis Principibus a Rudolpho I. usque ad Carolum V. gestarum etc. Halae Magdeburgicae, 1709.
Roscoe, William. The Life and Pontificate of Leo the Tenth. 4 vols. Philadelphia, 1805-1806.
Rymer, Thomas. Acta Regia; or an Account of the Treaties, Letters and Instruments between the Monarchs of England and Foreign Powers, publish'd in Mr. Rymer's *Foedera*, etc. Translated from the French of M. Rapin, as publish'd by M. Le Clerc. Vol. 3. London, 1727.
Schardius, Simon. Rerum Germanicarum Scriptores Varii. Vol. 1. Giessae, 1673.
Schmidt, Charles. Histoire littéraire de l'Alsace à la fin du XVe et au commencement du XVIe siècle. 2 vols. Paris, 1879.

Vehse, Eduard. Memoirs of the Court and Aristocracy of Austria. Translated from the German by Franz Demmler. Vol. 1. London, 1896.
Wegele, Franz X. von. Geschichte der deutschen Historiographie seit dem Auftreten des Humanismus. München und Leipzig, 1885.

2. SPECIFIC WORKS ON MAXIMILIAN AND HIS REIGN

Ammann, Hartmann. Versuch einer Charakteristik Kaiser Maximilians I., seiner Regierungsthätigkeit und äussern Politik. Brixen, 1892.
Birken, Sigmund von. Spiegel der Ehren des Höchstlöblichsten Kayser- und Königlichen Erzhauses Österreich . . . durch den . . . Herrn Johann Jacob Fugger. [Referred to in the footnotes as *Ehrenspiegel.*] Nürnberg, 1668.
Chmel, Joseph. Geschichte Kaiser Friedrichs IV. und seines Sohnes Maximilian I. Hamburg, 1843.
Chmel, Joseph. Habsburgische Chronik. "Monumenta Habsburgica," I, Abt. 1, xiii-cxliv. Wien, 1854.
Freher, Marquard, and Struve, Burcard. Rerum Germanicarum Scriptores. Vols. 2-3. [Referred to in footnotes as *Freher-Struve.*] Argentorati, 1717.
Grünpeck, Joseph. Die Geschichte Friedrichs III. und Maximilians I. Übersetzt von Th. Ilgen. "Geschichtschreiber der deutschen Vorzeit in deutscher Bearbeitung," XC. Leipzig, 1891.
Haltaus, Karl. Geschichte des Kaisers Maximilian des Ersten. Leipzig, 1850.
Hare, Christopher (pseud. for Mrs. Marian Andrews). Maximilian the Dreamer. London, 1913.
Hegewisch, D. H. Geschichte der Regierung Kaiser Maximilians des Ersten. 2 Bde. Hamburg und Kiel, 1782-1783.
Heyck, Eduard. Kaiser Maximilian I. Bielefeld und Leipzig, 1898.
Hormayr, Joseph Freyherr von. "Maximilian der Erste." "Österreichischer Plutarch," V, no. 10, 86-186. Wien, 1807.
Jansen, Max. Kaiser Maximilian I. München, 1905.
Klüpfel, Karl. Kaiser Maximilian I. Neue Ausgabe. "Deutsche National-Bibliothek," neue Ausgabe, X. Berlin, 1870.
Latomus, Bartholomaeus. "Vita et Obitvs Maximiliani I. Imperatoris." Vitae Summorum Dignitate et Ervditione Virorum ex Rarissimis Monumentis Literato Orbi Restitutae, cura Johannis Gerhardi Meuschenii, I, 1-25. Coburgi, 1735.
Seton-Watson, Robert William. Maximilian I. Holy Roman Emperor. Westminster, 1902.
Stang, William. "Emperor Maximilian I." *Catholic World*, XLII (Feb. 1886), 658-665.
Ulmann, Heinrich. Kaiser Maximilian I. 2 Bde. Stuttgart, 1884, 1891.

Van Dyke, Paul. Renascence Portraits. New York, 1905.
Walther, Andreas. "Die neuere Beurteilung Kaiser Maximilians I." *Mitteilungen des Instituts für österreichische Geschichtsforschung*, XXXIII (Innsbruck, 1912), 320-349.

3. CONTEMPORARY CHRONICLES, DIARIES, AND REPORTS

"Anonymi Monacensis Breve Chronicon Bavariae ab Anno Christi MCCCCLXXXVII. ad Annum MDVI." Andreas Felix Oefelius, Rerum Boicarum Scriptores," I, 47f. Augustae Vindelicorum, 1763.
"Anonymi Ratisbonensis Farrago Historica Rerum Ratisponensium ab Anno Christi DVIII. usque ad Annum Christi MDXIX." Andreas Felix Oefelius, Rerum Boicarum Scriptores, II, 498-523. Augustae Vindelicorum, 1763.
Anshelm, Valerius. Berner-Chronik. 6 Bde. Bern, 1884-1901.
Appenwiler, Erhard von. "Die Chronik Erhards von Appenwiler 1439-1471, mit ihren Fortsetzungen bis 1474." Basler Chroniken, hrsg. von der historischen und antiquarischen Gesellschaft in Basel, IV, 174-359. Leipzig, 1890.
Aventinus (Johannes Turmair). Kleinere historische und philologische Schriften. Bde. 1-5. München, 1880-1884.
Beheim, Michael. Das Buch von den Wienern. "Deutsche National-Literatur," hrsg. von Joseph Kürschner, X, 279-386. Berlin und Stuttgart, 1886.
Berlichingen, Götz von. Lebens-Beschreibung Herrn Gözens von Berlichingen, zugenannt mit der Eisern Hand. Mit einem vollständigen Indico versehen, zum Druck befördert, von Verono Franck von Steigerwald. Nürnberg, 1731.
Bonfinius, Antonius. Rervm Vngaricarvm Decades. Basileae, 1568.
Carion, Johann. Chronica. Ex lingua Germanica in Latinam, ab Hermanno Bono optima fide transfusa. Antverpiae, 1540.
Christophorus, Fr. "In Historiam Episcoporum Ratisponensium." Andreas Felix Oefelius, Rerum Boicarum Scriptores, I, 547f. Augustae Vindelicorum, 1763.
Commynes, Philippe de. Mémoires. Nouvelle Édition publiée avec une Introduction et des Notes ... par B. De Mandrot. 2 vols. Paris, 1901, 1903.
Cuspinianus, Johann. De Caesaribus atque imperatoribus Romanis. Basileae, n. d.
Cuspinianus, Johann. "Tagebuch." "Fontes Rerum Austriacarum," I, 411ff. Wien, 1855.
Cuspinianus, Johann. "Tagebuch." Nach dem Original herausgegeben und mit Erläuterungen versehen, von Hans Ankwicz. *Mitteilungen des Instituts für österreichische Geschichtsforschung*, XXX (1909), 280-326.

BIBLIOGRAPHY

Dandolo, Francia di Matteo. "Relazione." Eugenio Albèri, Le Relazioni degli Ambasciatori Veneti al Senato Durante il Secolo Decimosesto, Serie I, IV, 27-56. Firenze, 1860.

Deichsler, Heinrich. Chronik. "Die Chroniken der deutschen Städte," XI, 634. Leipzig, 1872.

de la Marche, Olivier. Mémoires. "Collection complète des Mémoires relatifs à l'Histoire de France . . . etc.," par M. Petitot, Série I, Tome X. Paris, 1825.

Delepierre, Octave. Chronique des Faits et Gestes Admirables de Maximilien Ier. durant son Mariage avec Marie de Bourgogne. Translatée du Flamand en Français pour la première fois, et augmentée d'éclaircissements historiques et de documents inédits. Bruxelles, 1839.

Despars, Nicolaes. Cronijcke van den Lande ende Graefscepe van Vlaenderen. Tweede Uytgaef, Vierde Deel. Te Brugge, By den Uytgever (J. De Jonghe), Te Rotterdam, by Mr. W. Messchert, 1840.

Dubravius, Ioannes. Historica Bohemica. Hanoviae, 1602.

"Etliche Geschichten (1489)." "Die Chroniken der deutschen Städte," XI, 722-732. Leipzig, 1872.

Faber, Felix. "Historia Sueuica." M. Goldast, Rerum Alamannicarum Scriptores, IV. Francofurti et Lipsiae, 1730.

Franck, Sebastian. Chronica, Zeytbuch vnd Geschichtbibel. 1565. Without place.

Franck, Sebastian. Germania. Von des gantzen Teütschlands/ aller Teutschen völcker herkomen Namen/ Händeln, etc. Bern, 1539.

Giustinian, Sebastian. Four Years at the Court of Henry VIII. Selection of Despatches written by the Venetian Ambassador, Sebastian Giustinian, and addressed to the Signory of Venice. January 12, 1515, to July 26, 1519. Translated by Rawdon Brown. London, 1854.

Goldast, Melchior. Reichshandlung, Tractaten/ Keyserliche/ Königliche und Fürstliche Mandaten, etc. Hanau, 1609.

Goldast, Melchior. Rerum Alamannicarum Scriptores. Francofurti et Lipsiae, 1730.

Guicciardini, Francesco. The History of Italy, from the Year 1490 to 1532. Translated by Austin Parke Goddard. 10 vols. London, 1753.

Hainhofer, Philipp. Des Augsburger Patriciers Philipp Hainhofer Reisen nach Insbruck und Dresden, von Dr. Oscar Doering. Wien, 1901.

Hedio, Caspar. Ein Ausserleszne Chronick von anfang der welt biss auff das jar nach Christi vnsers eynigen Heylands Geburt M. D. vliij. Strassburg, 1549.

Herberstein, Sigmund von. "Selbstbiographie." "Fontes Rerum Austriacarum," I, Abt. 1, 67-396. Wien, 1855.
"Histoire des Païs-Bas, depuis 1477 jusqu'en 1492, écrite en forme de journal par un auteur contemporain." Recueil des Chroniques de Flandre, publié sous la Direction de la Commission Royale d'Histoire par J.-J. De Smet, III, 689-742. Bruxelles, 1856.
Hochwart, Laurentius. "Episcoporum Ratisponensium Catalogi." Andreas Felix Oefelius, Rerum Boicarum Scriptores, I, 159-242. Augustae Vindelicorum, 1763.
Hug, Heinrich. Villinger Chronik von 1495 bis 1533. Hrsg. von Chr. Roder. "Bibliothek des Litterarischen Vereins in Stuttgart" (referred to hereafter and in footnotes as "Stuttgart. Lit. Ver."), CLXIV. Tübingen, 1883.
Jahrbücher des 15. Jahrhunderts. "Die Chroniken der deutschen Städte," X, 343, 377. Leipzig, 1872.
Kanzow, Thomas. Chronik von Pommern. In hochdeutscher Sprache hrsg. von L. B. von Medem. Anclam, 1841.
Kessler, Johann. Sabbata. Chronik der Jahre 1523-1539. Hrsg. von Ernst Goetzinger. St. Gallen, 1866.
Kirchmair, Georg. "Denkwürdigkeiten seiner Zeit. 1519-1553." "Fontes Rerum Austriacarum," I, Abt. 1, 417-534. Wien, 1855.
Knebel, Johann. Die Chronik des Klosters Kaisheim. Hrsg. von Franz Hüttner. "Stuttgart. Lit. Ver.," CCXXVI. Tübingen, 1902.
Krantz, Albert. Rerum Germanicarum Historici Clariss. Saxonia. Francofurti, 1621.
Lalaing, Antoine de. "Voyage de Philippe le Beau en Espagne, en 1501." Collection des Voyages des Pays-Bas, publiée par M. Gachard, I, 121-340, 387-480. Bruxelles, 1876.
Landshuter Rathschronik. 1439-1504. "Die Chroniken der deutschen Städte," XV. Leipzig, 1878.
Langius, Paulus. "Chronicon Citizense, De Illius Dioeceseos Gestis, et aliis etiam passim, juxta ejusdem praesulum annos et successiones, digestum, et ab anno domini DCCCCLXVIII perductum usque ad annum MDXV." Joannes Pistorius Nidanus, Rerum Germanicarum Scriptores, I, 1120-1291. Ratisbonae, 1726.
Lehmann, Christophor. Chronica der Freyen Reichs Stadt Speier. Franckfurth am Mäyn, 1698.
Leib, Chilian. "Historiarum sui temporis ab An. MDII. ad An. MDXLVIIII. Annales." Ioh. Chr. Freiherr von Aretin, Beyträge zur Geschichte und Literatur, VII, 535-560, 621-668. München, 1806.
Letters and Papers, Foreign and Domestic, of the Reign of Henry VIII. Arranged and catalogued by J. S. Brewer. (Referred to in footnotes as *Letters and Papers*.) Vols. 1-4. London, 1862.

Machiavelli, Niccolo. The Historical, Political, and Diplomatic Writings of Niccolo Machiavelli. Translated from the Italian by Christian E. Detmold. 4 vols. Boston, 1882.
Mair, Paul Hektor. Chronik von 1547-1565. "Die Chroniken der deutschen Städte," XXXII, 77. Leipzig, 1917.
Molinet, Jean. Chroniques. Publiées, pour la première fois, d'après les manuscrits de la bibliothèque du roi, par J.-A. Buchon. "Collection des Chroniques Nationales Françaises," vols. 43-47. Paris, 1827-1828.
Nauclerus, Johann. Memorabilium omnis aetatis et omnium gentium chronici commentarii. Tübingen, 1516.
Oldecop, Johan. Chronik. Hrsg. von Karl Euling. "Stuttgart. Lit. Ver.," CXC. Tübingen, 1891.
Pirckheimer, Wilibald. Bilibald Pirkheimers Schweizerkrieg und Ehrenhandel mit seinen Feinden zu Nürnberg. Nebst Biographie und kritischem Schriftenverzeichnis durch Ernst Münch. Basel, 1826.
Pirckheimer, Wilibald. Opera Politica, Historica, Philologica et Epistolica. Collecta, recensita ac digesta, a Melchiore Goldasto Haiminsfeldio. Francoforti, 1610.
Pirckheimer, Wilibald. Wilibald Pirckheimers Schweizerkrieg. Nach Pirckheimers Autographum im Britischen Museum. Hrsg. von Karl Rück. München, 1895.
Quirini, Vincenzo. "Relazione de Vincenzo Quirini, Tornato Ambasciatore dall'imperatore Massimiliano nel Decembre 1507." Eugenio Albèri, Le Relazioni degli Ambasciatori Veneti al Senato Durante il Secolo Decimosesto, Serie I, VI, 26f. Firenze, 1862.
Ranzanus, Petrus. "Epitomes Rervm Vngaricarvm." Io. Georg Schwandtner, Scriptores Rervm Hvngaricarvm Veteres, I, 326-422. Bibliopalae Vindobonensis, 1746.
Rem, Lucas. Tagebuch des Lucas Rem aus den Jahren 1494-1541. Ein Beitrag zur Handelsgeschichte der Stadt Augsburg. Mitgetheilt von B. Greiff. Augsburg, 1861.
Rem, Wilhelm. Cronica newer geschichten. "Die Chroniken der deutschen Städte," XXV. Leipzig, 1896.
Rhenanus, Beatus. Rervm Germanicarum. Basileae, 1551.
Rolewinck, Werner. "Fasciculus Temporum Omnes Antiquorum Chronicas Complectens." Joannes Pistorius, Rerum Germanicarum Scriptores, II, 397-576. Ratisbonae, 1726.
Schaumburg, Wilwolt von. Die Geschichten und Taten Wilwolts von Schaumburg. "Stuttgart. Lit. Ver.," L. Stuttgart, 1859.
Schedel, Hartmann. Libri Chronicarum. Nürnberg, 1493.
Schefftlar. "Breve Chronicon Schefftlariense Ord. Praemonstratensis ab anno MCLX. ad annum MDLXII. Anonymo Monacho Schefft-

lariense auctore." Andreas Felix Oefelius, Rerum Boicarum Scriptores, I, 639ff. Augustae Vindelicorum, 1763.
Schenk zu Schweinsberg, Eberhard Freiherr. Die Illustrationen der Chronik von Flandern—Handschrift nr. 437—der Stadtbibliothek zu Brügge und ihr Verhältnis zu Hans Memling. Strassburg, 1922.
Schradin, Nicolaus. "Kronigk diss Kriegs gegen den Allerdurchlüchtigisten Herrn Romschen Konig, etc. . . ." *Der Geschichtsfreund,* IV (Einsiedeln, 1847), 6-66.
Spalatin, Georg. "Friedrichs des Weisen Leben und Zeitgeschichte." Georg Spalatin's historischer Nachlass und Briefe, hrsg. von Chr. Gotth. Neudecker und Ludwig Preller. Jena, 1851.
Thoman, Nicolaus. "Weissenhorner Historie." Quellen zur Geschichte des Bauernkriegs in Oberschwaben, hrsg. von Franz Ludwig Baumann. "Stuttgart. Lit. Ver.," CXXIX. Tübingen, 1876.
Tichtel, Johannes. "Tagebuch, 1477-1495." "Fontes Rerum Austriacarum," I, Abt. 1, 1-66. Wien, 1855.
Tritheim, Johann. Joannis Tritheimij, Spanheimensis, Tomus II. Annalium Hirsaugiensium. S. Galli, 1690.
Tubero, Ludovicus. "Commentariorvm De Rebvs, Svo Tempore, Nimirvm Ab Anno Christi MCCCCXC. Vsque Ad Annvm Christi MDXXII." Io. Georg Schwandtner, Scriptores Rervm Hvngaricarvm Veteres, II, 107-381. Vindobonensis, 1746.
"Tucher'sche Fortsetzung der Jahrbücher bis 1469-1499." "Die Chroniken der deutschen Städte," XI, 503. Leipzig, 1872.
Unrest, Jacob. "Chronicon Avstriacvm." D. Simonis Friderici Hahni, Collectio Monumentorum, veterum et recentium, I, 537-803. Brunsvigae, 1724.
Vigneulles, Philippe von. "Gedenkbuch des Metzer Bürgers Philippe von Vigneulles aus den Jahren 1471 bis 1522." Hrsg. von Heinrich Michelant. "Stuttgart. Lit. Ver.," XXIV, 212f. Stuttgart, 1852.
"Viti Prioris Eberspergensis Ord. S. Benedicti Cronica Bavarorum ab Origine Gentis ad annum Christi MDIIII." Andreas Felix Oefelius, Rerum Boicarum Scriptores, II, 704-739. Augustae Vindelicorum, 1763.
Voisin, M. Auguste. Notice sur le seul exemplaire connu d'un livre intitulé: Die wonderlycke oorloghen van den doorluchtighen hooghgheboren prince, keyser Maximiliaen, hoe hy hier eerst int landt quam, ende hoe hy vrou marien trowde. Édition de 1577. Without date or place.
Weinrich, Caspar. "Danziger Chronik." Scriptores Rerum Prussicarum, IV, 727-800. Leipzig, 1870.
Westerstetten, von. "Auszug aus dem Bericht des v. Westerstetten d. d. Gengenbach 8. August 1504." Baierische Landtags-Handlungen in den Jahren 1429 bis 1513, XIV, 728. München, 1825.

Widmann, Leonhart. Chronik von Regensburg. 1511-1543. 1552-1555. "Die Chroniken der deutschen Städte," XV. Leipzig, 1878.

Zayner, Andreas. "Rerum Bello Bavarico Gestarum a Morte Georgii Divitis ad Laudum Coloniense Liber Memorialis incompletus." Andreas Felix Oefelius, Rerum Boicarum Scriptores, II, 345-468. Augustae Vindelicorum, 1763.

Zimmerische Chronik. Hrsg. von K. A. Barack. 4 Bde. "Stuttgart. Lit. Ver.," XCI-XCIV. Tübingen, 1869.

4. LETTERS

Ankwicz von Kleehoven, Hans. Johann Cuspinians Briefwechsel. Gesammelt, hrsg. und erläutert von Hans Ankwicz von Kleehoven. "Veröffentlichungen der Kommission zur Erforschung der Geschichte der Reformation. Humanistenbriefe," II. München, 1933.

Byrne, M. St. Clare. The Letters of King Henry VIII. A selection with a few other documents, edited by M. St. Clare Byrne. London, Toronto, Melbourne, and Sydney, 1936.

Currie, Margaret A. The Letters of Martin Luther, selected and translated by Margaret A. Currie. London, 1908.

Dürer, Albrecht. Tagebücher und Briefe. München, 1927.

Gachard, M. Lettres Inédites de Maximilien, Duc d'Autriche, Roi des Romains et Empereur, Sur Les Affaires des Pays-Bas. Première Partie. 1478-1488. "Europe: Historical Pamphlets," I. Bruxelles, Gant et Leipzig, 1851.

Geiger, Ludwig. Johann Reuchlins Briefwechsel. "Stuttgart. Lit. Ver.," CXXVI. Tübingen, 1875.

Herberger, Theodor. Sebastian Schertlin von Burtenbach und seine an die Stadt Augsburg geschriebenen Briefe. Mitgetheilt von Theodor Herberger. Augsburg, 1852.

Horawitz, Adalbert, und Hartfelder, Karl. Briefwechsel des Beatus Rhenanus. Gesammelt und herausgegeben von A. Horawitz und K. Hartfelder. Leipzig, 1886.

Kraus, Victor von. Maximilians I. vertraulicher Briefwechsel mit Sigmund Prüschenk Freiherrn zu Stettenberg, nebst einer Anzahl zeitgenössischer das Leben am Hofe beleuchtender Briefe. Innsbruck, 1875.

Kreiten, Hubert. Untersuchungen über den Briefwechsel Kaiser Maximilians I. mit seiner Tochter Margareta. Wien, 1907.

Le Glay, André J. G. Correspondance de l'empereur Maximilien Ier et de Marguerite d'Autriche, sa fille, gouvernante des Pays-Bas, de 1507 à 1519. Paris, 1839.

Luther. Dr. Martin Luthers Briefwechsel. Hrsg. von Enders, Kaweran, Flemming und Albrecht. 19 Bde. Calw und Stuttgart, Frankfurt a. M. und Leipzig, 1887-1932.

Luther. Dr. Martin Luthers Briefe, Sendschreiben und Bedenken. Hrsg. von Wilhelm Martin Leberecht de Wette. 6 Bde. Berlin, 1825-1856.
Rupprich, Hans. Der Briefwechsel des Konrad Celtis, gesammelt, hrsg. und erläutert von Hans Rupprich. "Veröffentlichungen der Kommission zur Erforschung der Geschichte der Reformation und Gegenreformation. Humanistenbriefe," III. München, 1934.
Sunthaim, Ladislaus. [Letter to Maximilian, in] Urkunden, Briefe und Actenstücke zur Geschichte Maximilians I. und seiner Zeit. Hrsg. von J. Chmel. "Stuttgart. Lit. Ver.," X, 486, no. CCCXXV. Stuttgart, 1845.
Sunthaim, Ladislaus. Letter to Gurk. *Jahrbücher der kunsthistorischen Sammlungen des allerhöchsten Kaiserhauses in Wien* (referred to hereafter, and in footnotes, as *Jahrb. k.-h. Samml.*), V (Wien, 1887), Teil 2, cxxi-cxxii, Regest nr. 4491.

5. *Volkslied* AND *Spruch*

Aretin, Joh. Chr. Freiherr von (ed.). "Das Lied von dem Benzenauer (1505)." Beyträge zur Geschichte und Literatur, IX, 1286-1291. München, 1807.
Baecker, Louis de. Chants historiques de la Flandre. 400-1650. Recuellis par Louis de Baecker. Lille, 1855.
Bechwinden, Haintz von. "Ein spruch von hertzog Albrecht vnd vonn dem pfaltzgraff Philippo. Anno dm̃. 1504." [In] "Zwei Flugschriften aus der Zeit Maximilians I." *Neue Heidelberger Jahrbücher*, XVII (Heidelberg, 1913), 139-218.
Ducis, Benedictus. Lofzangen ter eere van Keizer Maximiliaan. Benedictus de Opitiis [pseud. of Benedictus Ducis]. I's Gravenhage, 1925.
Frisch, Ernst von. "Jörg Pleyers Flugblatt von Kaiser Maximilians Abschied und Tod." *Gutenberg-Jahrbuch* (Mainz, 1935), pp. 150-153.
Goedeke, Karl, und Tittmann, Julius. Liederbuch aus dem sechzehnten Jahrhundert. Leipzig, 1867.
"Hie Nach Volget Die Grossen Krieg und Streit . . . zwischen . . . Kosamyrus von Brandeburg unnd . . . Nurmberg . . ." (Nürnberg, 1515) Dichtungen des sechzehnten Jahrhunderts nach den Originaldrucken hrsg. von Emil Weller. "Stuttgart. Lit. Ver.," CXIX, 14-21. Tübingen, 1874.
Hock, Stefan (ed.). Lyrik aus Deutschösterreich. Vom Mittelalter bis zur Gegenwart. "Amalthea-Bücherei," VII. Zürich, Leipzig und Wien, 1919.
Hoffmann von Fallersleben, Heinrich (ed.). Antwerpener Liederbuch vom Jahre 1544. "Horae Belgicae. Pars Undecima." Hannover, 1885.

Liliencron, Rochus von. Deutsches Leben im Volkslied um 1530. "Deutsche National Literatur," XIII.
Liliencron, Rochus von. Die historischen Volkslieder der Deutschen vom 13. bis 16. Jahrhundert. 4 Bde. Leipzig, 1865-1869.
Sahr, Julius. Das deutsche Volkslied. Ausgewählt und erläutert. Neubearbeitet von Paul Sartori. "Sammlung Göschen," nr. 25, Teil 1. Berlin und Leipzig, 1924.
Uhland, Ludwig. "Aus den Vorlesungen über Geschichte der deutschen Dichtkunst im fünfzehnten und sechzehnten Jahrhundert (1831)." [In] "Zur deutschen Poesie." Uhlands gesammelte Werke, VI, 148ff. Stuttgart und Berlin: Cotta, n. d.
Weller, Emil. Annalen der poetischen National-Literatur der Deutschen im XVI. und XVII. Jahrhundert. Nach den Quellen bearbeitet. Freiburg i. B., 1862.

6. Maximilian's Literary Activity

A. *General*

Jahrb. k.-h. Samml., I (Wien, 1883), Teil 2, xxxvi-xxxix, Regest nr. 219.
Redl, Franz. "Kaiser Maximilian I. von Habsburg in seinen Beziehungen zur Dichtkunst, Wissenschaft und Kunst." *Zeitschrift für die österreichischen Gymnasien*, LXIII (Wien, 1912), 693-723, 873-892.
Schlegel, A. W. Geschichte der deutschen Sprache und Poesie. Vorlesungen gehalten an der Universität Bonn seit dem Wintersemester 1818/1819. Hrsg. von Josef Körner. "Deutsche Literaturdenkmale des 18. und 19. Jahrhunderts," CXLVII, 3. Folge, nr. 27, 145f. Berlin, 1913.
Steinherz, S. "Ein Bericht über die Werke Maximilians I." *Mitteilungen des Instituts für österreichische Geschichtsforschung*, XXVII (1906), 152-155.
Van Dyke, Paul. "Literary Activity of the Emperor Maximilian I." *American Historical Review*, XI (October 1905), 16-28.
Wolff, Eugen. Reinke de vos und satirisch-didaktische Dichtung. "Deutsche National-Litteratur," hrsg. von J. Kürschner, XIX, 215-271, and the *Einleitung*.

B. *Individual Works*

Fischereibuch

Das Fischereibuch Kaiser Maximilians I. Unter Mitwirkung von Ludwig Freiherrn von Lazarini hrsg. von Dr. Michael Mayr. Innsbruck, 1901.

Freydal

Dodgson, Campbell. "An Unknown MS. of Freydal." *The Burlington Magazine for Connoisseurs*, LXII (London, June 1933), no. 363, 235-242.

Freydal. Des Kaisers Maximilian I. Turniere und Mummereien. Hrsg. von Quirin von Leitner. Wien und Nürnberg, 1880-1882.

Gebetbuch

Chmelarz, Eduard. "Das Diurnale oder Gebetbuch des Kaisers Maximilian I." *Jahrb. k.-h. Samml.*, III (Wien, 1885), 88-102.

Giehlow, Karl. "Beiträge zur Entstehungsgeschichte des Gebetbuches Kaisers Maximilian I." *Jahrb. k.-h. Samml.*, XX (1899), 30-112.

Lübke, W. [Reviewer of] "Albrecht Dürers Randzeichnungen aus dem Gebetbuche des Kaisers Maximilian I., mit eingedrucktem Originaltext." *Deutsches Kunstblatt*, I (Leipzig, Aug. 1850), 268-271.

Gedenkbuch

"Zwischen 1508 und 1515. Gedenkbuch Kaiser Maximilians I." *Jahrb. k.-h. Samml.*, V (1887), Teil 2, xix, Regest nr. 4023.

Genealogie

Harzen, E. "Maximilian des Ersten Stammbaum und dessen 'Zotende Mendl.'" *Deutsches Kunstblatt*, V (Leipzig, Juli 1854), 237-240.

Laschitzer, Simon. "Die Genealogie des Kaisers Maximilian I." *Jahrb. k.-h. Samml.*, VII (1888), 1-46.

Laschitzer, Simon. "Die Heiligen aus der 'Sipp-, Mag- und Schwägerschaft' des Kaisers Maximilian I." *Jahrb. k.-h. Samml.*, IV (1886), 70-289; V (1887), 117-262.

Jadgbuch

Baillie-Grohman, W. A. "An Emperor's Sporting Chronicle." *The Monthly Review*, Feb. 1901, pp. 149-162.

Das Jagdbuch Kaiser Maximilians I. In Verbindung mit Wm. A. Baillie-Grohman hrsg. von Dr. Michael Mayr. Innsbruck, 1901.

Teuerdank

Bernhart, I. B. "Bemerkungen über die Auflage des Theuerdanks von 1517 und über die in derselben vorkommenden Schreiberzüge." Joh. Chr. Freih. von Aretin, Beyträge zur Geschichte und Literatur, V, 67-98. München, 1805.

Biener, Clemens. "Die Fassungen des Teuerdank." *Zeitschrift für Deutsches Altertum und Deutsche Litteratur*, LXVII (Berlin, 1930), n. F. 55. Bd., 177-196.

Bürger, Otto. Beiträge zur Kenntnis des Teuerdank. "Quellen und

Forschungen zur Sprach- und Culturgeschichte der germanischen Völker," XCII, 92. Heft. Strassburg, 1902.

Misch, Georg. "Die Stilisierung des eigenen Lebens in dem Ruhmeswerk Kaisers Maximilian, des letzten Ritters." *Nachrichten von der Gesellschaft der Wissenschaften zu Göttingen aus dem Jahre 1930. Philologisch-Historische Klasse* (Berlin, 1930), pp. 435-459.

Strobl, Joseph. Kaiser Maximilians I. Anteil am Teuerdank. Eine kritische Untersuchung. Innsbruck, 1907.

Teuerdank in the following editions:

Die geuerlicheiten vnd einsteils der geschichten des loblichen streytparen vnd hochberůmbten helds vnd Ritters herr Tewrdannckhs. Nürnberg: Hans Schönsperger, 1517.

Die Geferlicheitẽ und geschichten des löblichen streytbaren vnnd Hochberiempten Helds vnd Ritters Teürdancks. Augsburg: Hainrich Stainer, 1537.

Theur-Danck etc. . . . Ulm: Matthäus Schultes, 1679.

Der aller-durchleuchtigste ritter, etc. . . . Augspurg: bey Mattåo Schultes, 1693.

Theuerdank. Hrsg. und mit einer historischen-kritischen Einleitung versehen von Carl Haltaus. Quedlinburg und Leipzig, 1836.

Teuerdank. J. Scheible, Das Kloster, IV, 13. Zelle. Stuttgart, 1846.

Teuerdank. Hrsg. von Karl Goedeke. Leipzig, 1878.

The Adventures and a Portion of the Story of the Praiseworthy, Valiant, and High-Renowned Hero and Knight, Lord Tewrdannckh. A Reproduction of the Edition Printed at Augsburg in 1519. Ed. by W. H. Rylands for the Holbein Society. London, 1884.

Der Theuerdank. Facsimile-Reproduction nach der ersten Auflage vom Jahre 1517 neu herausgegeben von Simon Laschitzer. *Jahrb. k.-h. Samml.,* VIII. Wien, 1888.

Triumph

Chmelarz, Eduard. "Die Ehrenpforte des Kaisers Maximilian I." *Jahrb. k.-h. Samml.,* IV (Wien, 1886), 289-320.

Dörnhöffer, Fr. "Ein Cyklus von Federzeichnungen mit Darstellungen von Kriegen und Jagden Maximilians I." *Jahrb. k.-h. Samml.,* XVIII (Wien, 1897), 1-55.

Ehrenpforte. 4. Aufl., Wien, 1799.

Giehlow, Karl. "Die Hieroglyphenkunde des Humanismus in der Allegorie der Renaissance, besonders der Ehrenpforte Kaiser Maximilians I." *Jahrb. k.-h. Samml.,* XXXII (Wien, 1915), Heft 1, 1-232.

Giehlow, Karl. "Dürers Entwürfe für das Triumphrelief Kaiser Maximilians I. im Louvre. Eine Studie zur Entwicklungsgeschichte des Triumphzuges." *Jahrb. k.-h. Samml.*, XXIX (Wien, 1910/1911), 14-84.

Schestag, Franz. "Kaiser Maximilians I. Triumph." *Jahrb. k.-h. Samml.*, I (Wien, 1883), 154-181.

Weisskunig

Der Weisskunig. Hrsg. von Alwin Schultz. *Jahrb. k.-h. Samml.*, VI. Wien, 1887.

Liliencron, Rochus von. "Der Weisskunig Kaiser Maximilians I." *Historisches Taschenbuch*, hrsg. von W. H. Riehl, 3. Jahrgang, 5. Folge, pp. 321-358. Leipzig, 1873.

Zeugbücher

Boeheim, Wendelin. "Die Zeugbücher des Kaisers Maximilian I." *Jahrb. k.-h. Samml.*, XIII (Wien, 1892), 94-201; XV (Wien 1894), 295-391.

C. Maximilian and Art

Baldass, Ludwig von. "Die Bildnisse Kaiser Maximilians I." *Jahrb. k.-h. Samml.*, XXXI (Wien, 1913/1914), 247-334.

Becker, C. "Hans Burgkmairs Turnierbuch." *Deutsches Kunstblatt*, I (Leipzig, Oct. 1850), 314ff.

Burkhard, Arthur. "Hans Burgkmair's Work for Emperor Maximilian I." "Harvard Studies and Notes in Philology and Literature," XV, 127-146. Cambridge, 1933.

Coursen, Charlotte H. "A Forgotten Renaissance Monument." *Catholic World*, LXXX (Nov. 1904), 225ff.

Dirr, P. "Eine Gedächtnisschrift von Johannes Faber über die Erbauung der Augsburger Dominikanerkirche." *Zeitschrift des historischen Vereins für Schwaben Neuburg*, 34. Jahrgang (1908), 164-178.

Haberditze, F. M. "Die Lehrer des Rubens." ("Tobias Verhaeght," p. 162.) *Jahrb. k.-h. Samml.*, XXVII (Wien, 1907/1909), 161-235.

Petz, H. "Urkundliche Nachrichten über den literarischen Nachlass Regiomontans und B. Walters 1478-1522." *Mitteilungen des Vereins für Geschichte der Stadt Nürnberg* (Nürnberg, 1888), 7. Heft, pp. 237-262.

Robinson, F. Mabel. "Art Patrons: Maximilian I." *Magazine of Art*, XII (1889), 307ff.

Schönherr, David. "Die Kunstbestrebungen Erzherzogs Sigmund von Tyrol." *Jahrb. k.-h. Samml.*, I (Wien, 1883), 182-212.

Scott, William Bell. Albert Durer: His Life and Works. London, 1869.

Sizeranne, R. de la. "Un Nouveau Profil de Femme au Louvre, Blanca Maria Sforza." *Revue des Deux Mondes*, Période VI, Tome 52 (1919), 341-361.
Thausing, Moritz. Dürer. Geschichte seines Lebens und seiner Kunst. Zweite verbesserte Auflage in zwei Bänden. Bd. 2. Leipzig, 1884.
Troyon, Pierre. "Les Trésors de Maximilien." *Revue des Deux Mondes*, Période VII, Tome 40 (1927), 692-697.
Zifferer, P. "Une Exposition Autrichienne au jeu de Paume. L'Époque de Maximilien Ier." *L' Illustration*, 85 ptl. (Je. 11, 1927), 618f.

7.. ANECDOTES AND LEGENDS

A. *General*

Bebel, Heinrich. Heinrich Bebels Facetien. Drei Bücher. Historisch-kritische Ausgabe von Gustav Bebermeyer. "Stuttgart. Lit. Ver.," CCLXXVI. Leipzig, 1931.
Bebel, Heinrich. Heinrich Bebels Schwänke, zum ersten Male in vollständiger Übertragung herausgegeben von Albert Wesselski. 2 Bde. München und Leipzig, 1907.
Erasmus, Desiderius. "The Fabulous Banquet." The Whole Familiar Colloquies of Desiderius Erasmus of Rotterdam. Translated from the Latin by Nathan Bailey. Pp. 223f. London, 1877.
Frey, Jakob. Gartengesellschaft. "Stuttgart. Lit. Ver.," CCIX. Tübingen, 1896. P. 82.
Kirchhof, Hans Wilhelm. Wendunmuth. "Stuttgart. Lit. Ver.," XCV-XCVII. Tübingen, 1869.
Lalebuch. Das Lalebuch (1597) mit den Abweichungen und Erweiterungen der Schiltbürger (1598) und des Grillenvertreibers (1603) herausgegeben von Karl von Bahder. "Neudrucke deutscher Litteraturwerke des xvi. und xvii. Jahrhunderts," CCXXXVI-CCXXXIX. Halle a. S., 1914.
Lindener, Michael. Michael Lindeners Rastbüchlein und Katzipori, hrsg. von F. Lichtenstein. "Stuttgart. Lit. Ver.," CLXIII. Tübingen, 1883. Pp. 72ff.
Luther. D. Martin Luthers Werke. Kritische Gesamtausgabe: Tischreden. 6 Bde. Weimar, 1912-1921.
Luther. The Table Talk of Martin Luther, translated and edited by William Hazlitt, Esq. London, 1857.
Sachs, Hans. "Historia, All römisch kayser nach ordnung, etc." "Stuttgart. Lit. Ver.," CIII, 353-372. Tübingen, 1870.
Thiele, Ernst. Luthers Sprichwörtersammlung. Weimar, 1900.
Wehrhan, Karl. Die deutschen Sagen des Mittelalters. "Deutsches Sagenbuch," hrsg. v. von der Leyen, 3. Teil, 1. Hälfte. München, 1919.

Zingerle, Anton. "Über Berührungen tirolischer Sagen mit antiken." *Beiträge zur Anthropologie, Ethnologie und Urgeschichte von Tirol. Festschrift* (Innsbruck, 1894), pp. 211-226.

Zingerle, Ignaz. Tirols Antheil an der poetischen National-Literatur im Mittelalter. Zweites Programm des k. k. akademischen Staats-Gymnasium zu Innsbruck. Innsbruck, 1851.

Zingerle, Ignaz V. Sagen aus Tirol. 2. Ausg. Innsbruck, 1891.

B. Individual Legends

Faustsage

The following *Faustbücher:*

Das Volksbuch vom Doctor Faust. 2. Aufl., hrsg. von Robert Petsch. Nach der ersten Ausgabe, 1587. "Neudrucke deutscher Litteraturwerke des xvi. und xvii. Jahrhunderts," VII. Halle a. S., 1911.

Spiess Faustbuch of 1587 in: Volksbücher des 16. Jahrhunderts, hrsg. und erklärt von Felix Bobertag. "Deutsche National-Litteratur," XXV, 147-295.

Fausts Leben, von Georg Rudolf Widmann. J. Scheible, Das Kloster, II (1846), 273-804.

Widmann's *Faust* edited by Nikolaus Pfitzer. Hrsg. von A. v. Keller, "Stuttgart. Lit. Ver.," CXLVI (1880), 431-439.

Das ärgerliche Leben und schreckliche Ende des vielberüchtigten Erz-Schwarzkünstlers Johannis Fausti. Erstlich vor vielen Jahren fleissig beschrieben von Georg Rudolph Widmann; hernach übersehen und wieder herausgegeben von Ch. Nikolaus Pfitzer, Med. D. Nürnb. A. 1674. Jetzo aber auf's Neue aufgelegt und mit 16 Holzschnitten verziert. Reutlingen, 1834.

Des Christlich Meynenden Geschichte Faust's. J. Scheible, Das Kloster, II (1846), 76-104.

The Life and Death of Dr. Johannes Faustus, Master of the Black Art, as played by the Kasperle Company, now first done out of German into English. London, 1893.

Lercheimer, Augustin. Augustin Lercheimer (Professor H. Witekind in Heidelberg) und seine Schrift wider den Hexenwahn. Lebensgeschichtliches und Abdruck der Letzten vom Verfasser besorgten Ausgabe von 1597. Hrsg. von Carl Binz. Strassburg, 1888.

Nagel, S. R. "Helena in der Faustsage." *Euphorion*, IX (1902), 43-69.

Palmer, Philip Mason, and More, Robert Pattison. The Sources of the Faust Tradition from Simon Magus to Lessing. New York, 1936.

Sachs, Hans. "Historia: Ein wunderbarlich gesicht keyser Maximiliani, löblicher gedechtnuss, von einem nigromanten." "Stuttgart. Lit. Ver.," CXCIII, 483-487. Tübingen, 1892.

Tille, Alexander. Die Faustsplitter in der Literatur des sechzehnten bis achtzehnten Jahrhunderts nach den ältesten Quellen. Berlin, 1900.
Wier, Johann. De praestigiis daemonum. Basel, 1583.
Wier, Johann. Von Schwarzkünstlern. J. Scheible, Das Kloster, II (1846), 188f.

Martinswandsage

Busson, Arnold. "Die Sage von Max auf der Martinswand und ihre Entstehung." *Sitzungsberichte der Kaiserlichen Akademie der Wissenschaften in Wien, Phil.-Historische Classe*, CXVI (Wien, 1888), 455-500.
Ernstinger, Hans Georg. Hans Georg Ernstingers Raisbuch, hrsg. von A. F. Walther. "Stuttgart. Lit. Ver.," CXXXV. Tübingen, 1877. P. 62.
Kiechel, Samuel. Die Reisen des Samuel Kiechel, hrsg. von K. D. Haszler. "Stuttgart. Lit. Ver.," LXXXVI. Stuttgart, 1866. P. 465.
Kirchlechner, K. [Reviewed by S. M. Prem] "Über Maximilian als Jäger und im besonderen über das Abenteuer des Kaisers auf der Martinswand." *Mitteilungen des Instituts für österreichische Geschichtsforschung*, VII (Innsbruck, 1886), 194.
Mayr, M. "Die geschichtliche Grundlage der Sage von Kaiser Max auf der Martinswand." *Forschungen und Mitteilungen zur Geschichte Tirols und Vorarlbergs*, 1. Jahrgang (Innsbruck, 1904), 66-75.
Sachs, Hans. "Die unütz fraw Sorg." "Stuttgart. Lit. Ver.," CV, 134. Tübingen, 1870.
Sachs, Hans. "Kampff-gesprech zwischen der Hoffart und der edlen Demut." "Stuttgart. Lit. Ver.," CIV, 149-157. Tübingen, 1870.
Zingerle, Reinhold von. "Zur Sage von Kaiser Max auf der Martinswand." *Forschungen und Mitteilungen zur Geschichte Tirols und Vorarlbergs*, 2. Jahrgang (Innsbruck, 1905), 164ff.

Miscellaneous

Delepierre, Octave. Chronique de L'Abbaye de Saint-André. Traduite pour la première fois d'après le manuscrit de la bibliothèque de Bruges; suivie de Mélanges Historiques et Littéraires. Bruges, 1839.
Doran, John. The History of Court Fools. London, 1858.
Flögel, Karl Friedrich. Geschichte der Hofnarren. Liegnitz und Leipzig, 1789.
Hill, Robert H. "Conrad of the Roses." *Blackwoods Magazine*, CCXXXV (Ja. 1934), 82-99.
Mander, Karel van. Het Leven der Schilders. Vol. 1. Amsterdam, 1764. P. 58.

Redlich, Oswald. "Zur Belagerung von Kufstein im Jahre 1504." *Mitteilungen des Instituts für österreichische Geschichtsforschung*, IX (Innsbruck, 1888), 104-113.

Sachs, Hans. "Historia: Die geschicht keyser Maximiliani löblicher gedechtnuss mit dem alchamisten." "Stuttgart. Lit. Ver.," CLXXIX, 422-426. Tübingen, 1886.

Sachs, Hans. "Die plinden mit der saw." Die Fabeln und Schwänke in den Meistergesangen, hrsg. von Edmund Goetze und Carl Drescher. "Neudrucke deutscher Litteraturwerke des xvi. und xvii. Jahrhunderts," CCVII-CCXII, 84f. Halle a. S., 1904.

Sachs, Hans. "Schwank: Der blinden kampf mit der säw." "Stuttgart. Lit. Ver.," CLXXXI, 343-348. Tübingen, 1888.

Sandrart, Joachim von. L'Academia Todesca della Architectura, Scultura & Pittura: oder Teutsche Academie der Edlen Bau-, Bild- und Mahlerey-Künste, etc. Bd. 1. Nürnberg, 1675. P. 224.

8. RELATIONS WITH THE EMPIRE

Adler, Sigmund. Die Organization der Centralverwaltung unter Kaiser Maximilian I. Leipzig, 1886.

Bachmann, Adolf. Zur deutschen Königswahl Maximilians I. Wien, 1890.

Baron, Hans. "Imperial Reform and the Habsburgs, 1486-1504." *American Historical Review*, XLIV (Ja. 1939), 293-303.

Braun, Anton. Die Verhandlungen zwischen Maximilian I. und den Reichsständen auf dem Reichstag zu Freiburg i. B. 1498. Freiburg i. B. 1898.

Chmel, Joseph. Urkunden, Briefe und Actenstücke zur Geschichte Maximilians I. und seiner Zeit. "Stuttgart. Lit. Ver.," X. Stuttgart, 1845.

Diederichs, Peter. Kaiser Maximilian I. als politischer Publizist. Heidelberg, 1932.

Erben, Wilhelm. "Maximilian I. und die Landsknechte." *Historische Zeitschrift,* der ganzen Reihe 116. Bd., 3. Folge, XX (München und Berlin, 1916), 48-68.

Haupt, Herman. "Ein oberrheinischer Revolutionär aus dem Zeitalter Maximilians I." *Westdeutsche Zeitschrift für Geschichte und Kunst, Ergänzungsheft* VIII (Trier, 1893), 76-228.

Ilwof, Franz. "Maximilian I. als Organisator der Verwaltung in Österreich." *Zeitschrift für allgemeine Geschichte, Kultur-, Litteratur- und Kunstgeschichte,* IV (Stuttgart, 1887), 75-80.

Jäger, Albert. "Der Übergang Tirols und der österreichischen Vorlande von dem Erzherzoge Sigmund an den Röm. König Maximilian von 1478-1490. Ein Bruchstück aus der Geschichte der Tiroler Landstände." *Archiv für österreichische Geschichte,* LI (1873), 297-448.

BIBLIOGRAPHY

Jäger, Albrecht. "Über Kaiser Maximilians I. Verhältnis zum Papstthum." *Sitzungsberichte der Kaiserlichen Akademie der Wissenschaften in Wien, Phil.-Historische Classe,* XII (Wien, 1854), 195-236, 409-441.

Kaser, Kurt. "Die auswärtige Politik Maximilians I." *Mitteilungen des Instituts für österreichische Geschichtsforschung,* XXVI (Innsbruck, 1905), 612-626.

Klaje, Hermann. Die Schlacht bei Guinegate vom 7. August 1479. Greifswald, 1890.

Krieger, Albert. Über die Bedeutung des 4. Buches von Coccinius' Schrift 'de bellis Italicis' für die Geschichte Kaiser Maximilians des I. Heidelberg, 1886.

Liske, Xaver. "Der Congress zu Wien im Jahre 1515. Eine kritisch-historische Studie." *Forschungen zur deutschen Geschichte,* VII (Göttingen, 1867), 463-558.

Liske, Xaver. "Der Wiener Congress von 1515 und die Politik Maximilians I. gegenüber Preussen und Polen." *Forschungen zur deutschen Geschichte,* XVIII (Göttingen, 1878), 445-467.

Lorenz, Ottokar. "Reichskanzler und Reichskanzlei in Deutschland." *Preussische Jahrbücher,* XXIX (Berlin, 1872), 474-505.

Nägle, August. "Hat Kaiser Maximilian I. im Jahre 1507 Papst werden wollen?" *Historisches Jahrbuch,* Jahrgang 1907 (München), XXVIII, 44-60, 278-305.

Priebatsch, F. "Die Reise Friedrichs III. ins Reich 1485 und die Wahl Maximilians." *Mitteilungen des Instituts für österreichische Geschichtsforschung,* XIX (Innsbruck, 1898), 302-326.

Rausch, Karl. Die Burgundische Heirat Maximilians I. quellenmässig dargestellt. Wien, 1880.

Schmeidler, Bernhard. "Das spätere Mittelalter als ein Zeitalter der Auflösung und der Vorbereitung." Welt als Geschichte, II (1936), 349-367.

Schmeidler, Bernhard. "Die Bedeutung des späteren Mittelalters für die deutsche und europäische Geschichte." *Historische Vierteljahrsschrift,* XXIX (1934), 93-108.

Schulte, Aloys. [Review by Kurt Kaser of] "Kaiser Maximilian I. als Kandidat für den päpstlichen Stuhl 1511." *Mitteilungen des Instituts für österreichische Geschichtsforschung,* XXIX (Innsbruck, 1908), 194ff.

Stälin, Christoph Fried. von. "Bericht über die Annahme der Kaiserwürde durch Maximilian im Jahre 1508." *Forschungen zur deutschen Geschichte,* I (Göttingen, 1862), 67-73.

Ulmann, Heinrich. "Der Traum des Hans von Hermansgrün. Eine politische Denkschrift aus d. J. 1495." *Forschungen zur deutschen Geschichte,* XX (Göttingen, 1880), 67-92.

Ulmann, Heinrich. "Die Wahl Maximilians I." *Forschungen zur deutschen Geschichte,* XXII (Göttingen, 1882), 131-158.
Ulmann, Heinrich. "K. Maximilians I. Absichten auf das Papstthum in den Jahren 1507-1511." [Reviewed by A. Huber in] *Mitteilungen des Instituts für österreichische Geschichtsforschung,* X (Innsbruck, 1889), 332f.
Ulmann, Heinrich. "Maximilian I. in dem Conflicte zwischen dem deutschen Orden in Preussen und Polen besonders in den J. 1513 bis 1515." *Forschungen zur deutschen Geschichte,* XVIII (Göttingen, 1878), 89-109.
Ziehen, Eduard. Mittelrhein und Reich im Zeitalter der Reichsreform 1356-1504. 2 Bde. Frankfurt a. M., 1934, 1937.

9. Miscellaneous

Aschbach, Joseph. Geschichte der Wiener Universität. 2 Bde. Wien, 1865, 1877.
Bauch, Gustav. Die Anfänge des Humanismus in Ingolstadt. München und Leipzig, 1901.
Bauch, Gustav. Die Reception des Humanismus in Wien. Breslau, 1903.
Bergmann, (Custos). "Lateinische Grammatik, moralische und diätetische Verse, sammt einer Vermahnung in Prosa, zum Unterrichte des Erzherzogs, nachherigen Kaisers Maximilian I. geschrieben." Ein Beytrag zur Geschichte der Lehr- und Lernweise des XV. Jahrhunderts, aus einer Handschrift der k. k. Ambraser-Sammlung, mitgetheilt vom Custos Bergmann. *Jahrbücher der Literatur,* LXXVIII (Wien, 1837), *Anzeige-Blatt,* 17-34.
Boeheim, Wendelin. Über einige Jagdwaffen und Jagdgeräthe." *Jahrb. k.-h. Samml.,* II (Wien, 1884), 129-144.
Boeheim, Wendelin. "Werke Mailänder Waffenschmiede in den Kaiserlichen Sammlungen." *Jahrb. k.-h. Samml.,* IX (Wien, 1889), cf. p. 379.
Brosch, Moritz. "Machiavelli am Hofe und im Kriegslager Maximilians I." *Mitteilungen des Instituts für österreichische Geschichtsforschung,* XXIV ((Innsbruck, 1903), 87-110.
Butler, Kathleen T. A History of French Literature. Vol. 1. London, 1923. Pp. 56, 61.
Chmel, Joseph. "K. Maximilians I. Ansichten über Regenten-Weisheit." (Gedicht: "Gespräch der Vögel.") *Archiv für österreichische Geschichte, Notizenblatt,* I (1851), 153-156.
Czerny, Albin. "Der Humanist und Historiograph Kaiser Maximilians I. Joseph Grünpeck." *Archiv für österreichische Geschichte,* LXXIII (1888), 315-364.

BIBLIOGRAPHY

Denis, Michael. Wiens Buchdruckergeschichte bis M.D.L.X. Wien, 1782.
Drei Frühdrücke zur Reichsgeschichte. Leipzig, 1938.
Drescher, K. "Nürnberger Meistersinger-Protokolle von 1575-1689." "Stuttgart. Lit. Ver.," CCXIII. Tübingen, 1897. P. 106.
Ebermann, Richard. Die Türkenfurcht, ein Beitrag zur Geschichte der öffentlichen Meinung in Deutschland während der Reformationszeit. Halle a. S., 1904.
Eckermann. Conversations of Goethe with Eckermann and Soret. Translated from the German by John Oxenford. New Edition. London, 1879.
Geiger, Ludwig. "Maximilian I. in seinem Verhältnisse zum Reuchlinschen Streite." *Forschungen zur deutschen Geschichte*, IX (Göttingen, 1869), 203-216.
Gess, Felician. "Habsburgs Schulden bei Herzog Georg." *Neues Archiv für sächsische Geschichte und Altertumskunde*, XIX (Dresden, 1898), nr. vii, 213-243.
Gundolf, Friedrich. Drei Reden: Hutten, Klopstock, Arndt. Heidelberg, 1924.
Headlam, Cecil. The Story of Nuremberg. London, 1901.
Herberger, Theodor. Conrad Peutinger in seinem Verhältnisse zum Kaiser Maximilian I. Augsburg, 1851.
Herder, Johann Gottfried. "Andenken an einige ältere deutsche Dichter." [In] "Zerstreute Blätter," Werke (Berlin, Gustav Hempel), XV, 283-336.
Ilwof, Franz. "Kaiser Maximilian I. und die Vertreibung der Juden aus Steiermark." *Forschungen zur deutschen Geschichte*, X (Göttingen, 1870), 654f.
Joachim, Erich. Johannes Nauclerus und seine Chronik. Göttingen, 1874.
Kautzsch, Rudolf. "Die Entstehung der Frakturschrift." *Beilage zum zwanzigsten Jahresbericht der Gutenberg-Gesellschaft*. Mainz, 1922.
Koch, Matthias. "Aus dem zum Unterricht Kais. Joseph's II. bestimmten Lehrbuch der deutschen Reichsgeschichte, verfasst vom Staatssecretär Baron Bartenstein," *Kais. Akad. d. Wissenschaften, Phil.-Hist. Classe. Denkschrift*, I (Wien, 1850), Teil 2, 168-186.
König, Erich. "Peutingerstudien." "Studien und Darstellungen aus dem Gebiete der Geschichte," IX (Freiburg i. B., 1919), Heft 1 u. 2, 1-178.
König, Karl F. A Record of Goethe's Belesenheit in the Pre-Weimar Period of his Life. Yale Dissertation, 1935. Unpublished.
Kraus, Victor von. "Itinerarium Maximiliani I. 1508-1518. Mit einleitenden Bemerkungen über das Kanzleiwesen Maximilians I."

Hrsg. von V. v. Kraus. *Archiv für österreichische Geschichte,* LXXXVII (1899), 229-318.
Lauterbecken, Georg. Regentenbuch. Wittemberg, 1581.
Liebenau, Th. von. "Dr. Conrad Türst als kaiserlicher Astronom." *Anzeiger für schweizerische Geschichte,* n. F., V (Bern, 1888), 243f., nr. 94.
Linden, Herman vander. Itinéraires de Marie de Bourgogne et de Maximilien d'Autriche (1477-1488). Bruxelles, 1934.
Matthisson, Friedrich. Tagebuch. [Published as "Anhang" to] Gedichte von 1795-1831, hrsg. von Gottfried Bölsing. "Stuttgart. Lit. Ver.," CCLXI. Tübingen, 1913. P. 208.
Panzer, Georg Wolfgang. Zusätze zu den Annalen der älteren deutschen Litteratur oder Anzeige und Beschreibung derjenigen Bücher welche von Erfindung der Buchdruckerkunst an bis MDXX in Deutscher Sprache gedruckt worden sind. Leipzig, 1802.
Pico della Mirandola. Gianfrancesco Pico Della Mirandola On The Imagination. The Latin text with an introduction, an English translation, and notes by Harry Caplan. "Cornell Studies in English," XVI. New Haven and London, 1930.
Rockwell, Leo Lawrence. Zur Wortstellung in der Zimmerschen Chronik, mit besonderer Berücksichtigung des Satzanfangs. Lancaster, 1928.
Schneegans, Heinrich. Geschichte der grotesken Satire. Strassburg, 1894.
Stälin, Christoph Friedrich. "Aufenthaltsorte Maximilians I. seit seiner Alleinherrschaft 1493 bis zu seinem Tode 1519." *Forschungen zur deutschen Geschichte,* I (Göttingen, 1862), 347-383.
Taylor, Archer. Problems in German Literary History of the Fifteenth and Sixteenth Centuries. New York and London, 1939.
Thommen, R. "Nachträge zu Türst." *Anzeiger für schweizerische Geschichte,* n. F., V (Bern, 1887), 8off., nr. 55.
Ward, Sir Adolphus William. The Collected Papers of Sir Adolphus William Ward. Vols. 3 (pp. 7f.) and 6 (p. 167). Cambridge, 1921.
Weller, Emil. Repertorium typographicum. Die deutsche Literatur im ersten Viertel des sechzehnten Jahrhunderts. Im Anschlusz an Hains Repertorium und Panzers deutsche Annalen. Nördlingen, 1864.
Wimpfeling, Jacob. Germania. Übersetzt und erläutert von Ernst Martin. Strassburg, 1885.
Zappert, Georg. "Über ein für den Jugendunterricht Kaiser Maximilians I. abgefasstes lateinisches Gesprächbüchlein." *Sitzungsberichte der Kaiserlichen Akademie der Wissenschaften in Wien, Phil.-Historische Classe,* XXVIII (Wien, 1858), 193-280.

BIBLIOGRAPHY

Zeibig, H. J. "Der Ausschuss-Landtag der gesammten österreichischen Erblande zu Innsbruck 1519." *Archiv für Kunde österreichischer Geschichts-Quellen,* XIII (1854), 201-366.

10. MAXIMILIAN IN LITERATURE

Arnim, Ludwig Achim von. Berthold's erstes und zweites Leben. Hrsg. von Max Koch. "Deutsche National-Litteratur," hrsg. von J. Kürschner, CXLVI, Teil 2, 1-303.

Arnim, Ludwig Achim von. Die Kronenwächter. Hrsg. von Alfred Schier. Werke, I. Leipzig: Bibl. Inst., 1911-1914.

Auersperg, Anton Alexander, Graf von (pseud., Grün, Anastasius). Der letzte Ritter—Romanzenkranz. Hrsg. von Eduard Castle. Werke, I, 1-112. Berlin: Bong & Co., 1909.

Bartholinus. "Ricardi Bartholini Pervsini, De Bello Norico, Ad Divvm Maximilianvm, Avstriados Libri Dvodecim: Cvm Scholiis Iacobi Spiegelij Selestadiensis, v. c." Justi Reuberi Vetervm Scriptorvm, I, 469-734. Francofvrti, 1584.

Bock, Hermann, und Weitzel, Karl. Der historische Roman als Begleiter der Weltgeschichte. Ein Führer durch das Gebiet der historischen Romane und Novellen. Leipzig, 1921.

Brant, Sebastian. Das Narrenschiff von Sebastian Brant. Hrsg. von Karl Goedeke. Leipzig, 1872.

Brant, Sebastian. Sebastian Brants Narrenschiff. Hrsg. von Friedrich Zarncke. Leipzig, 1854.

Celtis, Conrad. Conradus Celtis Protucius. Quattuor Libri Amorum. Secundum Quattuor Latera Germaniae. Edidit Felicitas Pindter. Lipsiae, 1934.

Collin, Heinrich J. von. "Epische und lyrische Gedichte." Sämmtliche Werke, IV. Wien, 1813.

Freytag, Gustav. "Die Brautfahrt oder Kunz von der Rosen. Lustspiel in fünf Acten. 1841." Dramatische Werke, I, 1-112. Leipzig, 1890.

Gengenbach, Pamphilus. Pamphilus Gengenbach, S R F. Hrsg. von Karl Goedeke. Hanover, 1856.

Glareanus, Henricus. "Glareani Descriptio Helvetiae." Hrsg. von Carl Christoph Bernoulli. *Denkschrift der hist. u. antiq. Gesellschaft zu Basel* (Basel, 1891), pp. 28-48.

Goethe, Johann Wolfgang von. Werke. Herausgegeben im Auftrage der Groszherzogin Sophie von Sachsen. Weimar: Böhlau, 1887-1919.

Hagen, August. Norica, das sind Nürnbergische Novellen aus alter Zeit. Nach einer Handschrift des sechzehnten Jahrhunderts. 6. Aufl., Leipzig, 1887.

Hans, Wilhelm. "Die Quellen und historischen Grundlagen von Arnims Kronenwächtern." *Euphorion,* X (1903), 153-159.

Hutten, Ulrich von. Des teutschen Ritters Ulrich von Hutten auserlesene Werke. Übersetzt und herausgegeben von Ernst Münch. 3 Bde. Leipzig, 1822-1823.
Hutten, Ulrich von. Ulrichs von Hutten Schriften. Hrsg. von Eduard Böcking. 7 Bde. Leipzig, 1859-1870.
Jensen, Wilhelm. Auf der Ganerbenburg. Eine tragikomische Historie. Weimar, 1896.
Ladd, Anna Coleman. Hieronymus Rides. Episodes in the Life of a Knight and Jester at the Court of Maximilian, King of the Romans. London, 1912.
Lemnius, Simon. Raeteis. Heldengedicht in acht Gesängen. Im Versmasz der Urschrift ins Deutsche übertragen von Placidus Plattner. Chur, 1882.
Mielke, H., und Homann, H. J. Der deutsche Roman des 19. und 20. Jahrhunderts. 6. Aufl., Dresden, 1920.
Miller, Artur Maximilian. Herr Jörg von Frundsberg. Der deutschen Landsknechte lieber Vater. Freiburg i. B., 1933.
Müller, Maler. Fausts Leben. "Deutsche Litteraturdenkmale des 18. Jahrhunderts." In Neudrucken herausgegeben von Bernhard Seuffert. III. Stuttgart, 1881.
Müller von Königswinter, Wolfgang. "Kaiser Max und Albrecht Dürer." Lieder- und Ependichter der Neuzeit, 2. Teil, "Bibliothek der Deutschen Klassiker," XXI, 484f. Hildburghausen, 1863.
Murner, Thomas. Thomas Murner und Ulrich von Hutten. "Deutsche National-Litteratur," hrsg. von J. Kürschner. XVII, 1. Abt.
Rauscher, Ernst. "Der Backenstreich." [In] E. G. Ricek, Die österreichischen Alpenländer im Spiegel deutscher Dichtung, pp. 5f. Wien, 1913.
Richter, Julius Wilhelm Otto. Hans Holbein der Jüngere. Eine altdeutsche Künstlergeschichte. Berlin, 1900.
Schenkendorf, Max von. Sämmtliche Gedichte. Erste vollständige Ausgabe. Berlin, 1837.
Thode, Henry. Der Ring des Frangipani. Ein Erlebniss. Frankfurt a. M., 1895.
Welschgattung. "Die Welsch-Gattung," von Friedrich Waga. "Germanistische Abhandlungen," 34. Heft, 170-272, Breslau, 1910.
Wickhoff, Franz. "Der zeitliche Wandel in Goethes Verhältnis zur Antike dargelegt am Faust." *Jahreshefte des österreichischen archäologischen Institutes in Wien*, I (Wien, 1898), 105-122.

INDEX

INDEX

Abimelech, 52.
Accellini, *see* Balbi, Girolano.
Achilles, 158f., 161, 163.
Achleitner, A., 185n.
Adam, 40, 139, 141, 142n.
Adelphus (Muling), Johann, 41f.
Adler family, 54n.
Adler, Sigmund, 208.
Aeacides, 42.
Aegidius, Petrus, 45.
Aemilianus, Quinctus, 38.
Aeneas, 161.
Agamemnon, 161, 163.
Ajax, 161, 163.
Albèri, Eugenio, 58n., 195, 197.
Albertus Magnus, 163.
Albrecht IV, Herzog von Baiern, 74, 92, 200.
Albrecht, Meister, 48, 146
Alexander the Great, 28f., 41f., 45n., 57, 111, 139, 152, 157, 160, 162f., 164n., 165; wife of, 162f.
Amaltheus, Paulus, 57.
Amman, Erasmus, 93.
Ammann, Hartmann, 19, 193.
Andreas, Willy, 191.
Andrews, Mrs. Marian (Christopher Hare), 20, 193.
Ankwicz von Kleehoven, Hans, 23n., 25n., 194, 199.
Anne, duchess of Brittany, 52, 56, 64, 67, 75f., 84, 90, 94f., 115f., 139, 152, 157, 160, 163.
Anshelm, Valerius, 18n., 55f., 65n., 76n., 194.
Appenwiler, Erhard von, 53n., 194.
Aretin, Johann Christian, Freiherr von, 77n., 141n., 196, 200, 202.
Arnim, Ludwig Achim von, 178-181, 186, 189, 213.
Aschbach, Joseph, 37n., 45, 118n., 210.
Auersperg, Anton Alexander, Graf von (Anastasius Grün), 174, 176n., 181ff., 189, 213.
Augustus, Emperor, 38, 47.
Aventinus, Johannes (Turmair), 28, 31, 34, 129, 138n., 194.

Bachmann, Adolf, 18n., 208.
Baecker, Louis de, 75n., 200.

Bakács, Thomas, 27.
Baillie-Grohman, William A., 98n., 112n., 202.
Balbi, Girolano, 57.
Baldass, Ludwig von, 204.
Barbarus, Hermolaus, 57f.
Bardentum, 176.
Baron, Hans, 20, 208.
Barre, Claude de (Claudio von Batre, Claudius Valdre, Claude de Vaudre, Cloi de Wadre), 6, 66, 130, 182, 184.
Bartenstein, Christoph, Freiherr von, 6in., 211.
Bartholinus, Ricardus, 57, 213.
Batre, Claudio von, 130; *see* Barre, Claude de.
Bauch, Gustav, 37n., 38n., 42n., 43n., 57n., 210.
Bavarian War, 29n., 77, 92, 140, 182, 186n.
Bebel, Heinrich, 42, 45f., 148, 205.
Bechwinden, Haintz von, 200.
Becker, C., 204.
Beheim, Michael, 141, 194.
Behr, Christian August, 165n.
Below, Georg von, 191.
Bergmann, (Custos), 210.
Berlichingen, Götz von, 48, 50n., 174ff., 186n., 189f., 194.
Bernd, M. Ambrosius, 138.
Bernhart, I. B., 202.
Bernheim, Ernst, 191.
Berthold von Henneberg, archbishop of Mainz, 20, 51.
Bezold, Friedrich von, 18f., 191.
Bibra, Siegmund, Freiherr von, 165n.
Biener, Clemens, 103n., 202.
Binz, Carl, 158n., 159n., 206.
Birken, Sigmund von: *Ehrenspiegel*, 6n., 12n., 129-132, 140-145, 149f., 153, 173f., 179, 181, 193.
Blangy, battle of, 75; *see* Guinegate, battle of.
Blattern, die bösen, 17, 101.
Bock, Hermann, 185n., 213.
Boeheim, Wendelin, 98n., 204, 210.
Bohemia, king of, 167.
Böhmenschlacht, 38, 42f., 77, 79, 91f., 117, 151, 173, 182, 186n.

[217]

Bonfinius, Antonius, 71n., 194.
Bonomus, Petrus, 130n.
Brant, Sebastian, 18n., 39f., 42, 45, 91, 213.
Braun, Anton, 208.
Bräuner, Jacob, 165n., 166.
Brautraub, see Anne, duchess of Brittany.
Brosch, Moritz, 61n., 65n., 210.
Bruges, revolt against Maximilian, 15n., 28, 30, 32, 38, 40, 49, 55, 69, 96n., 115ff., 133f., 144f., 151, 175, 182f., 186n.
Buchorn, councillors of, 146f., 155.
Bugslaff, duke of Pommerania, 28.
Burbank, 70n., 71n.
Burckhardt, Jacob, 62n., 191.
Bürger, Otto, 103n., 132n., 202f.
Burkhard, Arthur, 204.
Busson, Arnold, 105n., 121, 122n., 124f., 131, 173n., 207.
Butler, Kathleen T., 142n., 150n., 210.
Bütner, Wolffgang, 161.
Butsch of Innsbruck, 146.
Byrne, M. St. Clare, 199.

Caesar, Gaius Julius, 45n., 85, 111, 139, 152, 157, 160, 163.
Caesarius, Johann, 44n.
Cambray, League of, 51, 84.
Caplan, Harry, 58n., 212.
Carion, Johann, 29, 34n., 194.
Castile, king of, 65.
Castle, Eduard, 176n., 181n., 182n., 213.
Celtis, Conrad, 23n., 36, 39, 42ff., 130n., 187, 200, 213.
Charlemagne, 28, 42, 180.
Charles V, Emperor, 162-167; as Archduke, 24, 85; Maxmilian's "son," 180, "nephew," 186n.
Charles VIII, king of France, 52, 64, 67, 75, 84, 90; "Blue King," 116; "Carolus Gibbosus," 139; Dauphin, 69.
Charles the Bold, duke of Burgundy, 10, 15, 53, 67, 113, 160.
Chatillon, Gaultier de, 42n.
Chmel, Joseph, 17n., 24, 100n., 193, 200, 208, 210.
Chmelarz, Eduard, 97n., 119n., 202f.
Christlich Meynende, der, 167, 206.
Christophorus, Fr., 75n., 194.
Coccinius, Michael, 18n.
Collegium poëtarum of Vienna, 36n., 39, 42f.

Collenutius, Pandolphus, 57.
Collimitius, Georgius (Tanstetter), 34.
Collin, Heinrich Joseph von, 177f., 213.
Colman, Th., 70.
Commines, Philippe de, 10, 65, 68n., 194.
Constantine the Great, 42.
Cordua, Franciscus di, 165n.
Coursen, Charlotte H., 204.
Coxe, William, 12, 191.
Cronberger, the tailor, 141.
Crosses, the miracle of the, 17, 40, 100.
Currie, Margaret A., 199.
Cuspinianus, Johannes (Spiessheimer), 5, 10f., 12n., 23-35, 45n., 57n., 87n., 109, 118, 129, 130n., 141, 164, 194, 199.
Cyrus the Great, 57.
Czerny, Albin, 23n., 210.

Dagobert I, 42.
Dandalo, Francia di Matteo, 195.
David, King, 111, 159, 161.
Deichsler, Heinrich, 54n., 195.
de la Marche, Olivier, 6, 66ff., 130n., 143, 195.
Delepierre, Octave, 8n., 9n., 15, 68n., 69n., 75n., 195, 207.
Dendermonde, capture of, 143, 182f.
Denis, Michael, 211.
Denmark, king of, 138.
De Smet, J.-J., 196.
Despars, Jo^r Nicolaes, 68f., 143, 195.
Diederichs, Peter, 56n., 99n., 101n., 208.
Diet, at Augsburg, 53, 146, 168, 173; at Constance, 5, 49, 101f.; at Worms, 51, 101, 130.
Dietrichstein, Siegmund von, 103n.
Dirr, P., 37n., 204.
Disviri, 63n.
Dodgson, Campbell, 202.
Doll, Conrad, 118.
Doran, John, 145n., 207.
Dörnhöffer, Fr., 203.
Drescher, K., 211.
Droysen, Johann Gustav, 16f., 191.
Dubravius, Ioannes, 71, 129, 195.
Ducis, Benedictus, 200.
Dürer, Albrecht, 9, 38, 119f., 153, 182-185, 199, 202, 204f., 214.

Eberhard, count of Wurttemberg, 28n.
Ebermann, Richard, 41n., 211.
Eckermann, Johann Peter, 168, 211.
Egenolf, Franck. Chr., 132.
Ehrenpforte, see Maximilian, Works.

INDEX

Ehrenspiegel, see Birken, Sigmund von.
Elizabeth, queen of England, 167.
Endor, witch of, 139.
Engelbrecht, Peter, 33, 48, 109, 114, 182.
England, king of, 27, 96, 137f.
Ensisheim, the meteorite of, 40, 91, 99.
Erasmus of Rotterdam, Desiderius, 148, 205.
Erben, Wilhelm, 208.
Erich, Herzog von Braunschweig, 77, 173, 183, 186n.
Ernst, Jacob Daniel, 165f.
Ernstinger, Hans Georg, 207.
Esslingen, ambassador from, 56.
Eve, 141, 142n.

Faber, Felix, 32n., 195.
Faber, Johannes, 36, 37n., 44, 204.
Fassmann, 166n.
Fastnachtspiel, 61, 152.
Faust, 153, 156, 161-171, 187, 214.
Faustbuch, 153, 155, 167, 206; Berlin *Faustbuch* of 1590, 163; der Christlich Meynende, 167, 206; Pfitzer, Nikolaus, 164-167, 206; puppet plays of Dr. Faustus, 167, 206; Spiess, Johann, 161ff., 206; Widmann, Georg Rudolf, 163f., 206.
Fellner, Joseph, 182.
Ferdinand I, Emperor, 98, 158.
Ferdinand II, king of Castile and Aragon, 61, 65, 138n.
Ferrara, duke of, 57.
Fischereibuch, see Maximilian, Works.
Flanders, wars in, 56, 64, 95, 119.
Flemish chronicler, 8f., 15, 68, 145n.; Flemish poet, 78f.
Flögel, Karl Friedrich, 207.
Florence, Italy, ambassador from, 6f.; ridicule by, 61f., 136.
Flugblätter, 73, 100, 200.
Folksong, 72-90, 188; melody and its significance, 74ff., 79, 84; nature of historical folksong, 73ff., 89f.
Fouquesolles, Jacques de, 143.
France, king of, 52, 61, 96, 101, 137, 138n.
Francis I, king of France, 11, 61, 85f., 89.
Francis II, duke of Brittany, 115f.
Franck, Sebastian, 7, 9n., 104, 121-128, 130f., 135f., 141, 143, 149, 151, 168, 173f., 195.
Freher, Marquard, 36n., 37n., 38n., 39n., 41n., 42n., 44n., 45n., 57n., 58n., 64n., 100n., 193.
Frei, Peter, 78.
Freiburg i. Br., university at, 28, 44.
Frey, Jakob, 205.
Freydal, see Maximilian, Works.
Freytag, Gustav, 184f., 213.
Friedrich, Herzog zu Würzburg, 73.
Friedrich, Markgraf von Brandenburg, 37.
Friedrich III, Emperor, 4, 27, 30, 33, 37, 53, 57, 65n., 92, 94f., 109f., 117, 136, 141, 157f., 162, 209.
Friedrich Barbarossa, 52.
Friedrich der Weise, Elector of Saxony, 24f., 140, 173.
Frisch, Ernst von, 87n., 200.
Froissart, Pierre, 67n.
Forschauer, 81.
Frundsberg, Georg von, 81, 186n., 214.
Fueter, Eduard, 13n., 16n., 17n., 23n., 129n., 191.
Fugger family, 54n.
Fugger, Johann Jakob, 5f., 129f., 132, 134, 138n., 140f., 144n., 173, 193; *see* Birken, Sigmund von.
Fürstenberg, Graf von, 26.

Gachard, M., 49n., 124n., 199.
Gebetbuch, see Maximilian, Works.
Gedenkbuch, see Maximilian, Works.
Geiger, Ludwig, 37n., 38, 44n., 57n., 62n., 73n., 191, 199, 211.
Genealogie, see Maximilian, Works.
Gengenbach, Pamphilus, 41, 80, 84f., 89, 213.
Germania, see Franck, Sebastian.
Gern von Ems, Hans, 77.
Gess, Felician, 211.
Giehlow, Karl, 120n., 202ff.
Giessen, university at, 51n.
Gingerich, Virginia, 43n.
Giovio (Paulus Iovius), 63n.
Giustinian, Sebastian, 60f., 63n., 70n., 195.
Glareanus, Henricus (Heinrich Loriti), 38, 44, 129, 213.
Gluf, Heinz, 92.
Goedeke, Karl, 41n., 77n., 80n., 104n., 200, 203, 213.
Goethe, Johann Wolfgang von, 167-171, 174, 189f., 211, 213f.; father, 175; Works: "Colloquium," 175; *Dichtung und Wahrheit*, 174f.; *Egmont*, 175;

INDEX

Faust, 167-171, 174; *Götz von Berlichingen*, 174ff., 189f.; *Italienische Reise*, 175.
Goldast, Melchior, 31n., 32n., 195.
Goldschmidt, Peter, 166.
Gothein, Eberhard, 17, 20f., 99n., 100n., 101n., 191.
Gottlieb, Theodor, 97n.
Grabmal, Maximilian's, 98, 119.
Graff, Jörg, 85.
Greiff, B., 30n.,
Greiffenklau, Richard von, archbishop of Trier, 80f.
Grün, Anastasius, *see* Auersperg, A. A., Graf von.
Grünpeck, Joseph, 4n., 5, 9, 11, 12n., 18n., 23-35, 129, 143, 157, 182f., 193, 210.
Guicciardini, Francesco, 12n., 59f., 62f., 101f., 129, 195.
Guinegate, battle of, 66, 75, 84, 102, 182.
Gundel, Philipp, 44f.
Gundolf, Friedrich (Gundelfinger), 211.
Gurk, Cardinal of, *see* Lang, Matthäus.

Haberditze, F. M., 204.
Hagen, August: *Norica*, 133f., 185, 213.
Hainhofer, Philipp, 195.
Haltaus, Karl, 16, 101n., 104n., 128n., 131n., 133n., 174, 193, 203.
Hamilton, Comte Antoine, 167n.
Hanns, Meister, 147.
Hans, Wilhelm, 179n., 213.
Hans im finsteren tan, bruoder, 76n.
Hapsburg, House of, 3, 18n., 27, 33, 51, 118, 129, 172, 176, 181, 187.
Hare, Christopher, *pseud. for* Mrs. Marian Andrews.
Hartfelder, Karl, 57n., 199.
Harzen, E., 138n., 144n., 202.
Haselberg, Johann, 179.
Haupt, Herman, 51n., 208.
Hazlitt, William, 139n., 205.
Headlam, Cecil, 211.
Hector, 42, 152, 158-161, 163.
Hedio, Caspar, 27, 29, 30n., 32, 34n., 35, 195.
Hegewisch, D. H., 10-13, 193.
Heidelberg, university at, 41.
Helen of Troy, 152, 153n., 160, 162f., 168, 170.
Heller, Jacob, 185.
Henry VIII, king of England, 60, 70, 84f., 173, 199.

Herberger, Theodor, 49n., 199, 211.
Herberstein, Sigmund von, 6, 48n., 196.
Hercules, 161.
Herder, Johann Gottfried, 174, 211.
Hermannsgrün, Hans von, 52, 209.
Heuterus, Pontus (Huyter), 9n., 12n., 129, 191.
Heyck, Eduard, 19, 193.
Hill, Robert H., 207.
Historians, enlightened school of, 10, 12n.; philological school, 13, 18; Prussian school, 16.
Hochwart, Laurentius, 75n., 196.
Hock, Stefan, 200.
Hoffmann von Fallersleben, Heinrich, 76n., 79n., 200.
Hofkirche at Innsbruck, 98.
Hogel II, Zacharias, 161.
Hohenkrähen, castle of, 81f., 96.
Hohenleiter, Wolfgang, 98.
Hohenstaufen, 176, 180.
Holy Roman Emperor, 3, 4n., 50, 64, 90.
Hölzl, Blasius, 30n.
Homann, H. J., 214.
Homer, 161.
Höpp, Ulrich, 95.
Horawitz, Adalbert, 57n., 199.
Hormayr, Joseph, Freiherr von, 13, 176f., 181, 191, 193.
Huber, Alfons, 191, 210.
Huber, H., 18n.
Hug, Heinrich, 6n., 196.
Humanists, 18, 21f., 54, 100, 187f.; German, 35-48, 187f.; Italian, 56ff., 100.
Hume, David, 12, 191.
Hungary, king of, 86; *see* Wladislaw, king of Hungary.
Huss, Johannes, 140.
Hutten, Hans von, 47n., 50, 86.
Hutten, Ulrich von, 46ff., 50, 61, 67, 86, 143, 179n., 187, 211, 214.
Huyter, *see* Heuterus, Pontus.

Ilwof, Franz, 208, 211.
India, 30.
Ingolstadt, university at, 36n., 39, 42.
Italian wars, 46, 59f., 64, 90, 96, 100, 119, 170.

Jacob, Saint, 89.
Jagdbuch, see Maximilian, Works.
Jäger, Albert, 117n., 208.
Jäger, Albrecht, 209.
Jansen, Max, 19f., 97n., 193.

INDEX

Janssen, Johannes, 5n., 17-20, 49n., 67n., 191f.
Jensen, Wilhelm, 185n., 214.
Jesters, 31, 119, 126, 133f., 145, 186n.; see Rosen, Kunz von der.
Jews, and "Christus surrexit," 142, 148; bring Max golden eggs, 142, 149; gamble for Jesus' clothes, 81; in Regensburg, 93; in Styria and Carinthia, 56, 211.
Joachim I, Kurfürst von Brandenburg, 29n.
Joachim, Erich, 211.
Jöppel, Caspar, 76.
Joseph (II), archduke of Austria, 61n., 211.
Julius II, Pope, 7, 47n., 51f., 60, 127, 139f., 150.
Justinian the Great, 42.

Kalid, Sultan of Egypt, 151.
Kanzow, Thomas, 28, 196.
Karl, Herzog von Geldern, 86.
Karl Friedrich von Cleve, 131.
Kaser, Kurt, 20, 192, 209.
Kasimir, Markgraf von Brandenburg, 179, 200.
Kautzsch, Rudolf, 211.
Keisersperg, Johann Geiler von, 37n.
Kessler, Johann, 196.
Kiechel, Samuel, 207.
Kirchhof, Hans Wilhelm, 149ff., 205.
Kirchlechner, K., 105n., 207.
Kirchmair, Georg, 6, 8n., 9n., 54n., 55, 61, 196.
Klaje, Hermann, 65n., 209.
Klüpfel, Karl, 16, 101n., 156n., 193.
Knebel, Johann, 196.
Koch, Matthias, 61n., 211.
König, Erich, 30n., 211.
König, Karl F., 168n., 175n., 211.
Krafft, Peter, 176.
Krantz, Albert, 196.
Kraus, Victor von, 17, 25n., 26n., 27n., 50n., 107n., 115n., 199, 211f.
Kreiten, Hubert, 199.
Kreuzenstein, university at, 132n.
Kreuzwunder, see Crosses, miracle of the.
Krieger, Albert, 209.
Kronenwächter, Die, see Arnim, Ludwig Achim von.

Ladd, Anna Coleman, 186n., 214.

Lalaing, Antoine de, 49, 124, 196.
Lalebuch, Das, 155, 205.
Lambecius, Petrus (Peter Lambeck), 14.
Lamprecht, Karl, 192.
Landfriede, 82.
Landshuter Krieg, 77; see Bavarian War.
Landshuter Rathschronik, 196.
Landsknechte, 6, 31f., 55, 77, 85, 150, 186n., 208.
Lang, Apollonia, 185n.
Lang, Matthäus, 86, 200.
Lang, Vinzenz, 130n.
Langius, Paulus, 196.
Lanz, Karl, 192.
Laschitzer, Simon, 24n., 97n., 103n., 104n., 118n., 122n., 202f.
Latomus, Bartholomaeus (Steinmetz), 45, 193.
Lauterbach, Samuel Friedrich, 166.
Lauterbecken, Georg, 98n., 212.
Lazarini, Ludwig, Freiherr von, 98n., 112n., 201.
Lazius, Wolfgang, 39.
Le Glay, André J. G., 14, 68n., 199.
Lehmann, Christopher, 54n., 196.
Leib, Chilian, 196.
Leitner, Quirin von, 103n., 202.
Lemnius, Simon, 35n., 214.
Leo X, Pope, 46n.
Leonora of Portugal, 19, 88.
Leopold I, Emperor, 129.
Lercheimer, Augustin, 158n., 159, 206; see Witekind, Hermann.
Leszczynski, Raphael, 25.
Lettenhove, Kervyn de, 15f., 192.
Letzte Ritter, Der, see Auersperg, Anton Alexander, Graf von.
Lichtenstein, Paul von, 25, 81.
Liebenau, Th. von, 35n., 212.
Liebenfels, Hans von, 99.
Liège, bishop of, 100.
Liège, Guillaume de, 69.
Liliencron, Rochus von, 8n., 50n., 73n., 74n., 75n., 76n., 77n., 78n., 79n., 80n., 81, 82n., 84n., 85n., 86n., 87n., 88n., 89n., 91n., 92n., 93n., 94n., 95n., 96n., 103n., 104n., 108n., 201, 204.
Linden, Herman vander, 212.
Lindener, Michael, 149, 153n., 205.
Lindner, Th., 4n., 18n.
Liske, Xaver, 209.
Löbliche fruchtbringende Gesellschaft, die, 129.
Locher, Jakob (Philomusus), 39.

INDEX

Longinus, Vincentius, 39.
Lord High Treasurer of London, 70.
Lorenz, Ottokar, 209.
Loriti, Heinrich, *see* Glareanus, Henricus.
Louis XI, king of France, 10, 15, 68, 102, 143, 173, 184.
Louis XII, king of France, 51f., 84f., 96, 101, 173.
Lübke, W., 202.
Lucas, the priest, 63n.
Ludibilia of Venice and Florence, 61.
Ludwig I, count of Wurttemberg-Urach, 28n.
Luther, Martin, 7, 8n., 9, 24, 61, 127, 135-140, 142, 144n., 148f., 151ff., 157f., 160f., 163, 164n., 166, 181, 199f., 205.

Machiavelli, Niccolo, 8, 12n., 14, 18n., 58ff., 62f., 197, 210.
Maecenas, Gaius Cilnius, 38.
Mainz, Berthold von, *see* Berthold von Henneberg.
Mair, Paul Hektor, 53n., 197.
Malannoy, captain of, 56; *see* Mollennoy, captain of.
Malipiero, 62n.
Mander, Karel van, 153, 183f., 207.
Manlius, J., *see* Mennl, J.
Mantegna, Andrea, 118.
Margaret of Austria, 14, 52, 64f., 69, 95, 199.
Margaret of York, 113, 184.
Marie, queen of Hungary, 132.
Martinswand, legend of the, 104f., 121, 123ff., 130f., 173, 175, 177-180, 182, 184f., 207.
Mary, duchess of Burgundy, 3, 10, 15, 25, 30, 69, 78f., 113ff., 119, 139n., 152f., 160ff., 166, 182, 184f., 186n., 212.
Matthisson, Friedrich, 132, 212.
Maximilian I, Emperor, captivity in Bruges, *see* Bruges; characteristics as child, 5, 32, 109; councillors, 9, 19, 25ff., 29, 34, 50, 52, 55, 69, 101n., 115, 128, 136f., 143, 148, 158, 176, 186n.; death, 44f., 47, 87ff., 151, 182; duke of Burgundy, 64; epic figure, 184; father, *see* Friedrich III, Emperor; funeral, 36, 87f.; illegitimate children, 14; interest in astrology, 26, 109f., 157, 169; interest in genealogy, 33f., 37n., 117f., 144, 156; interest in history, 18, 33f., 37n., 54, 117f., 156f.; magic, 110, 139, 152f., 157-161; marriage to Anne, duchess of Brittany, 64, 75; marriage to Mary, duchess of Burgundy, 3, 10, 68, 78f., 119, 182, 184f.; mother, *see* Leonora of Portugal; plans to become pope, 179, 209f.; political policies, 13f., 16-19, 40, 46, 50ff., 91, 208ff.; product of the Renaissance, 17, 20, 97; propaganda, 22, 91, 94-104, 108-120, 153, 189; Roman king, 3, 27, 38, 40, 58, 64, 67, 69, 76f., 79, 90, 96, 142, 182; secretaries, 5, 30, 47, 54, 102n., 109f., 128, 136f., 142f.; threatened deposition, 25, 52; ANECDOTES: 13f., 16, 48f., 135-154, 188; Individual Anecdotes: abbot of Fulda, 146, 149; beggar, 138f., 144n.; blind men and sow, 128, 151f.; Butsch of Innsbruck, 146; capture of Dendermonde, 143, 182f.; capture of Vienna, 182; coffin, 88, 181f., 186; conjuration of spirits, 139, 151ff., 158-163, 168, 170; cook and Max' genealogy, 144; corrupt councillors, 136f., 148f., 186n.; council at Buchorn, 146f., 155; courtesan and royal seal, 147; gypsy girls at Augsburg, 182; hunting party, 150f.; Jews and the golden eggs, 142, 149; magician conjures for Max, 158f., 162f., 166; Meister Albrecht, 48, 146; Max and alchemist, 151; Max and Dürer, 153, 182-185; Max and lions, 107, 117, 122; Max and poor food, 147; Max attempts to escape from Bruges, 145n.; Max breaks lock, 141; Max called "Bürgermeister of Augsburg," 67f., 143; Max joins church processions, 181f.; Max outwits Venetians, 135f.; Max refuses picture, 142f.; Meister Hanns and poison plots, 147; minister from Denmark, 138, 142, 149; nervous petitioner, 138, 149; peasant's petition, 150; peasants of Vöcklipruck, 147, 155; retreat from Milan, 6, 55, 59, 186n.; rich man wants nobility, 142, 149, 153n.; rime of Nuremberg, 135; sacrifice in war, 139; secretary and mocking songs, 142, 148ff.; siege at Vienna, 141; singing birds, 112, 186n.; stag and pheasant pay homage, 17, 99f.; stupid man wants doctorate, 149, 153n.; thieving secretary, 136f., 149; Venice and the golden cradle, 136; women hide Max'

boots, 53, 182; see *Bömenschlacht*, Claude de Barre, Faust, Guinegate, Kunz von der Rosen, Martinswand, Pienzenau; CHARACTERISTICS: artistic skill, 110f., 175, 185, 204f.; bravery, 15, 32, 54, 58, 62, 68, 75, 77, 84f., 89, 92, 117, 122, 125f., 128, 186n.; builder, 111; corruption, 9, 27, 52, 55, 70f.; courtesy, 24f., 36, 69; dilatoriness, 11, 41f., 56, 63, 67, 70, 80, 83, 90, 110, 116; disposition, 7f., 11, 13, 16f., 21, 24ff., 29, 44n., 47ff., 53f., 57ff., 65f., 70, 140, 179, 187; disregard for human life, 140; education, 10f., 31, 33f., 48, 65, 109, 119, 148f., 151; eloquence, 5f., 33ff., 49, 55, 68, 101, 109; energy, 13, 26, 66, 68, 176, 186n.; fickleness, 8, 13, 63, 109; fidelity, 6, 16, 19, 30, 48f., 55, 57, 84, 93, 116f.; forgiving nature, 8, 52, 73, 77, 89, 127, 134, 137, 140, 148, 154, 182f.; generosity, 9, 13, 28, 35, 44, 58f., 62, 66, 68f., 71, 110, 135, 144, 148, 169f., 182f., 185; humility, 7, 29f., 48, 88ff., 150f., 186n.; humor, 13, 140, 146f., 150, 154, see Sayings; hunter, 12, 21, 26, 32f., 36, 43, 48f., 54, 60f., 98, 105ff., 112, 119, 123ff., 134, 139, 150f., 154, 177ff., 184; impecuniosity, 11ff., 15, 27, 40, 44n., 50, 54f., 57, 59ff., 65, 70f., 169; indecision, 6, 11, 15n., 19, 26f., 37, 41f., 49f., 52, 56, 60, 63f., 67, 70, 110; intellectual gifts, 9ff., 13, 19, 21, 33, 57, 109ff.; inventiveness, 13, 112f., 157; justice, 7f., 29, 36, 44n., 45n., 47, 49f., 55f., 58, 62, 69, 71, 88f., 89, 140, 169, 186n.; knowledge of languages, 10, 13, 34, 37, 46n., 58, 113ff., 119, 151, knowledge of men, 9, 13, 35, 49, 80; medical skill, 34, 108, 110; memory, 10, 13, 33; mercy, 7, 29, 35, 44n., 45n., 53, 55f., 62, 69, 71, 77, 89, 92, 96, 116f., 127, 140, 148, 182f., 186n.; military skill, 6, 12, 19, 21, 27, 31f., 36f., 44n., 45n., 48, 57, 62f., 66, 69, 71, 77, 79, 84-87, 101f., 108, 111f., 119, 127, 154, 170; modesty, 7, 29, 48, 54, 88; mummeries, 111, 169; music, 35, 67, 111, 119; patience, 7, 83, 89; patron of arts and learning, 21, 36, 42, 48, 54, 67, 110f., 185, 188; peace-loving, 7, 29, 35, 44n., 55, 62, 88f., 127, 148; personal appearance, 13, 30f., 48, 66, 70, 113, 143, 182, 184 (portraits, 42, 132, 175, 182, 204); physical strength, 11, 13, 26, 31f., 49, 57f., 62, 66, 102, 141, 151, 154; piety, 9, 15, 45n., 57f., 65, 68, 71, 81, 88ff., 96, 99, 164f., 180f.; pleasure-loving, 7, 21, 24, 49, 53, 93, 170, 179; popularity, 16f., 19, 21, 24, 31f., 56, 59, 66, 73f., 88, 170, 179, 188; prodigality, 9, 12n., 15, 32f., 52, 55, 59ff., 64, 70, 97, 110, 112, 115; reformer, 13f., 51f., 101, 208ff.; relations with women, 30, 33, 49, 53f., 57, 65; religion, 100, 109, 139, 156f., 170 (Max' relation to Protestantism, 140, 181); reticence, 7, 27, 63, 115; romantic nature, 15ff., 20f.; superstition, 9, 100, 139; temperance, 8f., 11, 29, 49, 70, 109, 111, 140, 176; tolerance, 46n., 56, 93; vanity, 12, 14n., 63; vivacity, 11, 19; OPINIONS OF MAX: American: 19; Bohemian, 71; English, 9-12, 20, 70f., 188; Flemish, 6, 8f., 15, 68ff.; French, 7, 10, 14, 64-68; German, 5-20, 23-56; Hungarian, 71; Italian, 6ff., 18n., 56-64, 188; SAYINGS: about *Landsknechte*, 150; answers scoffer, 141f.; comforts Philip, 138; on defeated nobility, 148; on Kaiser and pope, 139, 150; quotes proverb, 112; the kings, 137f., 149; young wife for old man, 147f.; WORKS: *Ehrenpforte*, 36, 38, 97n., 119f., 203; *Fischereibuch*, 98, 112, 201; *Freydal*, 98, 102n., 103, 119, 169, 202; *Gebetbuch*, 202; *Gedenkbuch*, 97n., 202; *Genealogie*, 97n., 98, 118f., 144n., 202; *Jagdbuch*, 98, 112, 202; *Teuerdank*, 16, 98, 102n., 103-108, 110n., 119-134, 153f., 157, 165, 168, 188f., 172-175, 181f., 184f., 202f., fusion with legend, 128f., historical foundation, 104f., synopsis, 105-108, 173; *Triumph*, 98, 119f., 145, 203; *Triumphwagen*, 119, 169; *Triumphzug*, 38, 119, 168, 182; *Weisskunig*, 9, 18n., 97f., 102n., 103n., 104n., 108-117, 119, 157, 174, 181, 185, 188f., 204; *Zeugbücher*, 98, 204.

Maximilian legend, 3f., 172, 183, 187, 188; development after 1600, 172f., 186, 189f.; in literature, 172-186; origins of, 22.

Maynus, Jason, 57.

Mayr, Michael, 98n., 104n., 105n., 112n., 201f., 207.

INDEX

Meiler (Müller) von Raperswil, Peter, 76.
Meistergesang, 152.
Meistersinger, 151, 211.
Melanchthon, Philip, 29n.
Menelaus, 163.
Mennl, Jacob (Manlius), 33f., 118, 144n., 170n.
Mephistopheles, 168, 170.
Middle Ages, 20, 174, 187.
Mielke, H., 214.
Miller, Artur Maximilian, 186n., 214.
Minnesang, 114n.
Misander (Adami), 166.
Misch, Georg, 97n., 103n., 203.
Modestus, Ioannes Antonius, 57.
Molinet, Jean, 7, 65-68, 143, 197.
Mollennoy, captain of, 69; *see* Malannoy, captain of.
Monrepas, Raoul von, 184; *see* Barre, Claude de.
More, Robert Pattison, 167n., 206.
Moreri, Louis, 166n.
Morienes, the Roman, 151.
Muling, *see* Adelphus, Johann.
Müller, J. von, 183.
Müller, Maler, 167, 214.
Müller von Königswinter, Wolfgang, 183f., 214.
Münch, Ernst, 26n., 46n., 157n., 192, 214.
Münster at Ulm, 132.
Murner, Thomas, 40, 214.
Muther, Theodor, 42n., 192.

Nagel, Siegfried Robert, 153n., 162n., 206.
Nagl, Johann Willibald, 192.
Nägle, August, 209.
Napoleonic period, 176.
Narcissus, 66.
Nauclerus, Johannes (Verge *or* Vergenhans), 28f., 129, 197, 211.
Netherlands, the, 29, 31.
Neumann, Johann Georg, 165n.
Noah, 118, 144.
Novel, historical, 172, 185, 190.
Nuremberg chronicler, 9.

Ochs, Peter, 55n., 192.
Oefelius, Andreas Felix, 29n., 75n., 194, 196ff.
Oldecop, Johan, 197.
Orendel, King, 81.
Ortenstain, Hans, 94.
Osiander, Johann Adam, 164.

Otto the Great, 42.

Pace, Richard, 9, 70f.
Palmer, Philip Mason, 167n., 206.
Panzer, Georg Wolfgang, 96n., 212.
Paris of Troy, 168, 170.
Parma, duke and duchess of, 167.
Pastor, Ludwig, 192.
Paullini, Kristian Frantz, 164f.
Perger, Sigmund Ferdinand von, 176.
Petter, Anton, 176.
Petz, H., 204.
Peutinger, Juliane, 185n.
Peutinger, Konrad, 29f., 30n., 186n., 187, 211.
Pfeffinger, Konrad, 140.
Pfintzing, Melchior, 103n., 104, 120-123, 125, 130f., 173.
Pfitzer, Nikolaus, 164-167, 206.
Philip, Pfalzgraf, 37, 53, 77, 140, 156, 200.
Philip (II), prince of Spain, 132.
Philip (der Schöne), archduke of Burgundy, 49, 65n., 69, 115, 124, 138; king of Spain, 78, 95.
Pico della Mirandola, Gianfrancesco, 58, 100, 212.
Pienzenau(er), Johann von, 52, 77f., 92f., 117, 183f., 185n., 200.
Pighius, Stephan Winand, 131, 173.
Pinicianus, Joseph, 45.
Pinturicchio, 118.
Pirckheimer, Wilibald, 7, 11, 26, 29, 31f., 34, 36n., 37n., 38n., 119n., 129, 157n., 185, 197.
Pistorius, Joannes, 31n., 196f.
Pleyer, Georg, 87f., 200.
Poeta laureatus, 36n., 38f., 185.
Poland, king of, 86; *see* Sigismund, king of Poland.
Polheim, Martin von, 50.
Polheim, Wolf von, 50.
Polymnius, Wilhelmus (Püelinger), 34.
Polyphemus, 161, 163.
Pompey the Great, 42.
Pope, the, 4n., 7, 40, 46, 51f., 60, 81, 100, 118, 137, 139, 179, 181, 209f.
Porta Honoris, see Maximilian, Works: *Ehrenpforte.*
Prem, S. M., 105n., 207.
Priam, 161, 163.
Priebatsch, F., 209.
Probst zu Schwaz, Hans, 79.

INDEX

Prüschenk, Sigmund, Freiherr zu Stettenberg, 106, 199.

Questenberg, 37n.
Quirini, Vincenzo, 58f., 60n., 62n., 63n., 197.

Ragor, Johann Huldr., 170n.
Ranke, Leopold von, 4, 13f., 20ff., 129n., 132n., 140n., 192.
Ranzanus, Petrus, 71n., 197.
Raphael, 118.
Räuberroman, 190.
Rausch, Karl, 209.
Rauscher, Ernst, 184, 214.
Redl, Franz, 103n., 138n., 201.
Redlich, Oswald, 78n., 208.
Reformation, German, 17, 19, 189.
Regensburg falls away from emperor, 74f.
Reinhardt, Herzog von Lothringen, 145f.
Rem, Lucas, 8, 30n., 55, 197.
Rem, Wilhelm, 7, 9n., 50n., 53n., 54n., 55f., 197.
Remigius, Nicolaus, 166.
Renaissance, 17, 20, 97, 108, 154, 172, 187.
Reuberus, Justus, 57n., 213.
Reuchlin, Johann, 37, 54, 156, 199, 211.
Reuter, Simon Henrich, 166.
Reutlingen, Martin (Maier) von, 96.
Revolution of 1848, 181.
Revolutionär, oberrheinischer, 51f.
Rhenanus, Beatus, 34, 57n., 197, 199.
Ricek, E. G., 184n., 214.
Richter, Julius Wilhelm Otto, 185n., 214.
Riedrer, Caspar, 112f.
Ritterdrama, 176, 190.
Ritterroman, 176.
Robertson, William, 10ff., 192.
Robinson, F. Mabel, 204.
Rockwell, Leo Lawrence, 158n., 212.
Roels, Fransoys, 69.
Rolewinck, Werner, 31n., 197.
Romantic School, 176, 178, 182, 189.
Romzug, 40, 78ff., 90.
Roo, Gerard de, 129, 141, 192.
Roscoe, William, 12, 192.
Rosen, Kunz von der, 128, 133f., 138, 145, 182, 184f., 213; advice to Max, 128, 143; breaks Venetian goblet, 143f., 150, 179; image of, 128; nearly causes explosion, 134; on Max' genealogy, 144; prank on blind men at Augsburg, 128, 152; pulls monks into well, 128, 179; uses Max as king in card game, 144f., 184f.; with abbot of Fulda, 146; with Max in Bruges, 133f., 144f., 182; with minister from Lothringen, 145f.; with poor priest, 135, 144, 149.
Rudolf von Habsburg, 178, 181.
Rupprich, Hans, 39n., 43n., 130n., 200.
Russ, Karl, 176, 182.
Rylands, W. H., 104n., 203.
Rymer, Thomas, 192.

Sabina, duchess of Wurttemberg, 86.
Sachs, Hans, 151ff., 158, 160, 162, 167f., 205-208.
Sachse, Michael, 163f., 165f.
Sadet, Captain, 69.
Sahr, Julius, 74n., 201.
Salten, Felix, 185n.
Samson, 122, 161.
Samuel, 139, 160ff.
Sandrart, Joachim von, 153n., 208.
St. Bastian's of Augsburg, 128.
Saul, King, 139, 160f.
Saurer, Laurenz, 25.
Sauromanus, Georgius (Sauermann), 44.
Scaliger, Julius Caesar, 18n.
Schardius, Simon, 38n., 45n., 46n., 192.
Schaumburg, Wilwolt von, 6, 49, 130n., 197.
Schedel, Hartmann, 31n., 118n., 197.
Schefftlar, monastery of, 197f.
Scheible, Johann, 104n., 159n., 163n., 167n., 203, 206f.
Schelhornius, J. G., 164.
Schenk zu Schweinsberg, Eberhard, Feiherr, 198.
Schenkenbach, der, 82n.
Schenkendorf, Max von, 178, 214.
Scherenberg, Bishop Rudolf II von, 73.
Schertlin von Burtenbach, Sebastian, 49, 199.
Schestag, Franz, 38n., 119n., 145n., 204.
Schiebel, Johann Georg, 165f.
Schier, Alfred, 178n., 213.
Schiller, Johann Christoph Friedrich von, 190.
Schlegel, August Wilhelm, 176f., 201.
Schmeidler, Bernhard, 51n., 209.
Schmidt, Charles, 40n., 42n., 192.
Schneegans, Heinrich, 212.
Schneider, Daniel, 163.
Schneider, Hans, 82n., 94ff.

Schönherr, David, 204.
Schönsperger, Hans, 104n., 203.
Schradin, Nicolaus, 35f., 198.
Schulte, Aloys, 209.
Schultes, Matthäus, 104n., 128f., 131n., 173f., 184, 203.
Schultz, Alvin, 97n., 103n., 108n., 109n., 204.
Schwandtner, Johann Georg, 71n., 197f.
Scott, William Bell, 119f., 204.
Scriptures, Holy, 101n., 109.
Sebourc, Baudoin de, 142n.
Selbitz, Hans von, 175.
Serntein, Cyprian von, 25f.
Seton-Watson, Robert William, 20, 193.
Sforza, Bianca Maria, Empress, 43, 50, 57, 61, 205.
Sforza, Lodovico (il Moro), 61f.
Sickingen, Franz von, 50n.
Sigismund, duke of Tyrol, 117, 204, 208.
Sigismund, king of Poland, 25, 86.
Sigmund, Emperor, 142.
Sizeranne, Robert de la, 205.
Spalatin, Georg, 24f., 198.
Spangel, Pallas, 41.
Spaur, Carl von, 98.
Spiess, Johann, 161ff., 206; *see Faustbuch*.
Sponheim, monastery of, *see* Trithemius, Johannes.
Spruch, 22, 72, 90-96, 99, 188.
Spurs, battle of the, 70, 84, 173.
Stabius, Johannes (Stöberer), 36, 37n., 38, 43, 118f.
Stainer, Heinrich, 104n., 203.
Stälin, Christoph Friedrich von, 4n., 209, 212.
Stang, William, 19, 193.
Stein, Eitelwolf von, 5, 49.
Steinherz, S., 97n., 103n., 201.
Strobl, Joseph, 103n., 132n., 133n., 203.
Struve, Burcard, *see* Freher, Marquard.
Sturm und Drang, 176.
Suden, Hermann, 165.
Sunthaim, Ladislaus, 118, 200.
Susanne of Bavaria, 179.
Swabian League, 56, 76, 81, 92.
Swiss Confederation, 76.
Swiss War, 26, 29, 32, 35, 52, 55, 66, 76, 90, 182f.
Syphilis, *see Blattern, die bösen*.

Taylor, Archer, 103n., 134n., 212.
Taylor, John, 70.

Tenremonde, *see* Dendermonde.
Teuerdank, *see* Maximilian, Works.
Thausing, Moritz, 120, 205.
Thermopylae, battle of, 38.
Thiele, Ernst, 135n., 205.
Thode, Henry, 185n., 214.
Thoman, Nicolaus, 198.
Thommen, R., 212.
Tichtel, Johannes, 198.
Ticiano, Ludovico, 57.
Tille, Alexander, 161n., 163n., 164n., 165n., 166n., 167n., 170n., 207.
Tittmann, Julius, 77n., 200.
Tolhopf, Johannes, 44.
Trajan, Emperor, 45n., 47.
Treitzsauerwein, family of, 112; Marx, 179ff.
Trier, Max' discovery of Christ's coat at, 80f., 88, 99.
Trithemius, Johannes (Tritheim), 18n., 64n., 100, 139, 152f., 156-161, 163-166, 198.
Triumph, Triumphwagen, Triumphzug, see Maximilian, Works.
Trivulzio, Gian Giacomo, 65.
Troyon, Pierre, 205.
Tubero, Ludovicus, 71, 198.
Tübingen, university at, 28n.
Turks, crusade against, 39ff., 46, 58, 83, 90-93, 95, 100f.
Turst, Conrad, 118, 212.

Uhland, Ludwig, 201.
Ulmann, Heinrich, 4, 18ff., 24, 52n., 94n., 193, 209f.
Ulrich, duke of Wurttemberg, 47f., 50, 86f., 89, 145.
Ulysses, 161, 163.
Umperlin, Hans, 86f.
Unrest, Jacob, 54n., 55f., 94, 98n., 198.

Valdre, Claudius, 130n.; *see* Barre, Claude de.
Van Dyke, Paul, 20, 52n., 97n., 103n., 114n., 194, 201.
Vaudre, Claude de, 66; *see* Barre, Claude de.
Vehse, Eduard, 193.
Venice, Doge of, 61n., 63n.; poison plots against Max, 62; prince of, 61; quarrels with, 79, 90, 96, 135f., 151; ridicule by, 61, 136.
Vettori, Francesco, 6f., 18n., 58f., 62f.

INDEX

Vienna, capture of, 182; congress at, 34f., 45, 86, 93, 209; siege at, 141; university at, 23n., 28, 36n., 42, 44f., 57, 118n.
Vigneulles, Philippe von, 198.
Vöcklipruck, peasants of, 147, 155.
Voisin, M. Auguste, 15n., 68n., 198.
Volkslied, 22, 72-90, 188; see Folksong.
Voltaire, François Marie Arouet de, 10, 12n.

Wadre, Cloi de, 130n.; see Barre, Claude de.
Waga, Friedrich, 41n., 214.
Waldauf von Waldenstein, Florian, 50.
Waldis, Burckhard, 104n., 132ff., 173.
Wallenstein, Albrecht von, 4.
Walther, Andreas, 4n., 18n., 194.
Ward, Sir Adolphus William, 212.
Watt, Joachim (Vadianus), 45.
Wegele, Franz X. von, 14n., 18n., 103n., 118n., 121n., 129n., 156n., 193.
Wehrhan, Karl, 205.
Weinrich, Caspar, 27n., 30, 198.
Weisskunig, see Maximilian, Works.
Weitzel, Karl, 185n., 213.
Weller, Emil, 75n., 200f., 212.
Welschgattung, 41, 214.
Welser, Anton, 30.
Welser, Bartolomaeus, 55.
Wendunmuth, see Kirchof, Hans Wilhelm.
Werdenberg, Graf Haug von, 92.
Westerstetten, von, 27n., 198.
Weyer, Johann (Wier, Wierus), 158f., 161, 207.
Weyler, Christoph, 87ff.
Wickhoff, Franz, 214.
Widmann, Georg Rudolf, 163, 206.
Widmann, Leonhart, 199.

Wier, Johann, see Weyer, Johann.
Wilcken, Hermann, see Witekind, Hermann.
Wilhelm, Kaiser, 163.
Wilhelm III, Herzog von Jülich-Cleve-Berg, 158.
Wimpfeling, Jacob, 18n., 37n., 46, 110n., 187, 212.
Wingfield, Sir Robert, 70.
Wirsing, Widow, 50.
Witchcraft, 158f.
Witekind, Hermann, 159ff., 163, 166, 206.
Wladislaw, king of Hungary, 26f., 86; see Hungary, king of.
Wolff, Eugen, 201.
Wolkenstein, Oswald von, 114n.
Wolsey, Thomas, 70.
Woodcuts, value of, 118f.
Wörnher, Johann, 49f.
Würzburg, monastery at, 156.

Zacher, Wolfgang, 178.
Zappert, Georg, 212.
Zarncke, Friedrich, 39n., 40n., 42n., 45n., 213.
Zasius, Ulrich, 44.
Zayner, Andreas, 199.
Zeibig, H. J., 8n., 54n., 213.
Zeisseler, Christoph, 166.
Zeugbücher, see Maximilian, Works.
Ziehen, Eduard, 5n., 20, 37n., 51n., 210.
Zifferer, Paul, 205.
Zimmerische Chronik, 7f., 9n., 48n., 49n., 50n., 53n., 136n., 145-148, 155, 158, 199.
Zingerle, Anton, 206.
Zingerle, Ignaz, 114, 206.
Zingerle, Ignaz V., 206.
Zingerle, Reinhold von, 207.